Studies in Empirical Economics

Aman Ullah (Ed.)
Semiparametric and Nonparametric Econometrics
1989. ISBN 3-7908-0418-5

Walter Krämer (Ed.)
Econometrics of Structural Change
1989. ISBN 3-7908-0432-0

Wolfgang Franz (Ed.)
Hysteresis Effects in Economic Models
1990. ISBN 3-7908-0482-7

John Piggott and John Whalley (Eds.)
Applied General Equilibrium
1991. ISBN 3-7908-0530-0

Baldev Raj and Badi H. Baltagi (Eds.)
Panel Data Analysis
1992. ISBN 3-7908-0593-9

Josef Christl
The Unemployment / Vacancy Curve
1992. ISBN 3-7908-0625-0

Jürgen Kaehler and Peter Kugler (Eds.)
Econometric Analysis of Financial Markets
1994. ISBN 3-7908-0740-0

Klaus F. Zimmermann (Ed.)
Output and Employment Fluctuations
1994. ISBN 3-7908-0754-0

Jean-Marie Dufour and Baldev Raj (Eds.)
New Developments in Time Series Econometrics
1994. ISBN 3-7908-0766-4

John D. Hey (Ed.)
Experimental Economics
1994. ISBN 3-7908-0810-5

Arno Riedl, Georg Winckler and Andreas Wörgötter (Eds.)
Macroeconomic Policy Games
1995. ISBN 3-7908-0857-1

Thomas Url and Andreas Wörgötter (Eds.)
Econometrics of Short and Unreliable Time Series
1995. ISBN 3-7908-0879-2

Steven Durlauf · John F. Helliwell
Baldev Raj (Eds.)

Long-Run Economic Growth

With 28 Figures

Physica-Verlag
A Springer-Verlag Company

Editors
Professor Steven Durlauf
Department of Economics
University of Wisconsin
1180 Observatory Drive
Madison, Wisconsin 53707-1376
USA

Professor John F. Helliwell
Department of Economics
University of British Columbia
Vancouver, B.C.
Canada V6T 1Y2

Professor Baldev Raj
Department of Economics
Wilfrid Laurier University
Waterloo, Ontario
Canada N2L 3C5

First published in "Empirical Economics"
Volume 21, Issue 1, 1996

ISBN-13:978-3-642-64747-5
CIP-Titelaufnahme der Deutschen Bibliothek

Long run economic growth / Steven Durlauf ... (ed.). -
Heidelberg : Physica-Verl. 1996
(Studies in empirical economics)
ISBN-13:978-3-642-64747-5 e-ISBN-13:978-3-642-61211-4
DOI: 10.1007/978-3-642-61211-4
NE: Durlauf, Steven [Hrsg.]

Softcover reprint of the hardcover 1st edition 1996

SPIN 10501210 88/2202-5 4 3 2 1 0 - Printed on acid-free paper

Contents

Contents

Long-Run Economic Growth[1]

STEVEN DURLAUF

Department of Economics, University of Wisconsin, 1180 Observatory Drive Madison, Wisconsin 53706-1363, USA

JOHN F. HELLIWELL

Department of Economics, University of British Columbia, Vancouver, B.C., V6T 1Y2, Canada

BALDEV RAJ

Department of Economics, Wilfrid Laurier University, Waterloo, Ontario, N2L 3C5, Canada

I Introduction

One of the primary goals of most national governments is to achieve sustainable growth of real income per person (hereafter economic growth), in the belief that it can help raise the economic well-being of the population as a whole. This widespread concern has been paralleled with the explosion of research on growth in the last decade. The macroeconomics of growth is concerned with questions such as: Why do growth rates differ over time in a given country? Do countries then become more similar in terms of income and productivity growth? Can growth rates be improved by designing economic policies? Answers to such questions are of obvious importance. We have put together a set of papers by distinguished growth researchers in order to survey the state of empirical work in this area.

II Background

The new developments in growth theory are driven by the desire to explain what was previously treated as exogenous to the neoclassical economic growth

[1] The editors express their sincere thanks to the referees for their invaluable help in reviewing the contributions in this monograph. The editors also greatfully acknowledge that financial support for this project was received from grants funded in part by the University of Wisconsin-Madison, Social Sciences and Humanities Research Council of Canada (SSHRC), a book preparation grant partly funded by Wilfrid Laurier University (WLU) Operating funds, and partly by the SSHRC General Research Grant awarded to WLU. Paul Carvalho, Vlasios George Melessankis and Paul Sop provided research assistance.

model – the sources of technological progress. The availability of new methods of theoretical analysis has also contributed to the increased interest. In addition, the interest in growth may correspond to the policy objective of finding new approaches to reversing the significant post-1973 slowdown of growth and productivity in the industrialized countries (see Raj and Slottje, 1995).

It might help to place this resurgence in the context of past contributions to growth theory since interest in growth theory dates back to the beginning of the study of economics. For instance, important contributions to the growth literature were made by the "classical" economists such as Adam Smith, David Ricardo, Thomas R. Malthus and Karl Marx, which are reviewed by Harris (1987). Similarly, a number of salient contributions were made by the "Keynesian" economists such as Harrod (1939), and Domar (1957), among others. Also, the "neoclassical" growth theorists such as Solow (1956) have made seminal contributions, which have provided a dominant framework for thinking about economic growth issues over the past three decades. Solow's framework will be briefly reviewed below to set the stage for highlighting the contributions by recent theorists.

As argued before, much of the new research in long-run economic growth has sought to explain what was previously unexplained; that is, what causes innovation? However, while recent growth theory has provided a richer structure with realistic attributes for modelling economic growth, it is important to recognize that the new growth theory has elements that both complement and substitute the orthodox neoclassical theory of economic growth. These features of the two theories might explain why some empirical studies support the new theory while other studies find support for the older neoclassical growth theory. The use of non-experimental heterogeneous data, as well as difficulties in controlling for unobserved country-specific factors and simultaneity or dual causality create additional complications in distinguishing between these two competing theories. Bernard and Durlauf (1995), in fact, demonstrate that along important dimensions, the neoclassical and new growth theories are observationally equivalent. New tools are continually being devised to overcome the known measurement problems and econometric difficulties with the objective of empirically comparing the two theories, as well as the availability of better quality data. This should make the task of testing the competing theories easier in the coming years.

Solow's (1956) growth theory, in its stripped-down model, asks the question: What are the determinants of sustainable growth of real income per person in an isolated economy producing a single product? This simple model assumes that the state of technology does not change over time, and that the labour force (or more generally natural resources; see Dasgupta and Heal (1974), Solow (1974) and Stiglitz (1974)) does not grow, and the capital stock does not depreciate. In such a model, the rate of growth of real income per person in the steady state equals the product of the saving rate and the marginal product of capital.

One of the implications of the above result is that the growth rate of real income per capita vanishes as the marginal product of capital approaches zero, which is an Inada (1963) condition. In other words, in Solow's economy, sustainable growth (beyond that provided by technical progress) is possible only if the marginal product is bounded from below by a positive constant. The analysis of equilibrium growth models that embody a positive bound for the marginal product is provided by Jones and Manuelli (1990) and Rebelo (1991).

Sustainable growth in the neoclassical growth framework, even in the absence of a non-vanishing marginal product of capital, can be guaranteed, provided that technical progress continues to take place. An important limitation of the neoclassical framework is that while it assigns innovation a central role in obtaining sustained growth in real income per capita, it does not explain why innovation takes place. One of the important features of the new growth theory has been to identify new channels for obtaining sustainable growth and to articulate how technological progress might result from purposive investment in R&D by commercial firms in search of profits. In order to set up a context for some of the contributions of the papers in this special issue, a brief overview of the main features of endogenous growth theory is provided below.

III Endogenous Growth Theory

The four major sources of economic growth are: (i) increases in the accumulation of capital goods or investment, (ii) increases in the quality of labour force, (iii) reallocation of resources from low-to-high growth/productivity sectors, and (iv) technological change.

The main motivation is to construct the new framework where the engine of growth is part of the model itself; that is, to formulate models in which sustainable growth is the result of the interaction of many optimizing agents. A critical empirical by-product of this endogenous growth literature is a body of new insights which can explain why persistent cross-country variations in growth rates are observed. It also lends new insight to the issue of whether the levels and/or growth rates of income and productivity across countries are converging; it suggests that convergence patterns are likely to be far more complex than may be captured by simple cross-country regressions. Empirical evidence of this may be found in Durlauf and Johnson (1995). While the debate about whether countries are converging is important, there are similar important issues with respect to regions and industries.

Another focus in endogenous growth theory has been to consider whether policy variables such as the provision of public services, trade policy, fiscal policy, social policy as it affects income distribution, legal and social norms such as property rights, and the provision of copyright laws, influence growth rates. These variables affect the level of the real income per capita rather than its growth rate in the neoclassical model. Endogenous growth theory also seeks a richer understanding of how economic growth is propagated across countries through channels such as international trade, capital flows, and the direct transfer of ideas and technology. These channels have important implications for answering questions concerning both convergence of growth across countries on the one hand and the broader issues of comparative growth on the other.

The resurgence of interest in growth theory may be linked to the twin contributions by Romer (1986) and Lucas (1988), who redirected the traditional focus on the accumulation of physical capital as a transitory source of growth to the accumulation of skills through education and training, or more generally through increasing returns in physical and human capital accumulation due to spillover effects. Building on the foundation that Solow had established a quarter of century earlier, these theorists incorporated technological change and imperfect competition to explain economic growth.

There are important interrelationships between the discovery and application of new technology on the one hand, and between competition and technology on the other. In order to acquire temporary market power, firms often invest considerable amounts of resources in the discovery and development of new ideas, products and processes. However, industries where R&D expenditure is important do not fit the economic model of competition since firms produce differentiated products using proprietary technologies sometimes unique to the firm. In addition, knowledge creation may involve spillover effects or positive externalities. However, the competitive advantage of knowledge can be quickly eliminated as other firms come out with their own version of the same products. Since some firms would be unsuccessful in the race for variety, they will simply bear the loss. Discovery of knowledge may be a no-win situation for many firms, unless firms are accorded patents on the creation of knowledge. Given that the spillover effects are important, there is an interrelationship between technological change and imperfect competition. While technological progress largely results from R&D expenditure or searches for new ideas, products, and improved ways of producing goods and services, there can be progress through experience or learning-by-doing. Indeed there may be important synergies between progress resulting from R&D expenditure and learning-by-doing.

In developing this new growth theory, Romer and Lucas relied on Arrow's mechanism of learning-by-doing as well as Uzawa's (1965) insight that skill acquisition augments the efficiency of labour. Accordingly, the long-run growth rate depends on both time spent on acquisition of skills and the effectiveness with which new skills are acquired. A critical feature of this framework is that the accumulation of skills may exhibit spillover effects, whether locally, nationally, or globally. Thus, learning-by-doing in a particular manufacturing plant can have important secondary effects for plants with similar technologies. Similarly, there can be important spillovers to society at large, from the collective acquisition of skills due to investment in education and training. The secondary benefits to society from either learning-by-doing or investment in education and training may even exceed the direct effects (Coe and Helpman, 1993). The existence of spillover effects provides a rationale for government subsidization of education and training, although it is unclear what form the policy intervention might take or what instruments would produce the desired results.

Another important channel for obtaining sustainable growth exists when an entrepreneur engages in developing new brands of horizontally differentiated products (cf. Romer, 1990, among others) and/or improves the quality of existing varieties of products (see Aghion and Howitt, 1992) by investing in firm-level, privately supported R&D. The use of this channel has been documented by economic historians such as Rosenberg (1963) for the machine tool industry, where companies chose to invest in the development of new technologies through investment in privately funded R&D expenditure. One of the principal motivations for expenditure on the R&D is to obtain temporary market power. R&D therefore provides an alternative to prices as a strategic variable for firms competing for a competitive edge.

It is important to note that innovation-based growth invariably involves risk-taking behaviour on the part of entrepreneurs in search of profits. The limited liability feature of incorporation provides a legal framework for risk sharing. The institution of patents grants firms investing in R&D temporary monopoly power to appropriate some part of the return on inventive activity. However, since patent systems are not exclusive, some firms try to keep their inventions as trade secrets. Investment in R&D not only adds to the knowledge of the firm, but also to the knowledge of society. Also, the accumulation of knowledge leads to a reduction of future costs for innovation. Thus, profitability can be sustained through R&D expenditure over a long time period. Growth in R&D driven models is constrained by resource availability (that is, on the margin, a variable worker can either be employed in the research labs or in manufacturing plants) on the one hand, and by market incentives on the other (cf. Helpman, 1992). This channel unleashes powerful forces that can either speed up or retard the growth rate, depending upon the relative strength of the two opposing effects. Also, when placed in an open world economy, country-specific economic policies can affect not only the home country but also the trading partners. The details about the mechanisms and a discussion of difficult policy issues are provided by Grossman and Helpman (1991, and references therein).

One of the predictions of the neoclassical growth theory is that the growth rate of real income per capita of countries with identical preferences, technologies, and population growth will converge over time due to higher rates of physical investment in the initially poorer countries, as capital moves in search of the higher rates of return. The recent resurgence of interest in convergence issues represents an extension of the comparative growth studies of Abramovitz (1979), Maddison (1982), Baumol (1986) and others, which were mainly based on data for the industrial countries. More recently, this resurgence has been extended to larger samples of countries by many researchers making use of the much broader sample of countries in the data set developed by Summers and Heston (1991) and their colleagues. Aside from the broader country coverage, perhaps the most important feature of this new data set is the measurement and application of purchasing power parities, thus permitting studies to compare levels as well as rates of growth of output per capita. To the extent that the initial set of studies that made use of the larger data samples had a theoretical agenda, it was driven by two apparently competing theoretical visions. On the one hand were those like Mankiw, Romer and Weil (1992) and Barro (1991), who took the evidence of convergence of growth rates of GDP per capita among the industrial countries and the evidence of conditional convergence in global samples (after adjusting for differences savings rates and other control variables) as support for the continued use of a simple version of the Solow (1956) model, in which each country is assumed to have equal access to the same set of production possibilities.

Taking a different tack were those who saw the evidence as showing either divergence (Romer 1986) or lack of sufficiently high investment flows from the rich to the poor economies (Lucas 1988). Studies such as Quah (1992; 1993a,b; 1996), Bernard and Durlauf (1995) and Durlauf and Johnson (1995) further deduced formal evidence against the convergence hypothesis, even when limited to OECD countries. This alternative view of the evidence was used to support the idea of nonconvexities at the national level to some form of accumulation, whether of R&D, skills, or physical capital, that would permit large or rich countries to grow faster than smaller or poorer countries. Subsequent more direct tests of the simple neoclassical production function, in which productivity residuals rather than simply rates of growth of GDP per capita are treated as the object of study, have shown [from the pioneering empirical work of Arrow, Chenery, Minhas and Solow (1961) through that of Dowrick and Gemmell (1991), Coe and Helpman (1993), Helliwell and Chung (1991) and others] that countries do not have equally efficient access to the same technologies, and that most of the convergence among the industrial countries over the post-war period has been in the rates of growth of the Solow residuals.

IV An Overview of Papers

Eight papers in this monograph provide a selection of contributions on empirical questions or empirical-related questions concerning long-run economic growth of aggregate and regional output or of productivity. A number of other symposia have appeared, and many more will undoubtedly appear in the future. For example, the *Journal of Political Economy* (1990S), the *Quarterly Journal of Economics* (May, 1991), the *Oxford Review of Economic Policy* (Dec. 1992), the *Journal of Economic Theory* (1992) and the *Scandinavian Journal of Economics* (1993) devoted either an entire regular or a supplementary issue to the topic of economic growth. In addition, a number of prominent lectures on economic growth have been published. A partial list of special lectures might include papers by Stern (1991), Helpman (1992), Hahn (1992), Solow (1993), among others.

The contributions in this collection are grouped into four broad themes: (i) the testable implications of various growth theories and modelling, and identification of common shocks (two papers); (ii) international trade and growth linkages (two papers); (iii) analysis of co-movements and convergence at regional levels of income (two papers); (iv) public services-growth, and money-growth linkages (two papers). An important caveat to this categorization is that in several instances the topics are interrelated.

The lead paper by Philippe Aghion and Peter Howitt derives and spells out some of the testable implications of a Schumpeterian theory of creative destruction. According to this theory, spillover effects may be positive for subsequent adopters, but are likely to be negative for those with prior investments in capital made obsolete by more recent innovations.

The second paper in this section, by Lucrezia Reichlin and Mario Forni, develops and uses a method to identify common shocks. They illustrate the usefulness of their method by providing estimates of the impact of shocks on 450 U.S. manufacturing sectors over the period 1958–86. They find that innovations tend, in the first year, to depress output and increase aggregate productivity, with subsequent effects positive for both output and productivity, but larger for productivity than for output. Aggregate non-technological ("demand") shocks are found to have a positive effect on output and a zero effect on productivity. Sectoral results, by contrast, show that non-technological shocks have a positive impact on both output and productivity, similar to the pattern found for technological shocks.

The two papers in the second section (Raymond Riezman, Peter Summers and Charles Whiteman; Richard Harris) consider various issues relating to international trade and economic growth. The paper by Richard Harris uses calibration and simulation techniques to illustrate the potential size of dynamic gains from trade. The basic argument is that opening to trade first raises income from the usual increases in static efficiency, and the higher income levels then induce greater investment in human capital, which in turn leads to higher rates of future growth. The simulations show that the dynamic effects are large relative to the static efficiency gains from trade liberalization, and the transitional dynamics are long lasting.

The article by Raymond Riezman, Peter Summers and Charles Whiteman addresses the long-studied question of whether exports are the source or the consequence of growth. Their initial bivariate results tend to support the results of previous researchers, in that only 16 of their 126 countries show evidence of export-led growth, as evidenced by unidirectional Granger causality from exports to growth. However, when they estimate a three-variable system with allowance for the roles of imports and the role of investment and human capital, they find that about half of the countries satisfy their export-led growth criterion. The results are sensitive to the time horizon used, and differ by horizon across countries as well as over time for individual countries.

The papers by Danny Quah, and Andrew Bernard and Charles Jones are concerned with co-movements and convergence issues relating to regional fluctuations and growth. Danny Quah develops and uses new tools for analyzing the significant two-way interaction that exists between disaggregate and aggregate behaviour: disaggregates affect aggregates, and aggregates affect disaggregates. Mainstream macroeconomics, in large part, has been concerned with the dynamic response of aggregate variables to aggregate shocks. The important interaction between the disaggregates and aggregates is not taken into account. He analyzes co-movements in aggregate and regional incomes. His technique is to work with the evolution of the cross-sectional distribution of per capita incomes and to analyze the relative importance of regional and aggregate disturbances. He finds some evidence of "waves" of regional dynamics, with the sources of the disturbances moving from one state, or group of states, to another.

Bernard and Jones use both cross-section and time-series methods to test for the convergence of levels of output per worker among U.S. states and industries. Like others, they find that the extractive industries pose special problems of measurement. However, they find more evidence of convergence in both mining and manufacturing than in other industries, while construction and trade show no evidence of convergence over the 1963–1989 data period. They find little indication that changes in industry shares have played an important role in convergence, two-thirds of which has taken place within manufacturing. They note the apparent contrast between these cross-state results and earlier cross-country research showing a bigger role for convergence in the service sectors.

The final section contains two papers. The paper by Steve Dowrick uses panel data for 116 countries to disentangle the simultaneous relations between government consumption and per capita GDP growth. He first confirms the simple correlation between the growth of real GDP per capita and the growth of government consumption, and then tries to factor out the effect stemming from higher incomes to higher demands for government services. This removes the significant positive influence running from government spending to growth. When he accounts separately for the price and the quantity of government services in the same simultaneous framework, he finds that higher prices of government services reduce growth, while higher quantities of government services increase growth.

The last paper by Paul Evans nests and tests admittedly special cases of exogenous and endogenous growth in a framework implying that if money is not neutral in the short run, and if growth is endogenous, money will not be neutral in the long run either. He uses data from 27 countries over the period 1960–1992 to show that money is not positively non-neutral in the long run, leading him to infer that growth cannot be endogenous, given his and other evidence that money is non-neutral in the short run.

V Concluding Remarks

While the new growth theory provides many new channels for achieving growth, empirical work that incorporates multiple features of the theory is still in its infancy. There is little doubt that the next few years will see a large expansion in our understanding of the econometrics and empirics of growth. We are hopeful that the selection of empirical papers in this monograph will serve as a source of inspiration to some empirical researchers and students of macroeconomics who are interested in participating in this endeavour.

References

Abramovitz M (1979) Rapid growth potential and its realization: The experience of capitalist economies in the postwar period. In: Malinvaud E (ed) Economic Growth and Resources. Macmillan, London 1–30

Aghion P, Howitt P (1992) A model of growth through creative destruction. Econometrica 60:323–51

Arrow KJ, Chenery HB, Minhas BS, Solow RM (1961) Capital-labour substitution and economic efficiency. Review of Economics and Statistics 43:225–50

Barro RJ (1991) Economic growth in a cross section of countries. Quaterly Journal of Economics 106:407–44

Baumol WJ (1986) Productivity growth, convergence and welfare: What the long-run data show. American Economic Review 76:1072–85

Bernard AB, Durlauf SN (1995) Convergence in international output. Journal of Applied Econometrics 10:97–108

Bernard AB, Durlauf SN (1996) Interpreting tests of the convergence hypothesis. Journal of Econometrics (forthcoming)

Coe DT, Helpman E (1993) International R&D spillovers. European Economic Review 39:859–887

Dasgupta P, Heal GM (1974) The optimal depletion of exhaustible resources. Review of Economic Studies (Symposium of the Economics of Exhaustible Resources) 3–28

Domar E (1957) Essays in the theory of economic growth. Oxford University Press, New York

Dowrick S, Gemmell N (1991) Industrialisation, catching up and economic growth: A comparative study across the world's capitalist economies. Economic Journal 101:263–275

Durlauf SN, Johnson PA (1995) Multiple regimes and cross-country growth behaviour. Journal of Econometrics (forthcoming)

Grossman GM, Helpman E (1991) Innovation and growth in the global economy. (Cambridge, MIT Press)

Hahn FH (1992) On growth theory. Forthcoming in Economics in a Changing World (Proceeding of the Tenth International Economic Association World Congress in Moscow). Macmillan, London

Harrod RF (1939) An essay in dynamic theory. Economic Journal 49:14–33

Harris DJ (1987) Classical theory growth. In the New Palgrave Dictionary of Economics. Macmillan, London

Helliwell JF, Chung A (1991) Macroeconomic convergence: International transmission of growth and technical progress. In: Hooper P, Richardson JD (eds) International Economic Transactions: Issues in Measurement and Empirical Research. Chicago, University of Chicago Press 388–436

Helpman E (1992) Endogenous macroeconomic growth theory. European Economic Review 36: 237–67
Inada K-L (1963) Endogenous technical progress and steady growth. Reivew of Economic Studies 36:99–107
Jones L, Manuelli RA (1990) A convex model of equilibrium growth: Theory and policy implications. Journal of Political Economy 98:1008–38
Lucas RE (1988) On the mechanics of economic development. Journal of Monetary Economics 22:3–42
Maddison A (1982) Phases of capitalist development. Oxford, Oxford University Press
Mankiw G, Romer D, Weil D (1992) A contribution to the empriics of economic growth. Quarterly Journal of Economics 107:407–37
Quah D (1992) International pattern of growth: Persistence in cross-country disparities. Working paper, London School of Economics
Quah D (1993a) Galton's fallacy and tests of convergence hypothesis. Scandinavian Journal of Economics 95(4):427–443
Quah D (1993b) Empirics cross-section dynamics in economic growth. European Economic Review 37(2/3):426–434
Quah D (1996) Convergence empirics across economies with (some) capital mobility. Journal of Economic Growth (forthcoming)
Raj B, Slottje DJ (1995) Productivity slowdown in the United States, unit root and trend: A peak through the structural break window. Wilfrid Laurier University
Rebelo S (1991) Long run policy analysis and long run growth. Journal of Political Economy 99:500–521
Romer PM (1986) Increasing returns and long-run growth. Journal of Political Economy 94:1002–37
Romer PM (1990) Endogenous technological change. Journal of Political Economy 98:S71–S108
Romer PM (1991) Increasing returns and new developments in the theory of growth. In: Barnett W (ed) Equilibrium Theory and Applications: Proceeding of the 6th International Symposium in Economic Theory and Econometrics Ch 5:83–110 Cambridge University Press
Rosenberg N (1963) Technical change in the machine tool industry: 1840–1910. Journal of Economic History 23:414–446
Schumpeter J (1942) Capitalism, socialism and democracy. Harper, New York
Solow RM (1956) A contribution to the theory of economic growth. Quarterly Journal of Economics 70:65–94
Solow RM (1974) Intergenerational equity and exhaustive resources. Review of Economic Studies (Symposium on the Economics of Exhaustive Resources) 29–45
Solow RM (1993) Learning from "Learning by doing." Third Annual Arrow Lectures, Department of Economics, Stanford University
Stern N (1991) The determinants of growth. Economic Journal 101:122–33
Stiglitz JE (1974) Growth with exhaustible natural resources: Efficient and optimal growth path. Review of Economic Studies (Symposium on the Economics of Exhaustible Resources) 123–37
Summers R, Heston A (1991) The penn world table (Mark 5): An expanded set of international comparisons, 1950–1988. Quarterly Journal of Economics 106:327–68
Uzawa H (1965) Optimal technical change in an aggregative model of economic growth. International Economic Review 6:18–31

I Testable Implications of Various Growth Theories and Modelling and Identification of Common Shocks

The Observational Implications of Schumpeterian Growth Theory

PHILIPPE AGHION

Nuffield College, Oxford OX1 1NF, England

PETER HOWITT

Institut D'Economie Industrielle, Université des Sciences Sociales, Place Anatole France, 31042 Toulouse cedex, France

Abstract: This paper obtains and discusses alternative testable implications of the Schumpeterian theory of creative destruction for economic growth.

Key Words: Growth theory, creative destruction, empirical implications

JEL Classification System-Numbers: O40

1 Introduction

Schumpeterian growth theory seeks to explain economic growth as arising from industrial innovations.[1] It differs from more aggregative human-capital based theories in being more specific about how knowledge grows, is used, and generates rents, and in emphasizing the reallocative aspect of the growth process, an aspect dramatized by Schumpeter's idea of "creative destruction." In the interest of isolating what are thought to be important effects, the theory has been developed so far in terms of highly stylized models that omit too much of reality to be taken seriously for purposes of empirical testing. Although empirical work has begun on calibrating and estimating Schumpeterian theory,[2] we still have no general systematic statement of the theory, indicating the observational implications that distinguish it from competing theories. Such a statement is necessary if the theory is ever to provide more than emotional gratification to its proponents. One does not have to be a strict Popperian to suspect that a theory that cannot indicate what empirical facts would refute it, other than facts that

---

[1] See Segerstrom, Anant and Dinopoulos (1990), Romer (1990), Aghion and Howitt (1992), and Grossman and Helpman (1991).

[2] Caballero and Jaffe (1993), Arroyo, Dinopoulos and Donald (1994) and Klenow (1994).

would also refute all its competitors, is saying nothing new and meaningful about how economies function.

The purpose of this paper is to make a first attempt to indicate such a set of observational implications. We take our (1992) model of creative destruction, extend it by introducing many sectors, less than perfect intertemporal substitutability of consumption, physical capital, and labour-market frictions, and draw out its corresponding observational implications. Because the Schumpeterian model has a more specific focus on industrial innovations, it implies that several variables should affect it in ways that are not visible from the more aggregative perspective of human-capital based theory. Furthermore, Schumpeterian theory has important implications for variables other than growth, in particular for gross flows in the labour market, unemployment, job creation and destruction, rates of entry and exit by firms, the rate of new product introduction, the rate of capital obsolescence, the level of R&D activity, and the rate of patenting.

Only closed economies are studied, and only long-run, steady-state equilibria are examined. Thus the implications drawn here could be tested by comparing long-run average data across several countries, or by looking at long historical eras within a given country. Of course this raises familiar problems of lack of homogeneity in the data. We leave the derivation of out-of steady state dynamics for a later exercise, while noting that there are too many features of business cycles omitted from this purely supply-side equilibrium analysis for us to take many short-run predictions seriously without a lot of further elaboration.

2 A Generalized Schumpeterian Model

In this section we present an extended version of our (1992) model of growth through creative destruction. In this model, there is a single final output, produced by a continuum of intermediate goods indexed on the unit interval, according to the production function:[3]

$$Y = \int_0^1 A_i F(y_i) di \tag{1}$$

where Y is gross output, y_i the flow output of intermediate good i, F is a production function with positive and diminishing marginal product, and A_i a

[3] Diminishing marginal product of the sole factor y_i can be rationalized by supposing that for each sector i there is another factor that must be combined with intermediate good i in order to produce final output, and which is in fixed supply. For simplicity we have suppressed the notation indicating the presence of these other sector-specific factors.

productivity parameter attached to the latest version of intermediate good i. Gross output can be used interchangeably as a consumption or capital good, or as an input into the transaction process in the labour market.

Each intermediate good is produced according to the production function:

$$y_i = G(K_i^p/A_i, N_i) \tag{2}$$

where K_i^p and N_i are the inputs of capital and labour into production in sector i, and G is a regular constant-returns production function. We divide K_i^p by A_i in (2) to indicate that successive vintages of the intermediate good are produced by increasingly capital-intensive techniques.[4]

Improvements in the productivity parameters come through an innovation process. In each sector the Poisson arrival rate of a new version of the intermediate good produced in that sector is:

$$\lambda\mu(K^r/A, H) \equiv \lambda\varphi(k^r) \;, \qquad \text{with } k^r \equiv K^r/A \;, \qquad \varphi' > 0 \;, \qquad \varphi'' < 0 \tag{3}$$

where K^r is the input of capital into R&D, H is the fixed supply of skilled labour that is supplied inelastically for R&D, λ is a parameter indicating the productivity of R&D, μ is a regular constant-returns production function, and A is the maximum of all the productivity parameters A_i in the economy. We refer to A as the leading-edge productivity parameter. We assume that the same resource mix is used in R&D in each sector, because the payoff is the same. Specifically, each innovation at date t results in a new intermediate good in that sector which embodies the leading-edge productivity parameter, regardless of how advanced or retarded the previous vintage was in that sector.

Growth in the leading edge occurs from innovations. Specifically, we suppose that:

$$\dot{A} = A\lambda\varphi(k^r) \tag{4}$$

Equation (4) indicates the research spillover common in Schumpeterian models, according to which each innovator's discoveries contribute marginally to the increase in the general knowledge that is available to everyone doing R&D in the future. One could imagine that there is an infinite list of techniques, each embodying a productivity parameter whose log equals that technique's number in the list, and that R&D consists of discovering these techniques one at a timc. Each discovery can be implemented only in the chosen sector of the innovator, but its discovery allows the next innovator to discover a slightly better technique in another sector.

We will be interested in a steady state in which capital, gross output, consumption, the real wage rate, and the leading-edge all grow at the same constant

---

[4] The obvious fact that more complex technologies require the use of more capital rationalizes a negative effect of A_i on G. The further assumption that G is homogeneous of degree zero in K_i and A_i is made in order to guarantee a steady state. Technically, if the production functions G and F were Cobb-Douglas, then a steady state would not require this additional homogeneity assumption.

rate g, and the distribution of relative productivities $F_a(A_i/A)$ is constant over time. It follows from (4) that the growth rate is directly determined by the flow of innovations:

$$g = \lambda\varphi(k^r) \tag{5}$$

To determine the level of R&D, note that the cost of capital to a research firm is $r + \delta_k$, where r is the rate of interest and δ_k is the proportional rate of depreciation of capital, an exogenous constant. This must equal the marginal expected return to research capital at each date t:

$$r + \delta_k = \lambda\varphi'(k^r)V_t/A_t \tag{6}$$

where V_t is the value of an innovation at date t.

A successful innovator uses his idea to set up a firm and produce the newly invented good, protected from competition by an infinitely lived patent. He drives out the previous incumbent in that sector by undercutting his price, and produces under a local monopoly until driven out by the next innovation in that sector. This is the central idea of creative destruction. He sells the good to a competitive final output sector, in which the price equals the marginal product $A_tF'(y)$. Thus if he is still surviving at date s, he will be earning a flow of monopoly rents equal to:

$$\pi_{s,t} = \max\{A_tF'(y)y - c_{s,t}y\} \tag{7}$$

where $c_{s,t}$ is his unit cost.[5]

When a monopolist is replaced, we assume that his capital has no second-hand value (in the language of growth theory we assume putty-clay capital). Hence his cost of capital is:

$$\bar{r} = r + \delta_k + \lambda\varphi(k^r) \tag{8}$$

where the last term is the expected rate of obsolescence resulting from being replaced by a new entrant.

To determine the cost of labour, assume that workers always bargain for a wage proportional to the leading-edge technology: $w_t = \omega A_t$, and that the firm must pay the setup cost ΓA_t each time it hires a worker. There is an exogenous rate δ_w at which workers quit for non-economic reasons, as in the literature on job-matching (Pissarides, 1990). Hence the cost of labour to the intermediate firm at any date s will be:

$$\overline{w}_s = A_s\overline{\omega} = A_s[\omega + [r + \delta_w + \lambda\varphi(k^r) - g]\Gamma] \tag{9}$$

where the creative destruction term $\lambda\varphi(k^r)$ is offset by the capitalization term g,

---

[5] We assume implicitly that the previous incumbent ceases to threaten the newly arrived firm once he has ceased production, which is why (7) includes no competitive constraint on the monopolist's choice of y.

which exists because the setup cost of hiring labour rises at the rate g, and hence confers a steady capital gain to the firm on its stock of workers.[6]

It follows from (2), (8), (9), and the fact that the intermediate firm's production function exhibits constant returns to scale, that the unit cost can be written as:

$$c_{s,t} = A_t \gamma(\bar{r}, \bar{\omega} e^{g(s-t)}) \ ; \qquad \gamma_1 > 0 \ , \qquad \gamma_2 > 0 \tag{10}$$

and the firm's profit and employment can be expressed as:

$$\pi_{s,t} = A_t \hat{\pi}(\bar{r}, \bar{\omega} e^{g(s-t)}) \ ; \qquad \hat{\pi}_1 < 0 \ , \qquad \hat{\pi}_2 < 0 \tag{11}$$

and

$$N_i = \hat{n}(\bar{r}, \bar{\omega} e^{g(s-t)}) \ ; \qquad \hat{n}_1 < 0 \ , \qquad \hat{n}_2 < 0 \ . \tag{12}$$

The value of an innovation at date t can be expressed as the expected present value of the rents that will accrue until the producer is replaced. The time until replacement is distributed exponentially with parameter $\lambda\varphi(k^r)$. Therefore:

$$\begin{cases} V_t = \int_0^\infty e^{-(r+\lambda\varphi(k^r))\tau} A_t \hat{\pi}(\bar{r}, \bar{\omega} e^{g\tau}) d\tau \\ \quad \equiv A_t v(r + \lambda\varphi(k^r), \bar{r}, \bar{\omega}, g) \ ; \qquad v_i < 0 \ , \qquad i = 1 \ldots 4 \ . \end{cases} \tag{13}$$

Finally, we assume that the economy is populated by infinitely lived individuals whose lifetime utility depends upon the path of consumption, c_t:

$$U = \int_0^\infty e^{-\rho t} \frac{c_t^{1-\sigma} - 1}{1-\sigma} dt \ , \qquad \sigma > 0 \ , \qquad \sigma \neq 1 \tag{14}$$

where ρ is the common rate of time preference and σ the common elasticity of marginal utility. It follows from the usual conditions of intertemporal utility maximization that in a steady state, with consumption growing at the rate g, the rate of interest must satisfy:

$$r = \rho + \sigma g \tag{15}$$

3 Empirical Determinants of Growth

From (3), (5), (6), (8), (9), (13), and (15) we find:

$$\rho + \sigma g + \delta_k = \lambda\mu_1(k^r, H) v(\rho + (\sigma + 1)g, \rho + \delta_k + (\sigma + 1)g, \omega + (\rho + \sigma g + \delta_w)\Gamma, g) \tag{16}$$

6 Pissarides (1990, ch. 2) has an extensive discussion of the capitalization effect in a similar context.

and

$$g = \lambda\mu(k^r, H) \ . \tag{17}$$

Equations (16) and (17) can be solved simultaneously for the productivity-adjusted level of R&D capital k^r and the rate of growth g in terms of all the exogenous variables of the model.

Equation (16) is a "research arbitrage" equation. On the left-hand side is the required steady-state expected rate of return on R&D, which is increasing in the growth rate of consumption g for the usual reasons of time preference. On the right-hand side is the actual rate of return, which is decreasing in the growth rate because (a) more growth raises the equilibrium rate of interest, which is the rate at which the returns from a successful innovation will be capitalized and which also has a positive effect on the costs of both capital and labour that determine the flow of profits to be capitalized (these effects correspond to the three places on the RHS of (16) where g is premultiplied by σ), (b) more growth will raise the rate of creative destruction, shortening the expected duration of any monopoly rents, which has a further positive effect on the rate at which a prospective innovator will discount the returns to a successful innovation and which further raises the cost of capital to the successful innovator (these correspond to the remaining effects of g in the first two terms of the $v(\ )$ function), and (c) more growth means that the wages that must be paid by someone wishing to exploit a successful innovation will rise at a faster rate (this is the reason for the fourth argument of the $v(\ )$ function). Moreover, the right-hand side of (16) is a decreasing function of the R&D intensity k^r because of diminishing returns to capital in research.

It follows that the research arbitrage equation (16) can be represented by a downward sloping curve as shown in Figure 1 below. As indicated above, more growth will raise the required rate of return and reduce the actual rate of return expected in R&D, hence reducing the steady-state equilibrium intensity of

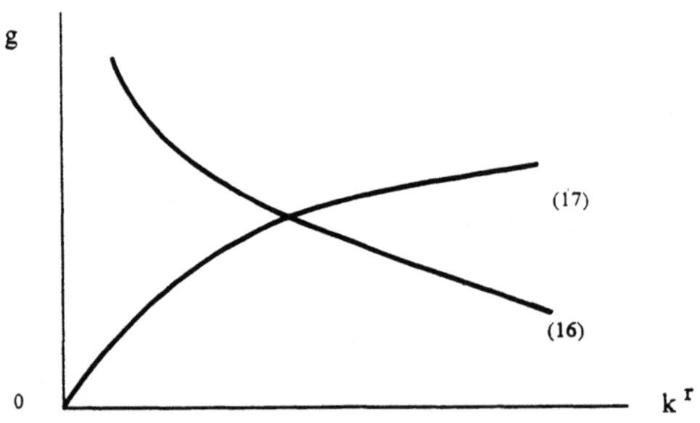

Fig. 1. The determination of growth (g) and R&D intensity (k^r) in steady state, by the intersection of the research arbitrage curve (16) with the growth curve (17)

R&D. Likewise, the "growth equation" (17) can be represented by an upward sloping curve, showing that more research will produce a faster increase in technological knowledge and hence a faster rate of growth. Using the above-indicated sign restrictions it is easy to verify:

Proposition 1:

(a) The long run growth rate g can be written as

$$g = \hat{g}(\rho, \sigma, \delta_k, \delta_w, \omega, \Gamma, \lambda, H) ,$$

where the function $\hat{g}$ is decreasing in its first six arguments and increasing in the last two.

(b) The productivity-adjusted level of R&D capital k^r can be written as

$$k^r = \hat{k}^r(\rho, \sigma, \delta_k, \delta_w, \omega, \Gamma, \lambda, H)$$

where the function $\hat{k}^r$ is decreasing in its first six arguments, and where $\partial\hat{k}^r/\partial\lambda$ has the same sign as one minus the (absolute) elasticity of the function:

$$V(g) \equiv v(\rho + (\sigma + 1)g, \rho + \delta_k + (\sigma + 1)g,$$
$$\omega + (\rho + \sigma g + \delta_w)\Gamma, g)/(\rho + \sigma g + \delta_k) .$$

The formal proof of Proposition 1 is relegated to the Appendix, since all of the effects on the growth rate can be understood intuitively in terms of Figure 1. That is, each of the first six arguments of the function $\hat{g}$ shifts the research arbitrage curve to the left, thus reducing the steady-state level of research and the growth rate. For example, an increase in the rate of time preference ρ discourages growth because, as indicated earlier, it raises the required rate of return while diminishing the actual rate of return. Each of the last two arguments of $\hat{g}(\ )$ shifts the research arbitrage curve to the right and the growth curve upwards.

All of the variables in Proposition 1 are measurable in principle, although in practice many of them are hard to measure accurately, especially the taste variables ρ and σ. The negative dependency of growth on these taste parameters, however, does not distinguish this from other endogenous growth models, most of which use the same intertemporal-utility maximization by an infinitely lived representative consumer as the basis for saving decisions. The fact that the productivity λ of R&D and the supply H of skilled workers have a positive effect on growth is also perhaps not surprising, but it does help to explain why it has been so hard to find cross-country evidence on the productivity of human capital. Specifically, to the extent that traditional empirical proxies for human capital such as years of schooling have a counterpart in the above model, it is in the supply of skilled workers. While the theory predicts that this variable has a positive effect on the growth of output it does not necessarily imply a significant effect on the level of output, as it would if it entered an aggregate production function like any other factor of production.

Proposition 1 also indicates that long-run growth will be affected, *ceteris paribus*, by various labour-market variables, such as the level of real wages, the rate of job-separation, ard the cost of hiring. An increase in any of these variables would reduce the profitability of monopolizing an intermediate good sector, which would reduce the profitability of R&D, the payoff to which is the prospect of gaining such a monopoly, and hence would reduce growth.

The empirical implications of Schumpeterian theory are not exhausted by Proposition 1, however, because the theory also has implications for how growth should covary with other endogenous variables. For example, it suggests that in the absence of changes in the taste variables σ and ρ, growth should be positively correlated with the rate of interest, although again, as discussed earlier, this would not distinguish Schumpeterian theory from other endogenous growth theories even if the taste variables were easily measurable.

An endogenous variable at the heart of Schumpeterian theory is the level of R&D. The (productivity-adjusted) value of resources (skilled labour and capital) put into R&D equals the flow of income in the R&D sector, which is the product of the flow of innovations $\lambda\mu$ and the value of each innovation v_t. From (13) we can express this as:

$$\overline{R\&D} = gv^*(g;\rho,\sigma,\delta_k,\delta_w,\omega,\Gamma)\ . \tag{18}$$

Equation (18) shows that although there is a relationship between growth and the level of R&D, it is not as straightforward as one might hope for. This is because an increase in growth will reduce the value of innovations, which in turn will reduce R&D if the elasticity of v^* with respect to g is greater than unity. We can however use (18) to characterize the relationship in terms of the following proposition:

Proposition 2: The equilibrium ratio of $\overline{R\&D}$ to g can be expressed as a function of g and the first six arguments of $\hat{g}(\ )$, and is decreasing in each argument.

There are three other endogenous variables that the theory says should covary positively with growth because their values equal g in the theory. The first of those is the flow of new patents. According to this theory, each innovation is accompanied by a new patent, and the flow-rate of innovations equals the long-run rate of growth. The second is the flow of entry of new firms. Each innovation is implemented by a new firm that takes over from the previous incumbent in one sector of the economy. The third is the flow of new products. (See Klenow, 1994, for an empirical study based on this variable.) Each innovation introduces a new product.

Of course it is easy to see that even a slight generalization of the theory would destroy the exact identity between these three variables and the rate of growth, because not all industries and countries have the same propensity to patent, because in practice some innovations are carried out by existing firms, and because some innovations can take the form of new processes rather than new products. A weaker but more robust testable implication is that:

Proposition 3: The long-run rate of growth should be positively correlated with the flow of patents, the flow of entry of new firms, and the flow of new product introduction.

The central role of creative destruction in Schumpeterian growth theory can be tested by looking at the correlation between growth and two other variables, the flow of exit of firms and the rate of obsolescence of capital. The former is identical to the flow of entry in a steady-state equilibrium, while the latter is the rate of arrival of new innovations, which we have seen is equal to the rate of growth. Hence:

Proposition 4: The long-run rate of growth should be positively correlated with the flow of exit of firms and with the rate of obsolescence of capital.

4 Labour Market Variables

Proposition 1 showed that a number of exogenous labour market variables should have a definite effect on the rate of growth. There are also a number of endogenous labour market variables that should be correlated in a definite manner with the growth rate. The first of these is the rate of job separation – the fraction of labour-market matches that break up per period. In the above model, this is just the fraction of those who leave for exogenous reasons δ_w plus the fraction working in firms that are replaced by an innovation. The latter is the fraction of sectors in which a new innovation arrives per period of time, which is just the rate of growth g. (We are assuming that δ_w is large enough that firms do not need to engage in layoffs in order to have employment decrease over time in response to the increase in real wages over time.) Because of this, we have:

Proposition 5: The long-run rate of growth should be positively correlated with the rate of job separation.

Another key endogenous labour market variable is the gross flow of job creation. As measured by Davis and Haltiwanger (1992) this is just the rate at which new employment increases within production establishments with positive employment growth during the period. In the above model, the only firms that increase their employment are those that have just arrived with a new innovation. The rate at which they do so is the rate of new firm creation g times the level of employment at each newly created firm $\hat{n}(\bar{r}, \bar{\omega})$. (Recall (12).) We have:

Proposition 6: The ratio of gross job creation to growth can be expressed as a function of the rate of growth and the first six arguments of the $\hat{g}$ function, and is decreasing in each argument.

The proof of Proposition 6 is given in the Appendix.

To discuss the rate of unemployment, we need to make use of the fact, which we also demonstrate in the Appendix, that the steady state distribution $F_A(A_i, t)$ of productivities across sectors at each date t is uniform on the interval (0, A). From this, we have that total employment in the economy will be:[7]

$$L = \int_0^1 \hat{n}[\rho + (1+\sigma)g + \delta_k, (\omega + (\rho + \sigma g + \delta_w)\Gamma)/a]\,da \tag{19}$$

and the rate of unemployment will be

$$u = 1 - L/N\ . \tag{20}$$

It follows directly from (19), (20), and the sign restrictions in (12) that:

Proposition 7: The rate of unemployment can be described as a function of the rate of growth and of the first six arguments of the $\hat{g}$ function. It is increasing in each argument.

The effect of the growth rate on unemployment is a direct consequence of the creative destruction at the heart of the Schumpeterian model. When growth goes up, so does the cost of capital and labour. Even in the limiting case of infinite intertemporal substitution, where $\sigma = 0$ and there is no effect on the rate of interest, an increase in growth will raise the cost of capital by increasing the rate of creative destruction. Since labour and capital are complements in production (that is, $G_{12} > 0$ because of concavity and constant returns), therefore the increase in the cost of capital alone is enough to cause the demand for labour to decrease when growth rises.

It should be mentioned that a somewhat deeper analysis of the relationship between growth and unemployment, such as the one we conducted in Aghion and Howitt (1994), would allow the possibility for this effect of growth on unemployment to be offset by a capitalization effect as described above. More

---

7 To verify that the expression for the cost of labour in (19) is the same as in (12) note that at date s the vintage of firms for which $A_i/A = a$ is t such that $e^{g(t-s)} = a$.

specifically, the capitalization effect would no longer be exactly offset by creative destruction in determining the cost of labour if we allowed innovations to move faster through the list of potential techniques; that is if we replaced the equation (4) above by:

$$\dot{A} = \Omega A \lambda \varphi(k^r) , \qquad \Omega > 1 \tag{4'}$$

Our earlier analysis, however, showed that there was always a range of growth rates over which creative destruction was the dominant force, and over which hence a rise in growth would lead to a rise in unemployment.

5 Conclusion

This paper has tried to identify a number of propositions arising from a general Schumpeterian model of endogenous growth, which are testable, at least in principle, and which we think are robust to reasonable extensions of the model. These propositions are all in the form of comparative-statics relationships across steady-states. The restriction to steady states severely limits their scope, but we believe that similar results will come out of a more dynamic analysis. While some of the results clearly depend upon some rather special features of our model, most lie at the heart of the Schumpeterian approach. Thus for example if it was demonstrated that growth in the long run was not correlated with R&D,[8] the productivity of R&D, the rate of patents, the rate of entry or exit of firms, the rate of introduction of new products, the rate of obsolescence of capital, or the rate of job creation, we would have to admit that the whole Schumpeterian approach to growth was a failure. While preliminary research by various authors along these lines appears promising, much remains to be done.

Appendix

Proof of Proposition 1: Define the function: $v^*(g; \rho, \sigma, \delta_k, \delta_w, \omega, \Gamma) \equiv v(\rho + (\sigma + 1)g, \rho + \delta_k + (\sigma + 1)g, \omega + (\rho + \sigma g + \delta_w)\Gamma, g)$. From (13), v^* is de-

[8] Clearly this list would have to be altered to take into account international trade and technology transfer in an open economy. In particular, for open economies not on the leading edge of technology, one would expect foreign investment and exports to play roles similar to the role played by R&D in the closed economy model examined above, since these channels, rather than R&D, are the most prevalent means by which new technologies are introduced into production in such countries.

creasing in each of its arguments. Then equation (16) can be reexpressed as:

$$\rho + \sigma g + \delta_k = \lambda\mu_1(k^r, H)v^*(g; \rho, \sigma, \delta_k, \delta_w, \omega, \Gamma) \ . \tag{16'}$$

The equilibrium values of g and k^r are determined by the pair of equations (16′) and (17), whose Jacobian determinant is: $\Delta \equiv \lambda[-\mu_{11}v^* + \mu_1(\sigma - \lambda\mu_1 v_g^*)] > 0$. Let x denote any of the first six arguments of the function $\hat{g}$ or $\hat{k}^r$. Express the LHS of (16′) as: $\hat{r}_k(g; \rho, \sigma, \delta_k, \delta_w, \omega, \Gamma)$. Then $\partial\hat{r}_k/\partial x \geq 0$, and:

$$\partial k^r/\partial x = \Delta^{-1}(\lambda\mu_1 v_x^* - \partial\hat{r}_k/\partial x) < 0$$

$$\partial g/\partial x = \Delta^{-1}(\lambda\mu_1)(\lambda\mu_1 v_x^* - \partial\hat{r}_k/\partial x) < 0$$

$$\partial g/\partial\lambda = \Delta^{-1}\lambda v^*[(\mu_1)^2 - \mu\mu_{11}] > 0$$

$$\partial g/\partial H = \Delta^{-1}\lambda^2 v^*[\mu_1\mu_{12} - \mu_2\mu_{11}] > 0$$

(concavity and constant returns imply $\mu_{12} > 0$)

$$\partial k^r/\partial\lambda = \Delta^{-1}\mu_1 v^*[1 - (\sigma\mu/\mu_1 v^*) + (\lambda\mu v_g^*/v^*)]$$

$$= \Delta^{-1}\mu_1 v^*\left[1 - \frac{\sigma g}{\rho + \sigma g + \delta_k} + (g v_g^*/v^*)\right] \quad \text{(by (16′) and (17))}$$

$$= \Delta^{-1}\mu_1 v^*[1 + gV'(g)/V(g)] \quad \text{(by the definition of } V(g))\|\ .$$

Proof of Proposition 2: From the preceding discussion, this ratio is $\hat{n}(\bar{r}, \bar{\omega})$. From (5), (8), (9), and (15):

$$\hat{n}(\bar{r}, \bar{\omega}) = \hat{n}(\rho + (\sigma + 1)g + \delta_k, \omega + (\rho + \sigma g + \delta_w)\Gamma) \ .$$

From the sign restrictions in (12) we can rewrite this equation as:

$$\hat{n}(\bar{r}, \bar{\omega}) = n^*(g; \rho, \sigma, \delta_k, \delta_w, \omega, \Gamma) \ , \qquad n_i^* < 0 \quad i = 1 \ldots 7.\| \ .$$

Proof that the distribution $F_A(A_i, t)$ is uniform on the interval (0, A).

To see this, first note that because the cumulative distribution F_a of the relative productivity A_i/A is stationary:

$$0 = \frac{d}{dt}F_A(xA, t) = (dA/dt)xf_A(xA, t) + \frac{\partial}{\partial t}F_A(xA, t) \qquad \forall x \in [0, 1] \ . \tag{21}$$

Also, the rate of decrease of the cumulative distribution of A_i evaluated at any fixed $X \leq A$ is just the total flow of innovations in all sectors i with $A_i \leq X$:

$$\frac{\partial}{\partial t}F_A(X, t) = -gF_A(X, t) \ . \tag{22}$$

From (21), (22), and the fact that $dA/dt = gA$:

$$Xf_A(X, t) = F_A(X, t) \tag{23}$$

for each X in $[0, A]$. It follows from (23) and the fact that A is the upper limit to A_i that for each t the distribution $F_A(X, t)$ must solve the following differential equation in X:

$$F'(X) = F(X)/X \qquad \forall X \in (0, A] \ , \qquad \text{and} \quad F(A) = 1 \ . \tag{24}$$

The unique solution to (24) is the uniform distribution. Therefore:

$$F_A(X, t) = X/A \qquad \forall X \in [0, A] \ , \qquad F_a(x) = x \qquad \forall x \in [0, 1].\| \ . \tag{25}$$

References

Aghion P, Howitt P (1992) A model of growth through creative destruction. Econometrica 60:323–51

Aghion P, Howitt P (1994) Growth and unemployment. Review of Economic Studies 61:477–94

Arroyo CR, Dinopoulos E, Donald SG (1994) Schumpeterian growth and capital accumulation: Theory and evidence. Unpublished

Caballero RJ, Jaffe AB (1993) How high are the giants' shoulders: An empirical assessment of knowledge spillovers and creative destruction in a model of economic growth. NBER Macroeconomics Annual 15–74. Cambridge, MA, MIT Press

Davis SJ, Haltiwanger J (1992) Gross job creation, gross job destruction, and employment reallocation. Quarterly Journal of Economics 107:819–64

Grossman GM, Helpman E (1991) Quality ladders in the theory of growth. Review of Economic Studies 58:43–61

Klenow PJ (1994) New product innovations. Unpublished, University of Chicago

Pissarides CA (1990) Equilibrium unemployment theory. Oxford, Basil Blackwell

Romer PM (1990) Endogenous technological change. Journal of Political Economy 98:S71–S102

Segerstrom PS, Anant TCA, Dinopoulos E (1990) A schumpeterian model of the product life cycle. American Economic Review 80:1077–91

First version received: March 1995
Final version received: December 1995

Dynamic Common Factors in Large Cross-Sections

Mario Forni

Dipartimento di Economia Politica, Universita di Modena, Via Berengario SJ,
41100 Modena, Italy

Lucrezia Reichlin

Université Libre Bruxelles, ECARE, 39 avenue F.D. Boosevelt, 1050 Bruxelles, Belgium

Abstract: This paper develops a method to analyze large cross-sections with non-trivial time dimension. The method (i) identifies the number of common shocks in a factor analytic model; (ii) estimates the unobserved common dynamic component; (iii) shows how to test for fundamentalness of the common shocks; (iv) quantifies positive and negative comovements at each frequency. We illustrate how the proposed techniques can be used for analyzing features of the business cycle and economic growth.

Key Words: Business cycle, sectoral comovements, factor analysis, principal components

JEL Classification System-Numbers: E32, O30, C51.

1 Introduction[1]

Many questions about growth and cyclical fluctuations can only be answered by looking at data which contain information on several nations, regions, sectors or firms, i.e., large cross-sections with time dimension large enough so as to be the object of dynamic analysis. Unfortunately, when the number of cross-sectional observations is large, traditional methods such as VAR or VARMA techniques are not appropriate, since the number of parameters to be estimated grows as the square of the cross-sectional dimension. A possible strategy to achieve parameter reduction is to use factor analytic models since, if the number of common factors is fixed, then the number of parameters to estimate grows only linearly with the number of cross-sectional observations. However, a large cross-sectional dimension poses problems for estimation (see, for example, the discussion in Quah and Sargent (1994) and the related comment by Geweke). The aim of this paper is to develop a method for the estimation and identifica-

[1] Thanks for helpful comments are due to Renato Flores, Marco Lippi, Marc Watson, and the participants to the ECARE-CEPR conference on empirical macroeconomics.

tion of a factor analytic model when the number of cross-sectional observations is large.

By exploiting results related to the Laws of Large Numbers, we show how to identify the number of common shocks in the data set and how to estimate them. The basic idea is as follows: since, by assumption, the idiosyncratic components are mutually orthogonal at all leads and lags, whereas the common components are not, if the number of cross-sectional observations is large, the former nearly die out relatively to the latter when averaging across sections. Therefore, the dimension of the common factor space h can be recovered by constructing a vector of aggregates with $q > h$ entries: since the rank of the spectral density matrix of this vector is equal to the number of common factors h, we can determine the latter by computing dynamic principal components as in Brillinger (1981). Moreover, we can estimate the common shocks by constructing h cross-sectional averages, estimating a VAR or a VARMA model and taking the residuals resulting from suitable identifying restrictions. Having recovered the common shocks, the model can be consistently estimated by applying OLS equation by equation. This is a great simplification with respect to what is suggested in the literature.

In order to get the structural parameters, the shocks have to be identified. As in the structural VAR literature, the problem is to find enough restrictions to select a particular Moving Average representation. The task is enormously simplified by assuming that the shocks belong to the space spanned by the present and the past values of the vector of the variables of interest, i.e., the shocks are fundamental. In structural VAR analysis, fundamentalness is generally assumed with no discussion. However, as noticed by Lippi and Reichlin (1993), this is arbitrary and can produce misleading results. Here we show that in factor analytic models, unlike in VAR models, fundamentalness can be tested. This provides a further motivation for our framework.

If either fundamentalness is rejected or we are not interested in the structural response functions, we can distinguish the common from the idiosyncratic component in each sector or region by regressing on the present, past *and future* of the q averages equation by equation. We can then remove the idiosyncratic components and analyze the common ones in order to see whether comovements between regions, nations or sectors are mainly positive, indicating a prevalence of complementarities in economic activity, or negative, indicating a prevalence of substitution effects. For this purpose we use an index for the relative weight of negative over positive covariances at all frequencies. This index is constructed from the computation of cospectra of the common components for all cross-sectional units.

The paper is organized as follows: the next three sections are devoted to identification of the number of common shocks, estimation and test for fundamentalness. In section five we illustrate the proposed methodology on a sample of manufacturing output and hours worked for 450 sectors in the US from 1958 to 1986. The paper ends with a discussion of open questions and possible developments.

2 Specification

Let us begin by assuming a countable infinity of sectors or regions $i = 1, \ldots, \infty$. We specify a dynamic factor analytic model, as for instance in Sargent and Sims (1977) and Geweke and Singleton (1981) and more recently, in Quah and Sargent (1994) and Forni and Reichlin (1995). Precisely, we assume that the vector of cross-sectional variables $y_t^i = (y_{1t}^i, y_{2t}^i, \ldots, y_{mt}^i)'$ can be written as

$$y_t^i = A^i(L)u_t + \varepsilon_t^i, \tag{1}$$

where

$$\varepsilon_t^i = (\varepsilon_{1t}^i, \varepsilon_{2t}^i, \ldots, \varepsilon_{mt}^i)'$$

is a vector of sector-specific factors – 'the idiosyncratic components' – possibly autocorrelated but mutually orthogonal at all leads and lags, with variances bounded above by the reals σ_h;

$$u_t^i = (u_{1t}, u_{2t}, \ldots, u_{qt})'$$

is a vector of unit variance white noises, the common shocks, identical for all sectors and variables, mutually orthogonal and orthogonal to ε_t^i for all i; $A^i(L)$ is a $m \times q$ matrix of rational functions in the lag operator L. All the variables are zero-mean, wide-sense stationary and linearly regular, with rational spectral density matrix.

The methodology proposed here exploits an important property of factor models: due to orthogonality, when aggregating across a large number of sectors the idiosyncratic component vanishes relatively to the common component $A(L)u_t$ (Granger [1987], Forni and Lippi [1995]).

To better clarify what we mean, let us introduce for each variable h a sequence of real numbers ω_h^i, $i = 1, \ldots, \infty$, such that we can find positive reals L_h and U_h fulfilling

$$L_h \leq \omega_h^i \leq U_h \ .$$

Now consider a strictly increasing sequence of positive integers i_k, $k = 1, \ldots, \infty$ and let $D_n = \{i_1, \ldots, i_n\}$. The variance of the aggregate idiosyncratic component

$$\bar{\varepsilon}_{ht}^n = \frac{\sum_{i \in D_n} \omega_h^i \varepsilon_{ht}^i}{\sum_{i \in D_n} \omega_h^i}$$

is bounded above by $n^{-1}(U_h^2 \sigma_h / L_h^2)$. Hence $\lim_{n \to \infty} \bar{\varepsilon}_{ht}^n = 0$.

On the other hand, the common components $y_{ht}^i - \varepsilon_{ht}^i$ are not mutually orthogonal, so that in general they will not vanish asymptotically. A positive lower bound for all but a finite number of cross-covariances between the common components is a sufficient (but not necessary) condition for this to be true.[2]

[2] Necessary conditions are given in Forni and Lippi (1995).

It follows that for n large the weighted average

$$\bar{y}_{ht}^n = \frac{\sum_{i \in D_n} \omega_h^i y_{ht}^i}{\sum_{i \in D_n} \omega_h^i}$$

is approximately equal to $B_h^n(L)u_t$, where

$$B_h^n(L) = \sum_{i \in D_n} \omega_h^i A_h^i(L) \Big/ \sum_{i \in D_n} \omega_h^i$$

and $A_h^i(L)$ is the h-th raw of the matrix $A^i(L)$. More precisely, as stated in the following proposition, the percentage of the total variance explained by the common component is close to unity.

Proposition 1: As $n \to \infty$, $\mathrm{var}(B_h^n(L)u_t)/\mathrm{var}(\bar{y}_{ht}^n) \to 1$.

The above result provides the justification for a method of identifying of the number of common shocks in a factor model having large cross-sectional dimension.

Let us consider a data set concerning n sectors. Now take a partition of s subsets $G_1, G_2, \ldots, G_s$, call $n_1, n_2, \ldots, n_s$ the number of elements in these sets and define the ms vector of aggregates:

$$Z_t = \begin{bmatrix} \sum_{i \in G_1} y_t^i/n_1 \\ \sum_{i \in G_2} y_t^i/n_2 \\ \vdots \\ \sum_{i \in G_s} y_t^i/n_s \end{bmatrix} \tag{2}$$

If the corresponding vector of idiosyncratic components is zero, Z_t has a (possibly infinite) moving average representation driven by u_t, say $C(L)u_t$. Hence it will be singular whenever the dimension of u_t, q, is less than ms; i.e., the spectral density of Z_t, $f_Z(\lambda) = C(e^{-i\lambda})C(e^{i\lambda})'$, will have reduced rank, equal to q.

But then, to identify the number of common shocks, we need only compute the ms dynamic principal components of Z_t and check how many we require to capture most of its variance at each frequency.

The proposed procedure consists of the following steps.

Step 1: Select randomly l different partitions of the sectors in the data set and compute the corresponding vectors $Z_t^j, j = 1, \ldots, l$.
Step 2: For each j, compute the spectral density of Z_t^j, and decompose it in the following way:

$$f_Z(\lambda) = P(\lambda)D(\lambda)\overline{P(\lambda)}'$$

where $D(\lambda)$ is a diagonal matrix with eigenvalues

$$[\mu_1(\lambda), \ldots, \mu_{ms}(\lambda)]$$

on the principal diagonal and

$$\operatorname{rank} D(\lambda) = \operatorname{rank} f_Z(\lambda)$$

(see Brillinger 1981).

Step 3: Order the $\mu_k(\lambda)$s from the largest to the smallest and compute the ratio between the variance of the sum of the first r principal components and the variance of the sum of all principal components:

$$\frac{\int_0^\pi \sum_{k=1}^r \mu_k(\lambda)\, d\lambda}{\int_0^\pi \sum_{k=1}^q \mu_k(\lambda)\, d\lambda} \tag{3}$$

for $r = 1, \ldots, ms$. This gives us the percentage of the trace of the covariance matrix of Z_t^j accounted for by the first r principal components.

Step 4: Set $q = r$ when r is such that the explained variance captures at least 95 percent of the total. If r components are sufficient and if this result is robust across the l experiments, conclude that there are $q = r$ common shocks in the data set.

3 Estimation and Diagnostic Checking

Another implication of Proposition 1 is that the common dynamic component of the model can be estimated by simply using sectoral averages. In particular, if the common shock u_t has dimension q, the common component can be estimated by using q aggregates. This is an estimation procedure much simpler than the one based on the EM algorithm, which has been suggested in this context (e.g., Quah and Sargent 1994).

Notice that in model (1) $A^i(L)u_t$ is the projection of y_t^i on the present, past and future of u_t since, by assumption, u_t is orthogonal to ε_t^i. Now take any vector of q averages Y_t such that the idiosyncratic component has died out. From Section 2, we know that the components of Y_t span the same linear space as the components of u_t. Hence, we can recover the common and the idiosyncratic components simply by regressing equation by equation the y_{ht}^i on thc present, past and future of Y_t.

Let us assume for simplicity that $m = q$ (this assumption will be relaxed below). Our proposed procedure is the following:

Step 1: Set

$$Y_t = [y_{1t}, y_{2t}, \ldots, y_{mt}]'$$

where

$$y_{ht} = \frac{\sum_{i=1}^n \omega_h^i y_{ht}^i}{\sum_{i=1}^n \omega_h^i}\ .$$

Then choose the weights ω_h^i so as to maximize the chance for the sector-specific component to go to zero. Under the orthogonality assumption, the weights minimizing the variance of the aggregate local component are:

$$\omega_h^i = 1/\sigma_h^i$$

where σ_h^i is the variance of the unobserved idiosyncratic component of sector i for variable h. To compute the $\sigma_h^i s$ proceed iteratively.

(i) As starting value for the estimate of σ_h^i take the sample variance of y_{ht}^i. Then compute the associated weights and Y_t.
(ii) Fix a K and, for each h, perform the n regressions of y_{ht}^i on the variables in Y_{t-k}, $k = -K, \ldots, K$, by OLS so as to obtain a first estimate of σ_h^i. Use the associated weights to get a new regressor Y_t.
(iii) Repeat step (ii) until all estimates of σ_h^i converge.

Step 2: After estimation verify (i) pairwise orthogonality between the local components by means of a Q test; (ii) whether the idiosyncratic component has died out in the sample. This can be done by computing, for each of the aggregates used in the estimation of the common shocks, the ratio of the variance of the local component to that of the aggregate. Under the orthogonality assumption this ratio can be estimated by

$$\sum_{i=1}^{n} \frac{1}{\hat{\sigma}_h^i} \bigg/ s_h \,, \tag{4}$$

where $\hat{\sigma}_h^i$ is the final estimate of σ_h^i and s_h is the sample variance of $\sum_{i=1}^{n} y_{ht}^i/\hat{\sigma}_h^i$.

Let us now come to the case $q \neq m$. In this case, we can still apply the above procedure, but *Step 1* must be modified in such a way to ensure that vector Y_t has q entries. If $q < m$, we can simply drop $m - q$ components from Y_t. If $q > m$, we must partition the sectors as in Section 2 for some or all of the variables h. The indeterminacy problems arising in both cases will be briefly discussed in the last section.

The sectoral response functions $A^i(L)$ cannot be estimated without recovering u_t. Identification of the common shocks will be discussed in the next section. However, independently of identification, we can analyzse the common component by spectral methods. Notice that the common components reflect both positive and negative comovements; a prevalence of the former over the latter would indicate that the propagation of shocks is mainly through complementarities, while the opposite would indicate a larger importance of substitution effects. In particular, we can estimate which effect prevails at all frequencies and obtain information on short- and long-run fluctuations. In a separate paper (Forni and Reichlin 1995) we analyze this issue in detail and propose a measure of substitution defined as the ratio between the sum of the negative values of the cospectra and the sum of the positive values for different frequencies.

To be more precise, let $s_{ij}(\lambda)$ be the co-spectrum of sectors i and j for variable h. We can decompose $s_{ij}(\lambda)$ as:

$$s_{ij}(\lambda) = s_{ij}(\lambda)_- + s_{ij}(\lambda)_+$$

where

$$s_{ij}(\lambda)_- = [s_{ij}(\lambda) - |s_{ij}(\lambda)|]/2$$

and

$$s_{ij}(\lambda)_+ = [|s_{ij}(\lambda)| + s_{ij}(\lambda)]/2 \ .$$

A measure of the substitution effect of the common shocks can be defined as the ratio:

$$SUBST(\lambda) = -\frac{\sum s_{ij}(\lambda)_-}{\sum s_{ij}(\lambda)_+} \tag{5}$$

4 Identification

As mentioned, estimation of the sectoral response functions requires identification of the vector of the common shocks u_t. We propose the following two-step procedure. The first step is to check whether the common shocks are fundamental, i.e. whether u_t belongs to the space spanned by the present and the past of Y_t. In traditional structural VAR analysis this cannot be tested and fundamentalness is just assumed. However, it has been pointed out by Lippi and Reichlin (1993) that this is an arbitrary assumption because, in general, we cannot ensure that u_t belongs to the larger set spanned by the future as well as the present and the past of Y_t. We will show here that, unlike VAR models, in factor models fundamentalness can be tested.

If fundamentalness is not rejected, the second step then consists in estimating a VAR or a VARMA model for Y_t, obtaining any vector of orthonormal residuals v_t and identifying u_t within the set of orthonormal transformation of v_t by imposing economically meaningful restrictions. Since this can be done by standard procedures, we do not discuss this point in detail here. (For a detailed discussion of this issue, see Forni and Reichlin [1995].)

Let us now show how to develop the first step.

From (2), we know that the vector of the q aggregate variables Y_t can be written to a good approximation as

$$Y_t = D(L)u_t$$

where the h-th raw of $D(L)$ is

$$D_h(L) = \frac{\sum_{i=1}^{n} 1/\sigma_h^i A_h^i(L)}{\sum_{i=1}^{n} 1/\sigma_h^i} \ .$$

The vector white noise u_t is fundamental if, and only if, $\det(D(L))$ does not vanish within the unit circle in the complex plane. An equivalent condition is that the past of u_t spans the same linear space as the past of Y_t (see Rozanov 1967). Assuming that the equality $Y_t = D(L)u_t$ holds exactly, we can state the following result:

Proposition 2: If u_t is fundamental for Y_t, then none of the sectoral variables y^i_{ht} Granger-causes Y_t.

Proof: Let us call $\mathbf{H}_t$ the Hilbert space spanned by all variables in Y_{t-k}, $k \geq 0$. Fundamentalness implies that $u_{h,t-k} \in \mathbf{H}_{t-1}$ $\forall h, k > 0$. Now, consider the orthogonal projection of Y_t on $\mathbf{H}_{t-1}$ and call η_t the vector of residuals. Clearly, η_t is orthogonal to $u_{h,t-k}$ $\forall h, k > 0$. Moreover, η_t is orthogonal to $\varepsilon^i_{h,t-k}$ $\forall i, h, k$ since it lies in $\mathbf{H}_t$. Hence η_t is orthogonal to $y^i_{h,t-k}$ $\forall i, h, k > 0$.

Therefore, while in VAR or VARMA framework fundamentalness of the structural shocks cannot be tested, in the factor model fundamentalness implies the testable implication that the macrovariables used for estimation cannot be Granger-caused by any of the sectoral variables.

5 Empirical Application

We now apply the ideas developed in Sections 1 to 4 to a data set containing output and hours worked of 450 manufacturing sectors in the US from 1958 to 1986.[3] As it will be illustrated, the factor analytic model can be used to capture essential features of short and long run fluctuations in manufacturing by reducing the parameter space in a data set of 26200 data points.

5.1 Number of Common Shocks

We reordered sectors by extracting randomly without replacement natural numbers from 1 to 450 to form the sequence i_k, $k = 1, \ldots, 450$. Then we partitioned the sectors in six groups of 75 sectors each by taking $G_1 = \{i_1, \ldots, i_{75}\}$, $\ldots$, $G_6 = \{i_{376}, \ldots, i_{450}\}$. We repeated the experiment 50 times to get the

[3] Further information on the data set is given in the Appendix.

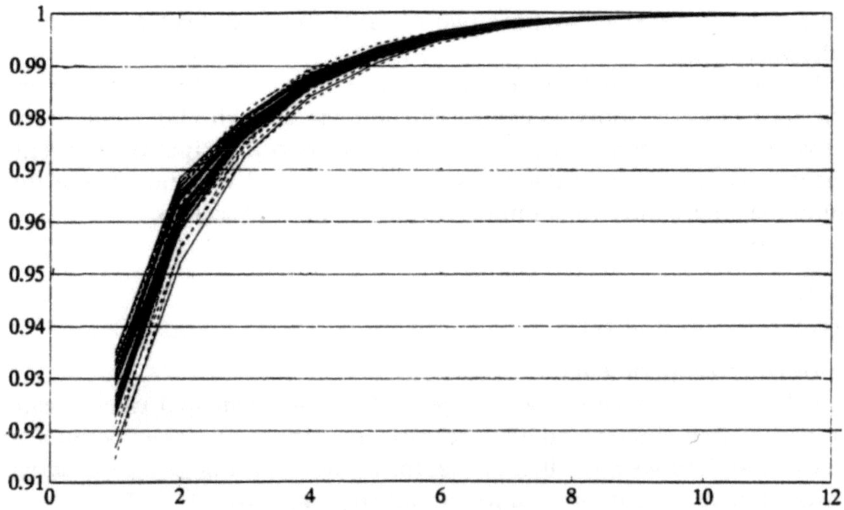

Fig. 1. Variance of Z_t explained by the first 12 principal components ($l = 50$ experiments)

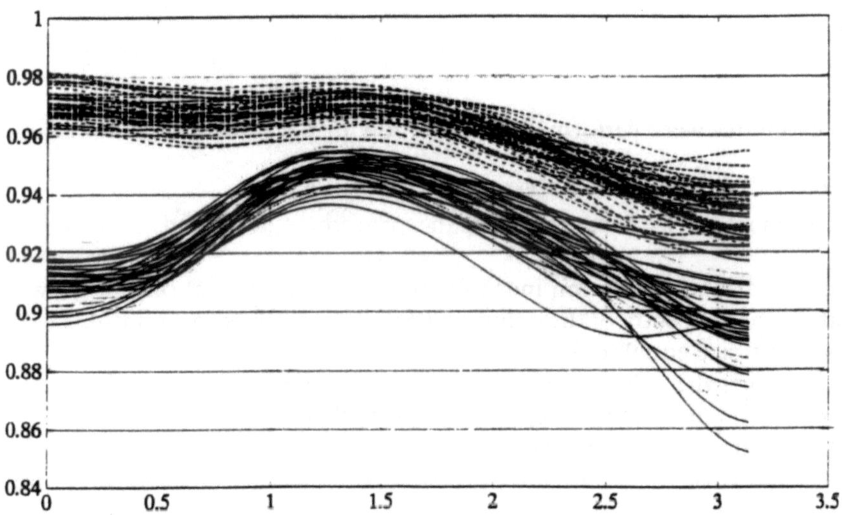

Fig. 2. Variance of Z_t explained by the first two principal components at different frequencies
Horizontal axis: λ

vectors $Z_t^j, j = 1, \ldots, 50$. Since we have two variables we have twelve aggregates forming the vector Z_t^j.

Figure 1 reports the estimated ratio (3) for $r = 1, \ldots, 12$ and for all experiments. The spectra were estimated using a Bartlett window with lag window size equal to five. For all experiments, the result is that two principal components are sufficient to capture more than .95 percent of the total variance. From this we conclude that there are two common shocks to our 450 sectors.

Figure 2 reports the ratios

$$\frac{\sum_{j=1}^{2} \mu_j(\lambda)}{\sum_{j=1}^{q} \mu_j(\lambda)} \quad \text{and} \quad \frac{\mu_1(\lambda)}{\sum_{j=1}^{q} \mu_j(\lambda)}$$

at each λ for the 50 experiments.

Observe that the variance explained by the first two principal components is similar across frequencies and that results are robust across experiments. Observe also that, had we modelled our factor model with one common shock only, we would have missed information about the long-run.

5.2 *Estimation Results*

The OLS estimates were performed on the following specification:

$$y_{ht}^i = \beta_h^i Y_{t+1} + \gamma_h^i Y_t + \delta_h^i Y_{t-1} + v_{ht}^i \ . \tag{6}$$

On this specification we have followed the procedure described in *Step 1* of Section 3.

We computed the substitution index for the panel of sectoral output growth by estimating the cospectra of the common components of sectoral outputs with Bartlett window size equal to 5.

Figure 3 reports the values of $SUBST(\lambda)$ for the common component.

Figure 4 reports positive and negative cospectra separately.

The figures illustrate nicely the business cycle features of our data: all the series of the sums of the positive cospectra have peaks at business cycle frequencies, while the series of the negative cospectra are rather flat.

5.3 *Diagnostic*

To verify the orthogonality between the sector-specific components, we performed a Q test on pre-whitened residuals from the sectoral regressions (6). For each pair of sectors we computed $T\sum_{k=-3}^{3} r_k^2$, where T is the time dimension of the residuals and r_k^2 denotes the sample cross-correlation of ε_{ht}^i and $\varepsilon_{h,t-k}^i$. Under

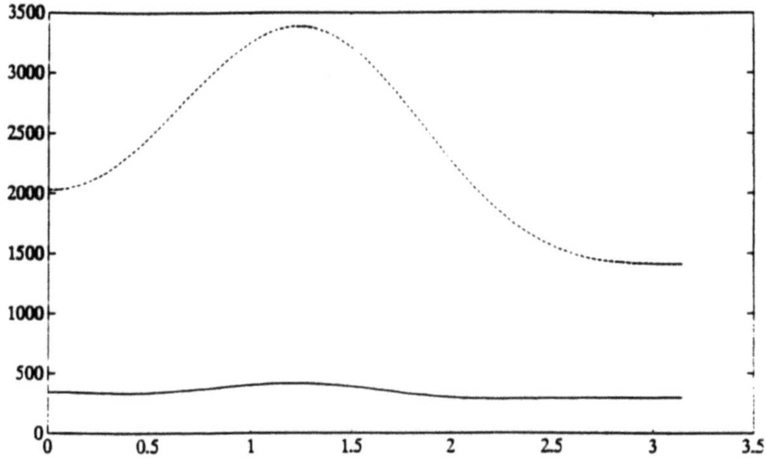

Fig. 3. Absolute sum of positive (dashed line) and negative (solid line) cospectra
Horizontal axis: λ

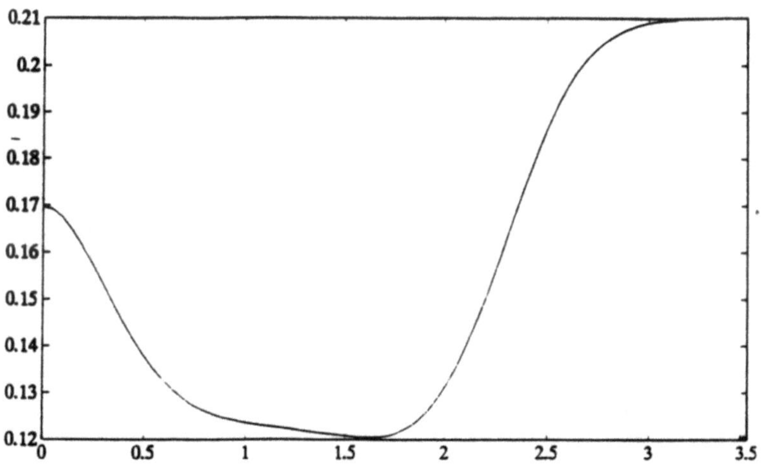

Fig. 4. Substitution index for the common component
Horizontal axis: λ

the null of pairwise orthogonality, the distribution of the test statistic is $\chi^2(7)$. Figure 5 reports both the theoretical and the empirical distributions for output residuals.

From the comparison we conclude that there is no evidence of large cross-correlations between the estimated idiosyncratic components.

To verify how rapidly the variance of the idiosyncratic component goes to zero for increasingly larger aggregates, we performed the following exercise. First, we reordered sectors by extracting randomly without replacement natural numbers from 1 to 450 to form the sequence i_k, $k = 1, \ldots, 450$. Second, we

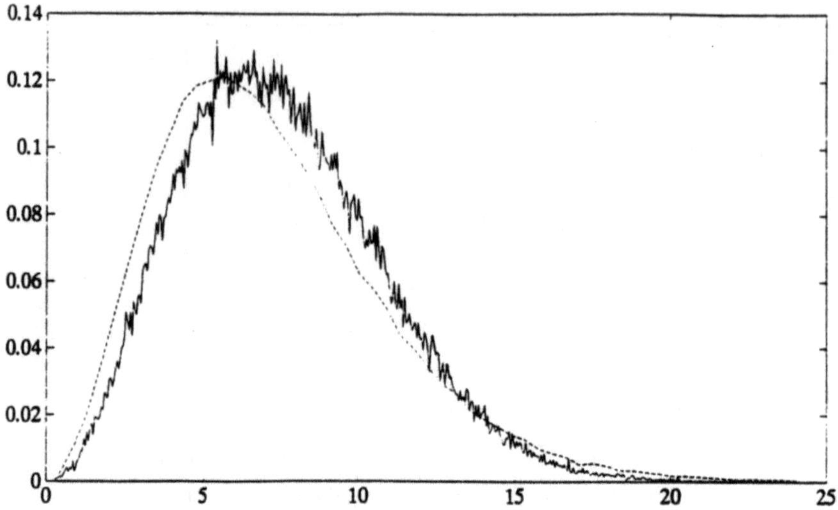

Fig. 5. Distribution of Q test for residuals of output regressions χ^2 distribution under the null (dashed line); empirical distribution (solid line)

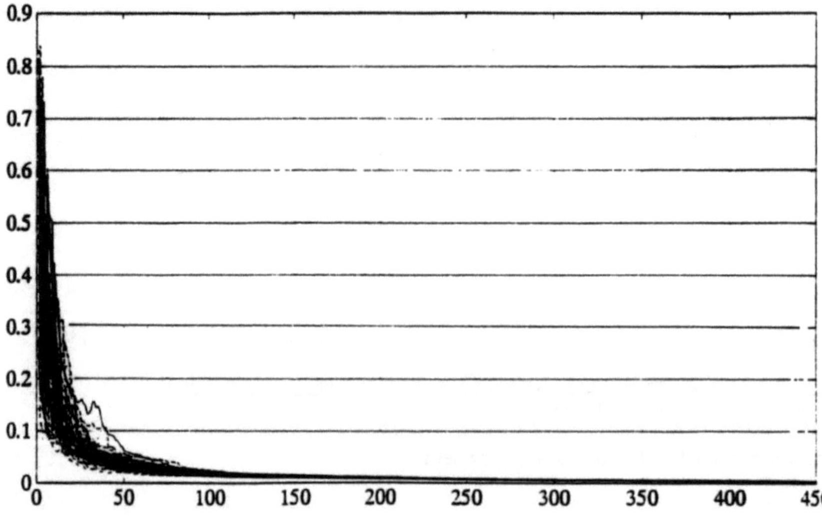

Fig. 6. Ratios of the variance of the idiosyncratic component to the variance of the sub-aggregates – 50 experiments – output data
Vertical axis: variance ratios
Horizontal axis: number of groups

computed the ratio (4) for the sets $\{i_1, \ldots, i_n\}$, $n = 1, \ldots, 450$. Lastly, we repeated the experiment for 50 different reorderings. Figure 6 illustrates the results for the sample of sectoral output.

The ratio reached is less than .01 for $n = 450$, which is the cross-sectional dimension of our data set. Notice that $n = 50$ is sufficiently large to get ratios of about .05. By imposing equal weights, the same figure is reached with 60–70 sectors; this provides a confirmation for the dimension of Z_t selected in Section 5.1. Similar results are obtained for hours worked.

5.4 *Test for Fundamentalness*

We test for fundamentalness by computing Geweke's measure of causation with one lag (Geweke 1982). Under the null of no causation this statistic multiplied by $T - 1$, where T is the time dimension of y^i_{ht}, is distributed as $\chi^2_{(1)}$. Figure 7 compares the distribution of Geweke's measure (solid line) with the theoretical $\chi^2_{(1)}$ distribution. Fundamentalness is rejected for 95 sectors out of 450 (21%).

We conclude that fundamentalness is rejected.

6 Summary and Open Questions

This paper has developed a simple method to analyze dynamic factor analytic models in data sets that contain a large number of cross-sectional units. We have shown how to identify the number of common shocks and how to estimate the model by using nothing more than OLS. Moreover, we have developed an index for measuring the importance of negative comovements over positive comovements at all frequencies. A final contribution of the paper is to show formally than in factor analytic models, unlike in VAR models, we can test whether the common shocks are fundamental, i.e., whether they belong to the space spanned by the present and the past of the variables of interest. This is a crucial step for the full identification of the model.

While our method provides a simple strategy for identification of the dimension and estimation of the common dynamic component in factor analytic models, there are at least two problems of indeterminacy in our strategy that should be further analyzed.

The first concerns the strategy for the determination of the number of common shocks. Notice that the vector Z_t can be constructed in a number of different ways and that this may lead to different results. In order to differentiate the entries in Z_t, we have suggested considering non-overlapping averages, that

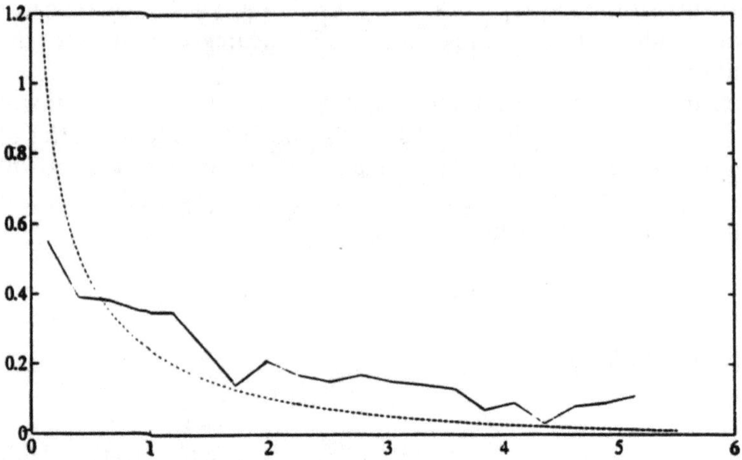

Fig. 7. Test for fundamentalness
Theoretical $\chi^2_{(1)}$ distribution (dashed line)
Geweke's measure (solid line)

is, a partition of the data set. This leads to the question of which partition should be chosen. In particular, we have to decide the number of aggregates s: s should be set as large as possible, since we need $sm > q$, and q is unknown. However, the larger s is, the smaller are the groups in the partition, and we need large groups in order to wash out the idiosyncratic components. A method for solving this trade-off is needed. The sample considered in our empirical application is very large, and the diagnostic of Section 5.3 indicates that for our choice of $s = 12$, the idiosyncratic component is safely dead (see Figure 6). However, for smaller data sets the tradeoff may be more troublesome.

The second problem concerns the estimation of the common component through sectoral averages. Here there are two issues: the choice of the weights in the computation of these averages and the choice of the partition.

As for the former, recall that any weighted average for which the idiosyncratic component goes to zero might be used. In Section 4, we have suggested choosing weights to follow the criterion of maximizing the chance of the idiosyncratic component going to zero. This is needed when we do not have many cross-sectional observations. However, when the number of sections is huge, other criteria, based on economic considerations, for example, might be chosen.

As for the latter, notice that, if $m = q$, as in our empirical application, it is natural to do as we have done and consider partitions over all the m variables; in this way we use all the information in the sample. However, if $m \neq q$, there is no obvious choice.

In general, we have two problems in the choice of the aggregates: (i) the idiosyncratic component must to go to zero; (ii) we want to choose aggregates for which the vector of shocks pass the test for fundamentalness suggested in Section 4. If the data set is large, problem (i) is easily overcome. Problem (ii), on the other hand, is likely to be more serious, and indeed, the empirical application shows this to be the case. One possible development of our analysis, which will be the scope of further research, is to devise a strategy for searching for those aggregates for which we can accept the fundamentalness hypothesis.

Appendix

Data Sources and Data Treatment

The data set used is the Annual Survey of Manufacturers (ASM) which is a survey of manufacturing establishments sampled from those responding to the comprehensive Census of Manufacturers. This database contains information for four-digit manufacturing industries from 1958 through 1986.

We have used value-added data for output and deflated them by the value of shipments.

Logs of sectoral data on output and hours worked were subject to unit root tests. For all data we were not able to reject the null of a unit root (results available on request) at the 5 percent level. We then took the differences and removed the mean.

The electronic computer sector (SIC 357) was found to have a unit root after being detrended by a segmented trend with change in drift in 1972.

References

Brillinger DR (1981) Time series data analysis and theory. Holt, Rinehart and Winston Inc

Forni M, Lippi M (1995) Aggregation and the micro foundations of macroeconomics. Oxford, Oxford University Press, forthcoming

Forni M, Reichlin L (1995) Let's get real: A dynamic factor analytic approach to disaggregated business cycle. CEPR working paper 1244

Geweke J (1982) Measurements of linear dependence and feedback between multiple time series. Journal of the American Statistical Association 77:304–13

Geweke J, Singleton KJ (1981) Maximum likelihood confirmatory factor analysis of economic time series. International Economic Review 22/1:37–54

Granger CWJ (1987) Implication of aggregation with common factors. Econometric Theory 3:208–22

Lippi M, Reichlin L (1993) The dynamic effects of aggregate demand and supply disturbances: Comment. American Economic Review

Quah D, Sargent TJ (1994) A dynamic index model for large cross sections. In: Stock J, Watson M (eds) Business cycles, indicators and forecasting. NBER and University Press of Chicago
Rozanov Y (1967) Stationary random processes. San Francisco, Holden Day
Sargent TJ, Sims CA (1977) Business cycle modelling without pretending to have too much *a priori* economic theory. In: Sims CA (ed) New methods in business research. Minneapolis, Federal Reserve Bank of Minneapolis

First version received: March 1995
First version received: November 1995

II International Trade and Growth Linkages

Human Capital and Measurable Dynamic Gains from Economic Integration:
An Application to the Economic Integration of North and South America

RICHARD G. HARRIS[1]

Department of Economics, Simon Fraser University, Burnaby, B.C. V5A 1S6, Canada

Abstract: The paper looks at the source of dynamic gains to trade liberalization using a two-country model with both physical and human capital accumulation. The model is calibrated and used to examine the effect of the economic integration of Canada and the United States with Latin America. The analysis assumes that differences in productivity levels between regions are due entirely to differences in human and physical capital endowments. Key assumptions are that capital is internationally mobile and human capital formation is income constrained. The simulated impact of moving to a hemispheric free trade area is significant. The long-run impacts are also different from the short-run efficiency effect predicted by conventional static triangle-rectangle analysis. The long-run *multiplier* effect on static output gains are on the order of 2.0 to 2.5 for the South – that is long-run output gains are 2.0 to 2.5 times predicted short-run static gains. In the case of the North, static predictions of gain are ambiguous in sign over the longer run; in some cases there are small dynamic gains – in others. small losses. Investment diversion toward Latin America is a prominent characteristic of the results.

Key Words: Trade liberalization, human capital, economic integration, foreign investment, Latin America.

JEL Classification System-Numbers: F15, O41

1 Introduction

The literature on measurable dynamic gains from trade is large on vision and short on actual numbers. The issue of whether the dynamic gains from trade are large was raised in the discussions of the 1992 Single European Market Pro-

---

[1] This paper is part of a project involving theories of economic growth and their implications for the economic integration of North and South America with research support of FOCAL/CIS *After NAFTA Research Program.* The hospitality of the University of New South Wales, where this research was originally undertaken, is gratefully acknowledged. Comments of two referees and seminar participants at the University of New South Wales, ANU, U. of Queensland, Monash U., U. of Melbourne, and the Universities of Adelaide and Flinders on earlier drafts were quite helpful. I am grateful for the able research assistance of Peter Robertson. All errors are the sole responsibility of the author.

gram, the Canada-U.S. Free Trade Agreement, and the North American Free Trade Agreement. The fact is, however, that there are few papers by economists which provide any numbers on "dynamic gains" of the same sort that are now routinely provided by calibrated applied general equilibrium models on static efficiency gains.[2] This paper looks at the potential dynamic gains to trade liberalization that arise from the long-run induced effects on physical and human capital accumulation. The model is used to examine the potential impact of economic integration of Canada and the United States with Latin America. The two regions of the Western Hemisphere are defined as *North* (Canada and the United States) and *South* (the rest of Latin America and the Caribbean). This integration can be regarded as a mix of domestic market liberalization in Latin America, including trade reform, and an extension of regional preferential arrangements in NAFTA to all of Latin America.

This paper picks up a theme suggested by the literature on human capital and growth.[3] Much of that literature has been concerned with the role of human capital accumulation as an explanation of differences in growth rates. Lucas (1990) drew attention to the point that differences in human capital endowments in a world of internationally mobile physical capital can also potentially explain *both* international differences in income levels and the absence of capital flows from rich to poor countries. The point of this paper is to draw out the quantitative significance of this observation for changes in trade policy in a fully calibrated dynamic two-country general equilibrium model of North and South America. In such a model, policy changes have potentially important effects on income, investment and international capital flows which lead to longer-term changes in relative and absolute factor endowments of both physical and human capital.

The simulated impact of moving to a hemispheric free trade area is significant. The long-run impacts are also different from the short-run efficiency effect predicted by conventional static triangle-rectangle analysis. The analysis estimates a Long-Run *multiplier* effect on static gains on the order of 2.0 to 2.5 for the South that is long-run output gains are 2.0 to 2.5 times predicted short-run

---

2 The older dynamic gains literature, following Scitovsky, simply defined these effects exclusion i.e., are not included in static efficiency calculations, but involve some reference to economies of scale or externalities. More recently the literature on "dynamic gains" and economic integration falls into roughly three categories. The first literature simply deals with induced accumulation effects of a once and for all policy change as articulated, for example, by Corden (1971). There is a second literature, largely from development economics, which attempts to relate productivity growth to indexes of openness or trade liberalization and surveyed recently by Havlryshyn (1990) and Pack (1988); recent contributions include Edwards (1992) and Helliwell (1994). Third, there is the literature which relies on true dynamic economies of scale, and/or externalities which can lead to actual changes in permanent growth rates. Recent endogenous growth models such as those developed by Grossman and Helpman (1990), Lucas (1985) and Romer (1986) fall into this category. Empirically getting a handle on the last sort of dynamic gain remains a major and unresolved empirical challenge.

3 See Barro (1991), Lucas (1988), Mankiw, Romer and Weil (1992), and Romer (1990).

static gains. In the case of the North, static predictions of gain are ambiguous in sign over the longer run; in some cases there are small dynamic gains – in others, small losses. These simulation results are "theory conditional." The theory however, unlike much of the new growth theory, is fairly traditional. Somewhat novel in the empirical analysis is the focus on dynamic transitions rather than steady-states. One conclusion is that "old theory," with some appropriate stylized facts, yields some surprising insights on dynamics gains and losses due to induced changes in factor accumulation.

The rest of the paper proceeds as follows: section 2 reviews the particular facts of economic integration in North and South America; section 3 discusses the significant differences in factor endowments and growth experience of the two regions; section 4 lays out the basic theoretical model and section 5 provides some details on the calibration procedure. Results are discussed in section 6.

2 Economic Integration in the Americas

With the signing of the NAFTA agreement there has been some discussion about the possibility of widening that arrangement to all of Latin America commonly referred to as a Western Hemispheric Free Trade Area (WHFTA).[4] For a trade policy analyst, WHFTA is unique in that the region has a number of characteristics not usually found in the more prominent free trade areas. First, trade barriers in Latin America have been very high and openness quite low. For example, in the largest economy of the region, Brazil, as of the mid-1980s the average level of tariff and para tariffs was approximately 80 percent and the ratio of trade volume to GDP less than 8 percent. Following a long history of Import Substitution policies in Latin America, a similar situation existed in many of the Latin American countries. Second, WHFTA provides a clear case of liberalizing between an industrialized North Canada and the United States and a much less developed South. Conventional indicators such as income per capita and GDP per worker indicate large developmental differences within the hemisphere that cast doubt on results from conventional general equilibrium models which take productivity differences between countries as given.

The static gains from the formation of a WHFTA have been estimated in a few studies using conventional methods. Table 1, taken from Harris and

---

[4] It is important to note there has already been substantial unilateral liberalization in a number of the Latin American countries mostly notably in Mexico and Chile. Furthermore some intra-regional Latin America trade has been liberalized although progress has been variable. The Mercosour is the most prominent and successful of the regional trade agreements within Latin America.

Table 1. Summary of static welfare gains of WHFTA

		Static welfare effect	Scale effect	Terms of Trade	Total
North		0.03	1.18	0.09	1.30
South		2.16	7.07	−0.79	8.43
	South Am.	1.85	7.41	−0.69	8.58
	Central Am.	4.74	2.21	−0.93	6.02
Argentina		0.59	6.92	−0.43	7.08
Bolivia		0.89	2.12	−0.72	2.29
Brazil		2.69	12.38	−0.38	14.68
Chile		3.38	5.72	−1.30	7.81
Colombia		11.07	8.39	−1.92	17.54
Ecuador		5.30	6.97	−1.51	10.77
Peru		4.46	8.08	−1.12	11.43
Uruguay		1.61	3.85	−0.85	4.61
Venezuela		2.08	5.89	−1.16	6.81

Source: Hams and Robertson (1993)

Robertson (1993), reports some partial equilibrium estimates of the gains to hemispheric trade liberalization for a number of countries in the region, and the two aggregates, North and South, relative to a 1988 base. The general result appears to be that the static gains to Latin America are fairly large by the standards of conventional estimates.

3 North-South Differences: Stylized Facts

The extent of the population growth differences between Canada-U.S. and Latin America is staggering. In figure 1 the past and future projected labor supplies for the region are indicated. Given that many of these workers have already been born, the projections are regarded as reasonably good by most demographic experts. From the point of view of the North, this raises the prospect of lowering wages in the North by integrating with a region with a fast growing and relatively unskilled labor force. One consequence of the large differences between regions in population growth rates is that multi-country general equilibrium models of North and South America must deal with growth transitions if they are to be relevant over time frames of less than 50 years.

Another important difference between the two regions is evident in relative rates of return to investment in physical and human capital. Although evidence is sparse in table 2, a summary of estimates for Latin America and the Advanced Countries for the 1960s and 1970s is provided. In the case of Latin America it appears these trends are still intact. There are two stylized facts. One, there is a much higher rate of return on education in Latin America than in the advanced

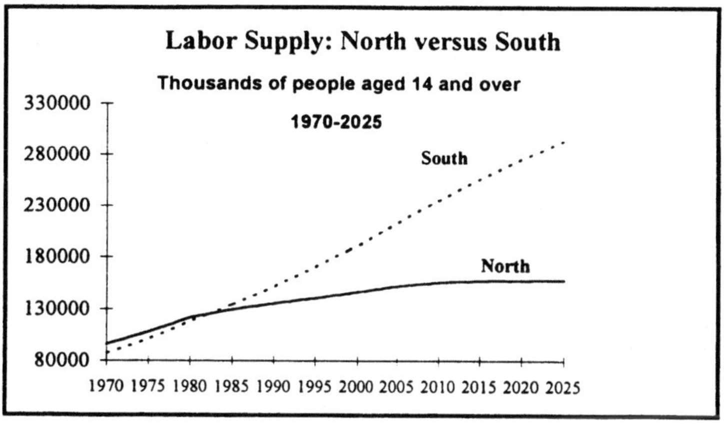

Fig. 1.

Table 2. North-south investment returns

	(percent) Returns on education					
	Social Primary	Secondary	Higher	Private Primary	Secondary	Higher
Latin America	26	18	16	32	23	23
Advanced	NA	11	9	NA	12	12
	Returns to physical and human capital					
	1960s Physical		Human	1970s Physical		Human
Developing	15		20	13		15
Advanced	10		8	11		9

Source: Psacharopoulos (1985)

countries. Two, unlike the advanced countries where the rate of return on education has been falling relative to that on physical capital, the differential in favor of human capital remains persistent in Latin America.

The other form of evidence on differences in factor endowment is somewhat more indirect but not less relevant and pertains to human capital stocks. Very little work on estimating human capital stocks has been done for developing countries. Table 3 data, from the United Nations' *Human Development Report*, 1992, displays several common indicators of human development, often taken as proxies for human capital stocks, for the South American countries, both in absolute terms and relative to the North. As one would expect, the social indicators for South American countries are lower. As the final row shows, however, there is some disparity as to how much lower. In particular, while schooling rates are about half that of the North, literacy rates and life expec-

Table 3. Human capital indicators

	Life expectancy (years) I	Adult literacy (percent) II	Mean years schooling III	Schooling per life (percent) III ÷ I
South	67.8	85.3	5.2	7.6
North	76.0	99.0	12.3	16.2
South/North (%)	89.3	86.2	42.2	47.2

Source: United nations development programme (UNDP), 1992

Table 4. Relative per capita incomes and relative human capital stocks, 1980

	Relative per capita income (percent)	Percentage income differential explained by human capital (percent)	Relative stock of human capital per person (percent)
Brazil	29.7	55.0	37.8
Canada	92.9	85.7	91.4
Ecuador	21.7	50.6	27.6
Honduras	9.7	49.4	22.8
Japan	63.8	32.5	82.3
New Zealand	61.0	5.9	96.7
Panama	23.3	37.5	54.4

Source: Gundlach (1994)

tancy rates are in the region of 85–90 percent lower. This reflects the trend, which was reported by the UN, of a declining gap between the developed countries and less developed countries with respect to basic human needs, but a widening disparity with respect to technological and high skill-level indicators, (United Nations, 1992, pp. 39–40).

Some more direct estimates of relative human capital stocks have recently been undertaken by Gundlach (1994); he estimates how much the per capita income of a number of countries relative to the U.S. can be attributed to human capital differences. Some of his results are reported in Table 4 below, using a sample of Latin American countries and some developed countries for comparison purposes.[5] Depending on the country, between 40 and 60 percent of the income difference relative to the developed country can be explained by human capital endowments alone. Given the large fraction of national income that accrues to labor, and given that much of that income is the return to human

[5] Gundlach weights various levels of educational attainment by a common set of wages across countries, thus getting an internationally comparable set of relative human capital stocks. More typical are the methods used by Barro and Lee (1993), who use completed schooling data to impute relative human capital stocks. For a few countries there are some estimates using cumulative educational expenditures; see Schultz (1988). In the latter two cases, the methods ignore the experience of the workforce and international differences in the quality of formal education.

capital, a broad policy change such as economic integration is bound to affect both the returns to human capital and the subsequent accumulation of human capital.

4 A Two-Country Growth Model

In this section a basic two-country model of economic growth is outlined which attempts to accommodate some of the broader facts on international differences in human capital stocks together with a view that physical capital is at least partially mobile internationally. The model is a two-country version of the closed economy augmented Solow model developed by Mankiw, Romer and Weil (1992). Human capital is non-traded and investment in new physical capital is internationally mobile but subject to taxation. There are two major endogenous accumulation decisions in each region one on human capital and another on physical capital.

The key assumption, following Lucas (1988), is that technology in each country is virtually identical; differences in income and productivity are thus entirely attributable to differences in relative factor endowments, human capital and physical capital stocks per worker. In the tradition of trade theory, of course, this description of technology accords well with the Heckscher-Ohlin model in which technology is identical but factor endowments are different. Unlike the Heckscher-Ohlin theory, one wants a theory that is capable of accommodating observed differences in factor prices.[6] As is the case with most of the modern growth literature, technology is described in each country by an aggregate GDP function; while useful from a number of perspectives, including data and parameter availability, this specification has the disadvantage that trade flows cannot be modeled explicitly. Given the focus on factor endowment changes though, the model captures some important features necessary to examine long-term changes in relative income levels. In particular, relative international factor price differences in the single good framework are attributable to relative factor endowment differences.[7]

---

6 H-O theory is consistent with non-equalization of factor prices by assuming either specialization occurs or trade distortions are present.

7 There are a number of ways in which a multi-good trade model gives rise to these types of endowment effects on factor prices outside of the strict H-O framework. See Leamer (1984), chapter 1, for a discussion.

Model Details

Physical and human capital are both accumulated via exogenous Solow-style saving functions. Physical capital is not traded, but output is tradable (at least in part), while human capital is internationally immobile. The limitations on physical capital movements are modeled as one in which new investment may be allocated to either region but once in place is irreversible. This specification, while reasonable, does lead to results different from these in which the capital stock is completely mobile internationally as will become clear below. The technology exhibits constant returns to scale Conventional Total Factor Productivity (TFP) growth[8] is driven by one or a combination of a) shifts in a Hicks Neutral technology parameter; and b) the accumulation of human capital. The former is presumed to be identical in both countries.

The following are the basic equations of the model.

Each region $i = N, S$ has an aggregate GDP function given by

$$Y_i = A_i(d_L L_i^\rho + d_K K_i^\rho + d_H H_i^\rho)^{-1/\rho} \tag{1}$$

with given factor endowments L, K, and H. It will be convenient in some cases to write (1) as

$$Y_i = AF(L_i, K_i, H_i) \ . \tag{2}$$

A is the common Hicks Neutral technology shift parameter assumed to grow at the exponential rate θ. The marginal product of physical capital, which equals the gross rate of return on capital, is given by

$$r_i = AF_K^i(L_i, K_i, H_i) \ . \tag{3}$$

Income in each country is defined as M_i, and given capital flows, will be different from GDP. Aggregate saving functions for non-human capital follow the conventional Solow-Swan specification,

$$S_i = s_i M_i \ , \tag{4}$$

and "World Savings," or the sum of savings in both regions, is given by

$$S_W = S_N + S_S \ . \tag{5}$$

Aggregate physical capital accumulation equations for each region i, given gross investment rates I_j, is

$$\dot{K}_i = I_i - \delta_K \dot{K}_i \ , \tag{6}$$

where the depreciation rate, δ_K, is assumed to be identical across regions.

Human capital accumulation follows Mankiw, Romer and Weil (1992) and uses an augmented Solow-Swan specification with

[8] Defined as output growth less the weighted growth in labor and capital inputs.

$$\dot{H}_i = g_i Y_i - \delta_H H_i \ . \tag{7}$$

The mechanism for the generation of human capital plays a critical role in this model. The parameters g_i should be interpreted more broadly than simple "savings" rates of human capital they represent the combined effect of all factors on the rate at which market income is converted into gross human capital.[9] The specification matches well with the observed evidence on schooling and income levels reviewed by Schultz (1988). There is a strong presumption that, with highly imperfect credit markets for financing human capital, income is a principal determinant of spending on human capital formation. Given similar g parameters, and the assumption that human capital is non-tradable, differences in market income levels are therefore the principal determinant of international differences in the rate of human capital formation.

The net foreign asset position in region i is denoted by B_i; income on these assets is given by $r_{k_j}(1 - t_j)B_i$ where r_{k_j} is the rate of return on physical capital located in the other country, j, and t_j is the appropriate tax rate on the income from foreign-owned capital. For simplicity, it is assumed that foreign-owned capital is taxed only in the South. Total income in countries N and S is therefore given by

$$\begin{aligned} &\text{if } B_N \geq 0 \qquad M_N = Y_N + r_S(1 - t)B_N \\ &\text{if } B_N \leq 0 \qquad M_N = Y_N - r_N B_S \end{aligned} \tag{8}$$

$$\begin{aligned} &\text{if } B_N \geq 0 \qquad M_S = Y_S - r_S B_N \\ &\text{if } B_N \leq 0 \qquad M_S = Y_S + r_N B_S \ . \end{aligned} \tag{9}$$

The 'tax' on foreign-owned capital income in the South is not to be interpreted in the usual sense of a factor tax. Income in the South does not include the implicit tax revenues on foreign capital. There are two possible interpretations of the factor market distortion parameter, t. One, t may represent the expected loss factor on foreign-owned capital in the South. Thus, on average, a dollar of rental income in the South has an expected value of $(1 - t)$ due to random expropriation or destruction. Two, t may measure rent-seeking, bureaucratic costs, and other forms of resource-using activity, that foreign ownership in the

9 In a Ben-Porath (1967) style model we would have an explicit production function for gross human capital given by

$$\dot{H} + \delta H = G(x, y, H)$$

where x and y represent respectively market and non-market resources devoted to the production of human capital. Market resources devoted to human capital formation reflect training costs, education costs and health costs in part. Non-market resources reflect time inputs into schooling and household production that contribute to human capital formation. The stock of H enters the human capital production function for the simple reason that past human capital formation many contribute to the rate at which new human capital can be produced. This complex specification is replaced by the much simpler one adopted here.

South attracts. The model is set up such that capital exports always equal capital imports and thus $B_N = -B_S$.

Total non-human capital savings must be allocated as physical investment between the two regions. The allocation of investment in each period to the South is given by

$$I_S = \alpha S_W \tag{10}$$

with the investment share *function* $\alpha(\cdot)$ defined implicitly by

$$1 - \alpha = \left(\frac{K_N}{K_N + K_S}\right)[(r_N - \delta_K)/(r_S(1 - t) - \delta_K)]^\gamma \ . \tag{11}$$

The tax on northern-owned capital located in the South is at an ad valorem rate t. Each region's share of total investment is presumed proportional to the relative share of world capital held by each region, conditional on equal rates of return. The parameter γ is the elasticity of the share of investment in the region with respect to relative rates of return. The allocation of investment to the North is given by

$$I_N = (1 - \alpha)S_W \ . \tag{12}$$

The microfoundation for the investment allocation rule is consistent with the portfolio balance literature of international finance, but is not explicitly grounded in optimizing behavior. Investment allocation reflects both relative rates of return and the size of both economies as reflected in their respective shares of the world capital stock. The relative size factor is quite important; it is consistent with the existence of steady-states, and imparts a strong persistence to any shock that raises one region's share of the total capital stock.[10]

The dynamics of B_N are given by the difference between saving and investment in the North.

$$\dot{B}_N = S_N - (1 - \alpha)S_W \ . \tag{13}$$

Population Growth

It is necessary to specify the evolution of the labor force in both regions. These time paths of $L_i(t)$, are taken as exogenous to the model, and vary as illustrated

[10] Modelling asset allocation has been a long-standing problem in the applied general equilibrium literature, particularly in models without explicit uncertainty, and in integrating stocks with flows. One approach, for example, is to induce preferences over the asset mix as in Eichengreen and Goulder (1992). An alternative approach would be to model allocation of new investment goods as subject to quadratic costs of adjustment, but without asset preferences. Decision rules derived from such a framework would require additional assumptions on expectations, but would be broadly consistent with the specification in (11).

in figure 1. In the calibration, the labor force assumptions correspond to past and actual projections of labor force growth given demographic patterns in Canada, the United States and Latin America. Immigration is treated as exogenous and is contained in the labor force assumptions. Given the large differences over time of labor force growth between regions, the model is a non-steady transition path for virtually all of the simulations conducted.

Theoretical Properties of the Model

The two-country dynamics are potentially very complicated. In the appendix it is shown that if population growth rates and other parameters were taken as similar in N and S, and technological change were Harrod neutral, the model would have a well-defined steady state.[11] In the steady-state, rates of return are equalized across regions, income per worker is equalized, factor ratios are identical and growth rates are equal. The speed at which this steady state is approached, however, is an empirical matter. In figures L.1 through L.3, simulation paths of the model's benchmark are shown, using the calibrated parameter values, but taking out the effect of changes in population growth rates between North and South after 2025. As these figures indicate, the dominant impression is one of extremely slow convergence of North to South in level terms.

There appear to be essentially two reasons for the slow convergence. First, in the closed economy context, the speed of convergence in a model with diminishing returns is related to how the marginal productivity of accumulating factors diminishes in response to capital deepening. That is approximately equal to the elasticity of output with respect to the broadly defined capital stock both physical and human. In this model, that number is approximately 0.60 to 0.65 much closer to unity than in the usual physical capital-only model. This implies that convergence is much slower than would otherwise be the case.[12] The half-life of convergence to steady state in such a world is about 30 to 35 years. There is another effect at work here that serves to slow down the movement of capital from North to South substantially this is the presence of non-traded human capital. The marginal product of capital is an increasing function of the H/L ratio. This is the explanation in the Base Case as to why rates of return on physical capital in North and South are quite close, although factor ratios are very different. Once capital (or more accurately new gross investment) stops flowing disproportionately to the South, the rate at which the levels converge

[11] The closed economy for such a model does not have a well-defined steady state unless $\sigma = 1$ as exogenous technological change is Hicks-Neutral.

[12] Even within the Solow model the half-life of convergence time is in the order of 17 years. See Mankiw, Romer and Weil (1992) and Barro and Sali-Martin (1992) for a discussion of this issue and its empirical implications for testing the Solow-Swan model.

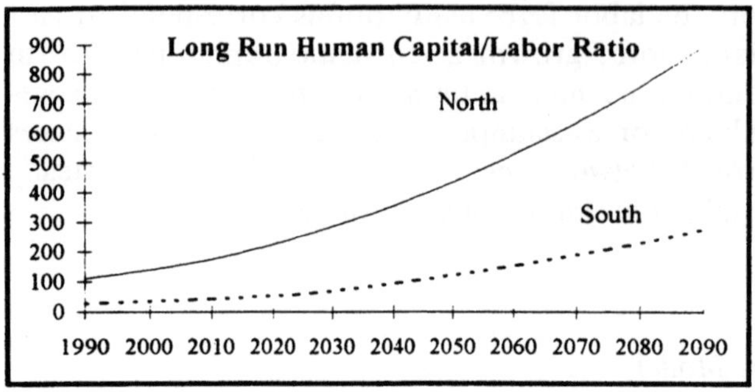

Fig. L1

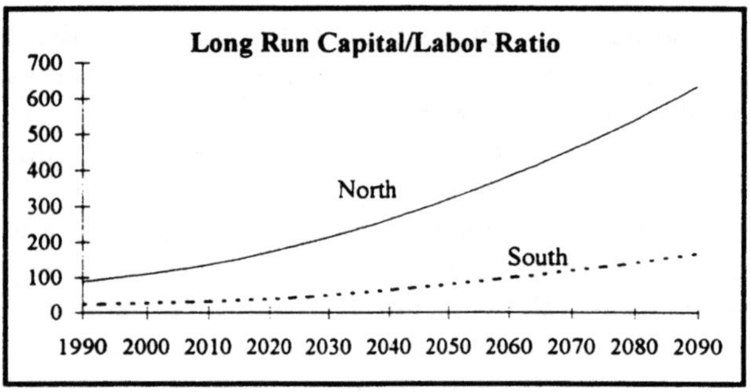

Fig. L2

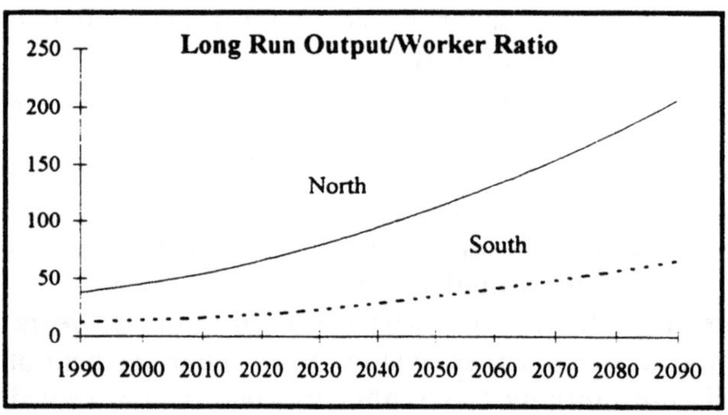

Fig. L3

Benchmark growth path

slows down considerably. Given that population growth rates differ between regions, the dynamics of the model are fairly complicated with elastic capital flows. For example, faster growing labor raises the return to capital in the South, thus attracting capital, while a lower rate of human capital accumulation tends to slow it down. It appears that for practical purposes the transition dynamics are the whole story.

5 Model Benchmarking and Policy Shocks

In the dynamic general equilibrium literature it has been customary to use steady-state conditions to scale certain key ratios such as capital output ratios to savings rates, and then to be sure that all shares and level variables match the appropriate benchmark data source.[13] It is also conventional to use estimates from the literature on elasticities in order to calibrate key parameters on technology and preferences. Parameters for the policy variables are either assumed or derived from the literature. The major difference in this paper, from that of the conventional approach, is that, for reasons alluded to earlier, a steady-state benchmarking procedure is not used. Currently there is no generally agreed on methodology of calibrating dynamic GE models on out of steady-state benchmarks.

The approach adopted is to calibrate the model so as to reproduce the approximate growth experience of the two regions over the period for which there is available data. For the North there is fairly detailed data on factor inputs and the key aggregates in constant PPP dollars going back to 1970. For the South, using the recent capital stock estimates of Hofman (1992) for the major Latin American countries, a series on capital and labor inputs was constructed for the years 1970–1988. There was no explicit human capital series available for Latin America and therefore calibration involved imputing a human capital series for the South. Work in the field of conceptualizing and quantifying "human capital" stocks is controversial. Recent estimates of human capital stocks in the United States, based on the summation of investment costs, show human capital stocks to be approximately equal in value to physical capital stocks, (Kendrick[14], 1976, p. 105, McMahon, 1991, p. 294). The recent

---

[13] The technique of using steady-state restrictions to calibrate the benchmark in dynamic applied GE analysis was pioneered by Ballard, Fullerton, Shoven and Whalley (1985). The technique is now common in much dynamic policy analysis. A recent example in the trade policy context is Eichengreen and Goulder (1992).

[14] Kendrick's (1976) "The formation and stocks of total capital" contains useful but dated estimates of physical and human capital stocks in the USA. Kendrick estimates human capital using expenditure data on education and training, health, safety (intangibles) and accumulated child-rearing costs (tangibles). He finds that education accounts for 61% of the net human capital total, and child rearing 31%. The remaining 8% is due to medical, health and mobility factors.

estimates by McMahon have the advantage, for the purposes here, of being consistent with the physical capital estimates produced by the US Bureau of Economic Analysis, and thus broadly consistent with the Summers and Heston data set discussed above (McMahon, 1991, p. 284). According to these estimates, the ratio of gross human capital to gross physical capital in the U.S. averaged 1.24 over the period 1979–89.

Conditional on the data, a number of the parameters were chosen to get reasonable fits to the time-series properties of the data in North and South. Two free parameters were calibrated to the initial levels data for 1970. These were i) the level of total factor productivity $A(0)$ and ii) the human capital stock in the South, $H_S(0)$. $A(0)$ is a scaling variable, chosen so that, given production function parameters and factor inputs for the North, the calibrated output matches observed output. $H_S(0)$ was chosen so that observed GDP (real) in the South matched the predicted model output given the presumed identical production function in North and South and factor inputs of physical capital and labor in the South. The trend rate of technological change was derived by estimating the trend in the augmented TFP residual for the North, given assumed parameters for the CES production function and observed factor inputs.

"Goodness of fit" criteria were used in calibrating the savings rates on physical and human capital. Setting the initial values of the state variables, the model is simulated over the 1970–88 period. The predicted series on GDP, human capital, physical capital in the North, and GDP and physical capital in the South are compared with the actual series on the same variables. Four key parameters were then chosen so as to get the best "fit" possible, in the sense that the model picked up the major trends and predicted RMSE were 'small'.[15] These parameters are referred to as "dynamically calibrated"; they are the gross savings rates on physical and human capital in North and South and the tax on foreign capital in the South. It is important to emphasize that these parameters are calibrated to reflect the average time series properties of the data, conditional on the theoretical model.

A major non-trending characteristic of the data was the collapse in growth in Latin America beginning in 1982. This particular episode, which many people associate with the debt crisis, corresponds to the collapse of the terms of trade in Latin America; Cohen (1993) and Warner (1992) both have noted that, with the resulting 20 percent deterioration in the terms of trade, the drop in investment in these countries was largely predictable. To account for this "shock," an 8 percent negative shock to A_S spread over three years beginning in 1982 was fed into the model to account for the terms of trade shocks to Latin America prior to dynamically calibrating the savings and tax rates. The interpretation of

[15] Actually the parameter values were chosen by minimizing the weighted sum of the RMSE. Some different weighting factors on the series were tried, but it appeared to make little difference to the resulting parameter values.

A_S therefore is a terms of trade adjusted TFP coefficient relative to the North. All simulations are reported under the assumption that the $A(t)$ functions for both North and South are exogenous.

This calibration procedure produces a human capital series for the South, $H_S(t)$, which is used as a starting point for subsequent simulations. The method used is essentially to attribute (relative) income levels and growth in the South, after accounting for capital and labor growth, to an unobserved human capital stock. One 'check' on this procedure is to compare the relative human capital stocks imputed by the calibration procedure to an alternative measure of relative capital stocks. An alternative indicator of relative human capital stocks between the North and South is a ratio measure of educational attainment, similar to that used by Barro (1991) in his construction of comparative indexes of human capital. Using weighted primary and secondary schooling rates in the countries of the North and South in 1960, an index of approximate average educational attainment of the labor force in 1970 in each region is used to proxy comparable indexes of human capital stocks per worker in North and South. Taking the ratios and using the respective labor forces in each region, the aggregate ratio of human capital in the South to the North was computed at 0.566. This ratio applied to the McMahon estimates of the human capital stock in the North[16] to give a comparable estimate of the aggregate human capital stock in the South of $4,282,260. This compares with the calibrated estimate in the model of $1,280,000. The implication, then, is that the two methods give fairly different estimates of the human capital stocks in the two regions. The calibration method imputes a much lower level of human capital than does application of the Barro methodology. The fairly low estimates of human capital derived from the calibration procedure stem in part from forcing income differences between regions to be explained entirely by differences in endowments. There is also the likelihood that the series used for human capital in the North, based on cumulating educational expenditures, leads to an underestimate of the human capital stock in the North due to job training and on-the-job experience. The net effect of the calibration method, however, is to overstate the differences in human capital between the regions.

Table 5 sets out the base case parameters and initial values either derived from searches of the literature or determined by the calibration procedure. Some features of the parameter values are as follows:

1) Production Function: The common elasticity of factor substitution is set at 1.2. This feature corresponds well to a number of studies on long time series; the major problem it poses is that the estimated capital share in the South falls between 24 and 28 percent, which is considerably below reported capital shares for Latin America. See DeGregorio (1992). The factor weighting coefficients, d_i, were chosen in order to reproduce observed factor shares in the North given endowments and the elasticity of factor substitution.

---

[16] In 1985 PPP$ the McMahon method gives an estimate of H in the North at $7,565,830.

Table 5. Parameter values

Human capital in S		Net foreign assets-S		Net foreign assets-N			
H_S 1970		B_S 1970		B_N 1970			
1280000		0		0			
Savings rates on physical and human capital				Growth rate of		Efficiency levels	
s_s	s_n	g_s	g_n	Hicks Neutral TFP		A	
0.18	0.18	0.151	0.151	0.0017		2.03	
Tax rate-depreciation rates and capital flow							
tax	δ_K	δ_H	γ				
0.20	0.04	0.02	1.3				
CES share weights			CES share weights			Substitution	
South			North			parameter	
d_K	d_H	d_L	d_K	d_H	d_L	ρ	σ
0.237	0.2996	0.463	0.237	0.2996	0.463	0.1667	1.2

2) Comparative Human Capital Stocks: The calibrated human capital stock per worker in the South is 18.7 percent of that in the North; alternatively, human capital per worker in the North was more than 5 times higher than in the South.
3) The model calibrated tax on foreign investment in the South is 20 percent given an assumed rate of return elasticity on investment shares of 1.3.
4) The gross saving rates on human capital for the South and the North were, surprisingly, almost identical. In light of the small difference in the free calibration, both were set equal to a common value of 0.151. Recall that these are not true "savings" parameters, but reflect the properties of the production function for human capital. Similarly, the calibrated rate of gross saving on physical capital was 0.18 for both regions.
5) The rate growth of total factor productivity, θ, was estimated from the growth experience of the North. Not surprisingly, trend productivity growth in the Hicks efficiency parameter is very low at 0.17 percent per annum.

For a given set of starting values, the model is solved numerically, using the fourth order Runge-Kutta method for solving systems of continuous non-linear differential equations. This technique numerically integrates the model forward from the base year, using an integration procedure based on a successive Taylor Series expansions around each estimated point, (see Press et al., 1990). The model is simulated for the period 1970 to 2090 given the assumed evolution of the demographic variables.[17]

[17] The parameter values give reasonable fits to all level variables through the end of 1988. The model is intended only for long-term analysis and does not produce business cycle fluctuations. Thus short-term movements in growth rates are not picked up by the model or the calibration procedure.

Characteristics of the Base Case

There a couple of features of the benchmark growth path worth noting. First, the capital labor ratio is gradually increasing in the South but not at as rapid a rate as in the North population growth weighs heavily on per capita income growth in the South. The South's share of investment increases slowly from 26 percent of the total to 36 percent of the total over the 35-year period. Total cumulative investment flows between regions are very weak as indicated by the share of the North's ownership of physical capital located in the South. There is remarkably little convergence in the base – the per capita income gap actually widens slightly from 65 percent to 69 percent by 2025. Capital output ratios grow in both regions, but quite slowly. Returns to both human and physical capital remain higher in the South than in the North. This base generally fits the view of a world in which capital is not flowing from the North to the South and income convergence is crawling along at an imperceptible pace.

Productivity Shocks and Regional Economic Integration

Static production gains to economic integration are approximated by assuming that trade liberalization has an impact similar to a once-off change in the efficiency of factors of production within an aggregate GDP function following a procedure used by Baldwin (1992)[18] in a one-country model. Trade liberalization can be thought of as enhancing the productivity of either all factors (a 'neutral' productivity increase) or of one of the factors (a biased productivity increase). Consider a general production function

$$Y = AF(\tau_L L, \tau_K K, \tau_H H) \ . \tag{14}$$

The shift parameters τ_f index factor efficiency levels, which are changed by reducing trade barriers or other policies. If it is assumed that the productivity effects are predominantly neutral, then this is modeled as a proportionate increase in all τ. For example, suppose in the case of the North it is estimated that the static efficiency impact of WHFTA is 1.0 percent of GDP. This would imply that all τ_i would increase by 1.0 percent with increases spread over an appropriate period reflecting how long it takes the assumed productivity change

[18] This procedure can only be justified as an approximation given that, with the changes in relative prices that accompany trade reform, conditions for exact aggregation across sectors cannot be satisfied. The aggregate production function, however, is useful in that it provides a convenient way of keeping track of both factor price changes in response to changes in aggregate inputs and as shifts in production possibilities due to trade reform.

to work through the economy. The assumption made in this paper is that the productivity effects of trade liberalization are spread evenly over five years after the initial "integration" shock in both the North and the South. At the end of this phase-in period the cumulative level effect on factor efficiency is assumed to be permanent.

Three sets of productivity 'bias' in integration shocks are explored. The first assumes all productivity changes are factor neutral and is modeled as proportionate changes in all τ. Two others explore the possibility that the productivity bias is toward either unskilled labor or physical capital. Standard theories suggest that trade liberalization tends to raise the efficiency of some sectors differentially relative to others. A 'New Trade Theory' view of protection, for example, would lead to the prediction that the factors used intensively in the protected sectors are those whose efficiency is raised most by a trade liberalization.[19] In the case of liberalizing trade in the Americas, the pattern of protection is fairly clear. In the North, labor intensive-manufactures and agricultural products are protected, while in Latin America the long history of Import Substitution in manufacturing raised protective barriers against capital-intensive manufacturing. In table 3.2 Harris and Robertson (1993) report 77 percent of total welfare gains fall on the manufacturing sector in the South.[20]

The alternative to the 'new trade theory' view is that suggested by a conventional Heckscher-Ohlin two-factor model. Protection tends to reduce productivity of the export sector. Given the pattern of North-South protection in the Western Hemisphere, a WHFTA would raise productivity of labor-intensive goods in the South and raise productivity of capital-intensive exports in the North. Via the Stolper-Samuelson theorem, these effects would be reflected in factor prices. A WHFTA integration shock in the Heckscher-Ohlin model should raise real wages in the South and raise real returns to capital in the North. This will be referred to as the Heckscher-Ohlin bias in the WHFTA integration shocks. In the reported simulations, all increases in labor productivity will be attributed to an improvement in the efficiency of unskilled labor rather than to an increase in the returns to human capital.

To highlight the effect of alternative bias in integration shocks, in the non-neutral cases it is assumed efficiency gains fall entirely on one factor in each

---

[19] In models with imperfect competition and economies of scale, import protection tends to reduce the absolute productivity of all factors used in the protected sector. See Harris (1985). The bias assumed here is that the reduction in efficiency falls entirely on the factor used intensively in the protected sector.

[20] A related literature supporting this view is that on the "inappropriate capital intensity of developing countries" summarized by Pack (1988) (section 6.3). A set of country studies by Kreuger (1983) emphasizes the strong potential employment effects of shifting away from import substitution that tends to encourage the artificial expansion of capital-intensive sectors. In a sample of eight countries, for example, she finds that with a fixed capital stock reduction of protection total employment could increase by an average of 47 percent. In the model used here, employment is viewed as exogenous, but clearly the move away from protection of capital-intensive sectors would raise productivity substantially.

region. Thus under the new trade theory view this results in an increase in τ_L in the North and in an increase in τ_K in the South. To achieve a given increase in the total output level approximately equal to an assumed efficiency gain of x, given that the s_f is the input share of factor f, the factor-biased change in efficiency units is approximately equal to $\hat{\tau}_f = s_f/x$.[21]

The magnitude of the static productivity change used in the trade liberalization simulations of WHFTA are taken from Harris and Robertson (1993) (see table 1 in section 2); approximately 8.5 percent of GDP for the South and 1.3 percent of GDP for the North – this includes both static welfare triangles, gains in productivity due to achievement of economies of scale and welfare changes due to induced shifts in the terms of trade.

The calibrated model is used to investigate two policy counterfactuals. Each is related to the potential impact of WHFTA relative to the situation as it existed at the end of the 1980s. The first policy experiment is a regional free trade area, or a general broadening of NAFTA to include all of the Americas. This is considered under three alternative assumptions on factor bias: a) a neutral productivity shock of 1.3 percent in the North and 8.5 percent in the South;[22] b) a biased productivity shock with all of the positive impact on unskilled labor (L) in the North and on capital (K) in the South (the 'New trade theory' bias); and c) a biased productivity shock with all of the impact on capital in the North and on labor in the South (Heckscher-Ohlin bias). The second policy experiment adds to the trade liberalization an investment liberalization that involves phased in removal of the differential taxation of foreign investment in the South – equal to 20 percent ad valorem in the Base case. For comparison purposes the effect of removing only the tax on foreign investment, while leaving factor efficiencies unchanged, is also reported. The levels shocks commence in 1995 and are spread evenly over a five-year period. By the year 2000 all levels effects of the integration shocks on the efficiency of factor inputs cease. All subsequent changes in output are due to indirect effects which are induced through factor accumulation. It will be convenient to refer to the 'dynamic multiplier' as the ratio of the long-term GDP gains, indexed by the date on which they occur, relative to the assumed initial static gains. Thus a 30-year dynamic multiplier value of 2, for example, would mean that a 1 percent static increase in GDP due to the increased efficiency of factor inputs would result ultimately, in 30 years time, in a 2 percent overall gain in GDP relative to the base.

---

21 The formulae is exact only for small changes. Errors caused by using this first-order approximation to the levels productivity shocks are quite small – on the order of 0.01 percent.

22 Strictly speaking, the consumption gains should not be included in a "productivity shock" – however, the actual consumption gains are a minor fraction of overall welfare effects. The numbers are only approximate in any case.

6 Policy Simulation Results

In table R.1 results for the case of a neutral efficiency shock to North and South covering a 30-year period are summarized. Recall that this case involves permanently raising the efficiency level of all factors simultaneously, but spread evenly over the first five years from 1995 to 2000 by the appropriate amount. In total, factor efficiency is raised by 1.3 percent in the North and 8.5 percent in the South.

The neutral shock gives rise to an ultimate gain in both aggregate and per capita income in the South of 20 percent. The multiplier effects run fairly smoothly through time with total gains at 13.4 percent after 10 years, 17.25 percent after 20 years and 20 percent after 30 years. Dynamic effects in the North, however, are relatively minor; a 1.3 percent increase in efficiency levels ultimately increases income by only 1.56 percent. 'Hemispheric' GDP, with the Hemisphere defined as the aggregate of North plus South, rises by about 8 percent over the 30-year period. The long-run impact is almost exactly twice the short-run impact. The mechanism at work is fairly clear – both increases in physical and human capital in the South result in a rising share of total invest-

Table R1. Impact of factor unbiased liberalized trade shock changes in selected variables 1999–2025
Efficiency increase: 1.3 percent in North and 8.5 percent in South
(% change over base)

	2000	2005	2010	2015	2020	2025
Y_s	10.79	13.43	15.51	17.25	18.75	20.06
Y_n	1.29	1.31	1.36	1.43	1.50	1.56
Y_w	4.02	4.93	5.76	6.54	7.27	7.96
alpha	13.48	13.05	13.12	13.39	13.72	14.05
GNP_s	10.36	12.67	14.57	16.21	17.64	18.92
GNP_n	1.04	0.95	0.92	0.92	0.94	0.95
MPK_s/MPK_n	7.55	4.36	2.71	1.81	1.29	0.98
Incgap	−4.18	−5.20	−5.92	−6.43	−6.85	−7.25
H/L_s	1.62	4.25	6.68	8.89	10.88	12.67
H/L_n	0.15	0.33	0.46	0.56	0.63	0.69
Y/L_s	10.79	13.43	15.51	17.25	18.75	20.06
Y/L_n	1.29	1.31	1.36	1.43	1.50	1.56
K/Y_s	−6.13	−3.95	−2.73	−2.00	−1.55	−1.25
K/Y_n	−1.53	−1.72	−1.77	−1.76	−1.72	−1.68
W_s/W_n	1.88	3.93	6.15	8.55	9.06	9.54
MPH_s/MPH_n	2.09	4.25	6.48	8.77	8.86	8.91
B_n/K_s*	0.00	0.00	0.00	0.02	0.02	0.03

* Figures represent the absolute differences in the share of foreign-owned capital in the South. Variable definitions: K physical capital stock; H human capital stock; W wage of unskilled labor; MPK marginal product of K net of depreciation; MPH marginal product of H net of depreciation; *Incgap* is per worker income gap of North-South over North; Y/L is average labor productivity; B_n is net foreign assets of the North; K/Y is the physical capital to output ratio; Alpha share of total investment going to S; subscripts s, n and w refer to South, North and Western Hemisphere respectively.

ment allocated to the South. Increases in human capital are directly related to changes in income. Explaining movements in investment is more complicated. In the 1990 Benchmark, the marginal product of capital is about 18 percent higher than that in the North and the capital/labor ratio in the South is less than one-third that of the North with the relative situation worsening over time in the Benchmark path due to both population growth and the limits on capital flows in the model. The integration shock does nothing to population growth but it does facilitate movement of capital over time by raising relative returns to capital in the South. This effect is diluted over the longer term as higher rates of capital accumulation in the South give rise to diminishing returns. The marginal product of human capital in the *base* is about 30 percent higher in the South than in the North, with the difference diminishing slowly over time. The WHFTA shock causes the relative return to the South's marginal product of human capital to rise in the long-run by about 9 percent; this is accompanied at the same time by increasing ratios of human capital to labor. The explanation for this change is income growth which facilitates accumulation of non-tradable human capital by the South.

The basic economics behind these results are illustrated in figures 2, 3 and 4. These are drawn for the productivity bias assumed under the new trade theory but the pictures are similar in the case of the alternative assumptions on factor bias of an integration shock. In figure 4 the sharp rise in the returns to capital in the South relative to the North following the integration shock are shown over the 1995–2000 period. Figure 3 indicates the effect this has on the share of total investment that is allocated to the South. Notice the strong persistence in this share at the end of the shock period. The impact on productivity levels is shown in figure 2; slowly but surely, productivity in the South (and hence income) rises with the absolute impact effect increasing over the entire 25 years following the initial productivity shocks.

In table R.2 results on WHFTA integration are provided under the 'New Trade Theory' factor bias assumption. Recall that the basic idea here is that trade liberalization, given the patterns of protection in the two regions, has differential factor efficiency consequences in the North and South – efficiency gains in this scenario are assumed to fall on capital in the South and labor in the North. In the South the results are qualitatively and quantitatively similar to the neutral case – the long-run multiplier is 2.4 and the mechanism responsible is a larger share of new investment going to the South, which results in a much larger capital stock. Human capital to labor ratios move about the same in this scenario as with the neutral trade shock.

The impact on the North of the different factor bias is noticeable however. Long-run income actually falls by 0.2 percent with total capital stocks falling relative to the base by 1.6 percent in 10 years and 3.1 percent in 30 years. The factors at work here are clear. With the total savings rate on physical capital in the region fixed, investment capital tends to shift more rapidly toward the South than does income growth; this implies over the long-run that the capital stock is lower in the North than it would have been without WHFTA. It is important to

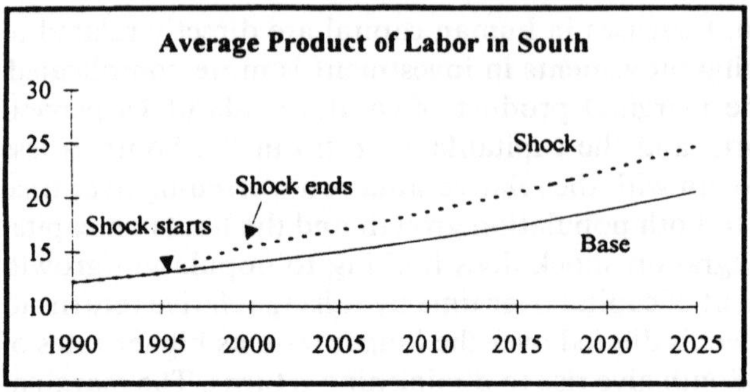

Fig. 2.

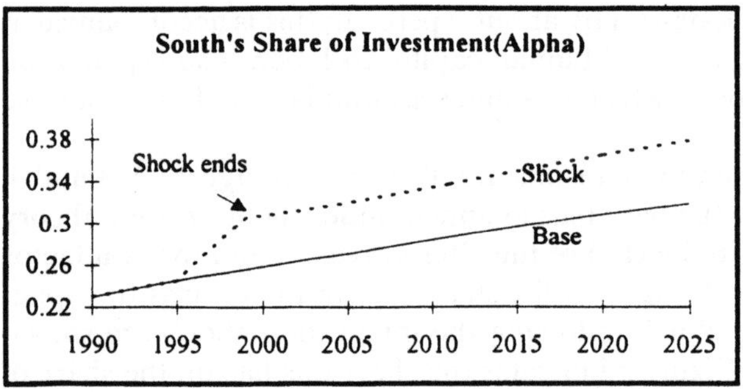

Fig. 3.

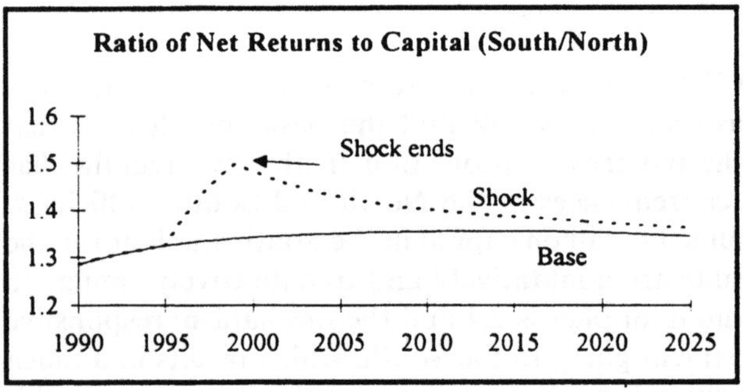

Fig. 4.

Table R2. Impact of factor biased liberalized trade shock changes in selected variables 1999–2025
Efficiency increase: 1.3 percent in North and 8.5 percent in South
Bias: labor in the North and capital in the South
(% change over base)

	2000	2005	2010	2015	2020	2025
Y_s	10.43	13.40	15.64	17.44	18.95	20.27
Y_n	0.86	0.59	0.38	0.19	−0.00	−0.20
Y_w	3.60	4.41	5.12	5.76	6.35	6.88
alpha	18.98	17.94	17.75	17.93	18.27	18.66
GNP_s	9.77	12.16	14.05	15.63	17.01	18.22
GNP_n	0.49	−0.01	−0.42	−0.78	−1.13	−1.48
MPK_s/MPK_n	10.39	5.74	3.44	2.24	1.59	1.21
Incgap	−4.22	−5.54	−6.44	−7.10	−7.65	−8.16
H/L_s	1.54	4.05	6.40	8.54	10.47	12.20
H/L_n	0.09	0.12	0.04	−0.09	−0.27	−0.48
Y/L_s	10.43	13.40	15.64	17.44	18.95	20.27
Y/L_n	0.86	0.59	0.38	0.19	−0.00	−0.20
K/Y_s	−4.62	−1.76	−0.29	0.48	0.88	1.09
K/Y_n	−1.63	−2.21	−2.50	−2.68	−2.79	−2.88
W_s/W_n	1.48	3.06	4.74	6.51	7.16	7.76
MPH_s/MPH_n	1.82	3.64	5.45	7.25	7.51	7.71
B_n/K_s*	0.00	0.00	0.02	0.03	0.04	0.05

* Figures represent the absolute differences in the share of foreign-owned capital in the South. Variable definitions: K physical capital stock; H human capital stock; W wage of unskilled labor; MPK marginal product of K net of depreciation; MPH marginal product of H net of depreciation; *Incgap* is per worker income gap of North-South over North; Y/L is average labor productivity; B_n is net foreign assets of the North; K/Y is the physical capital to output ratio; Alpha share of total investment going to S; subscripts s, n and w refer to South, North and Western Hemisphere respectively.

note, however, that capital per worker is vastly higher in the North than in the South, even 30 years after the initial shock.

In table R.3 the results for a combined trade and investment liberalization are reported. The assumed factor bias of the integration shock is the same as in the last policy experiment. Results in table R.3 can therefore be compared with those in table R.2. The 20 percent tax on investment by the North in the South is removed over the five-year period 1995–2000. By 2025 the combined removal of trade barriers and the foreign investment tax gives rise to a capital stock in the South that is 40 percent greater than otherwise. Income levels in the North are hurt more significantly – income falls by 6.3 percent over the 30-year period. Investment diversion appears to be quite possible. The negative dynamic GDP multiplier for the North in this case is approximately −4.8. Of course the numbers on GNP are marginally different for the North than those on GDP. The impact of a progressively stronger movement in capital towards the South is evident in the last row of Tables R.2 and R.3. The North's share of investment in the South is increased quite significantly by the trade liberalization and investment liberalization shocks. The North's absolute ownership share of the South capital stock rises by 15 percentage points in the case of the combined

Table R3. Impact of combined trade and investment liberalization changes in selected variables 1999–2025
Full removal of tax on foreign investment
Bias: labor in the North and capital in the South
Efficiency increase: 1.3 percent in North and 8.5 percent in South
(% change over base)

	2000	2005	2010	2015	2020	2025
Y_s	12.99	18.35	21.57	23.68	25.16	26.25
Y_n	−0.01	−1.54	−2.82	−4.00	−5.15	−6.30
Y_w	3.72	4.40	4.76	4.94	5.00	4.96
alpha	53.34	46.25	43.30	42.14	41.76	41.75
GNP_s	11.03	14.25	16.19	17.51	18.47	19.20
GNP_n	−0.87	−3.45	−5.58	−7.47	−9.26	−10.99
MPK_s/MPK_n	1.30	−10.24	−15.05	−17.26	−18.35	−18.90
Incgap	−5.79	−8.79	−10.64	−11.89	−12.89	−13.82
H/L_s	1.68	4.62	7.38	9.78	11.81	13.51
H/L_n	−0.02	−0.51	−1.38	−2.46	−3.68	−4.97
Y/L_s	12.99	18.35	21.57	23.68	25.16	26.25
Y/L_n	−0.01	−1.54	−2.82	−4.00	−5.15	−6.30
K/Y_s	0.43	7.59	10.39	11.26	11.27	10.89
K/Y_n	−3.38	−5.96	−7.48	−8.50	−9.27	−9.90
W_s/W_n	1.60	3.54	5.83	8.47	10.02	11.41
MPH_s/MPH_n	1.95	4.17	6.65	9.38	10.56	11.51
B_n/K_s*	0.00	0.02	0.05	0.09	0.12	0.15

* Figures represent the absolute differences in the share of foreign-owned capital in the South. Variable definitions: *K* physical capital stock; *H* human capital stock; *W* wage of unskilled labor; *MPK* marginal product of *K* net of depreciation; *MPH* marginal product of *H* net of depreciation; *Incgap* is per worker income gap of North-South over North; *Y/L* is average labor productivity; B_n is net foreign assets of the North; *K/Y* is the physical capital to output ratio; Alpha share of total investment going to *S*; subscripts *s*, *n* and *w* refer to South, North and Western Hemisphere respectively.

form of liberalization. The investment boom in the South, triggered by the integration shock, is driven to a considerable degree by foreign investment. Clearly the North, while losing its relative attractiveness as a location for investment, benefits as an owner of capital in the South.

The impact of liberalizing investment alone is illustrated in table R4. Most noteworthy is the completely opposite effects of this tax removal on the North and South. North GDP falls in the long-run by 5 percent while South GDP rises by 5 percent. For the "world," total GDP falls by 1.6 percent. This result is accounted for by the negative effect on investment on human capital formation in the North – it falls by almost 4 percent over a 40-year period. Given the relative size of the North in the region, this has quite a strong impact on total output over the long-run. In general this result should be treated with considerable caution, given the uncertainty as to the probable "true" ad valorem distortion on foreign-owned capital in the South.

The Heckscher-Ohlin model of international trade provides an alternative view on the probable factor price and productivity effects of trade liberalization.

Table R4. Impact of investment liberalization changes in selected variables 1999–2025
Full removal of tax on foreign investment
(% change over base)

	2000	2005	2010	2015	2020	2025
Y_s	1.99	3.90	4.76	5.10	5.15	5.05
Y_n	−0.74	−1.77	−2.67	−3.51	−4.32	−5.14
Y_w	0.05	−0.08	−0.36	−0.73	−1.15	−1.61
alpha	29.05	24.60	22.47	21.40	20.83	20.53
GNP_s	0.93	1.62	1.76	1.63	1.39	1.07
GNP_n	−1.21	−2.91	−4.35	−5.66	−6.91	−8.12
MPK_s/MPK_n	−7.58	−14.23	−17.20	−18.60	−19.28	−19.61
Incgap	−1.22	−2.51	−3.24	−3.68	−4.00	−4.27
H/L_s	0.10	0.43	0.76	1.00	1.13	1.15
H/L_n	−0.10	−0.54	−1.21	−2.01	−2.89	−3.82
Y/L_s	1.99	3.90	4.76	5.10	5.15	5.05
Y/L_n	−0.74	−1.77	−2.67	−3.51	−4.32	−5.14
K/Y_s	4.81	9.10	10.73	11.15	11.00	10.61
K/Y_n	−1.49	−3.17	−4.22	−4.95	−5.52	−5.98
W_s/W_n	0.11	0.43	0.93	1.59	2.29	2.90
MPH_s/MPH_n	0.12	0.48	1.02	1.73	2.45	3.05
B_n/K_s*	0.00	0.02	0.03	0.06	0.08	0.10

* Figures represent the absolute differences in the share of foreign-owned capital in the South. Variable definitions: K physical capital stock; H human capital stock; W wage of unskilled labor; MPK marginal product of K net of depreciation; MPH marginal product of H net of depreciation; *Incgap* is per worker income gap of North-South over North; Y/L is average labor productivity; B_n is net foreign assets of the North; K/Y is the physical capital to output ratio; Alpha share of total investment going to S; subscripts s, n and w refer to South, North and Western Hemisphere respectively.

That theory, and in particular the Stolper-Samuelson theorem, suggests that bilateral liberalization of imports would raise the wage of unskilled labor in the South and the returns to capital in the North. The impact of a trade liberalizing WHFTA, given this type of assumed factor bias, is reported in table R5. There are two interesting features of these results. First, the general magnitude of the long-run gains are similar for the South as estimated under alternative assumptions on factor bias; GDP rises by about 19 percent in the long-run, which is very close to the results reported in the other productivity shock experiments. In this case, however, the North does not lose – North GDP rises about 2 percent in the long-run as capital does not tend to flow to the South as strongly as it does under the alternative assumptions. The world aggregate effect of this factor productivity shock are remarkably similar to the other experiments in all cases world GDP rises in the long-run by about 8 percent.

The similarity of results on GDP changes under alternative assumptions on factor bias is misleading. The underlying economics are somewhat different in this case from the opposite factor bias assumed in new trade theory view. Because unskilled labor productivity rises in the South and unskilled labor is faster growing in the South, this carries some dynamic benefits that would

Table R5. Impact of factor biased liberalized trade shock changes in selected variables 1999–2025
Efficiency increase: 1.3 percent in North and 8.5 percent in South
Bias: capital in the North and labor in the South
(% change over base)

	2000	2005	2010	2015	2020	2025
Y_s	11.00	13.29	15.11	16.61	17.87	18.94
Y_n	1.25	1.38	1.54	1.72	1.90	2.08
Y_w	4.05	4.94	5.76	6.53	7.25	7.92
alpha	10.64	10.43	10.52	10.69	10.88	11.03
GNP_s	10.68	12.80	14.54	16.01	17.26	18.35
GNP_n	1.07	1.16	1.31	1.48	1.68	1.88
MPK_s/MPK_n	5.94	3.50	2.18	1.43	0.96	0.66
Incgap	−4.29	−5.11	−5.66	−6.04	−6.32	−6.57
H/L_s	1.72	4.38	6.79	8.94	10.85	12.53
H/L_n	0.15	0.36	0.54	0.72	0.90	1.07
Y/L_s	11.00	13.29	15.11	16.61	17.87	18.94
Y/L_n	1.25	1.38	1.54	1.72	1.90	2.08
K/Y_s	−6.81	−4.98	−3.88	−3.17	−2.67	−2.31
K/Y_n	−1.28	−1.28	−1.20	−1.09	−0.97	−0.85
W_s/W_n	2.11	4.17	6.20	8.19	8.61	9.00
MPH_s/MPH_n	2.05	3.99	5.82	7.55	7.52	7.46
B_n/K_s*	0.00	0.00	0.00	0.00	0.01	0.02

* Figures represent the absolute differences in the share of foreign-owned capital in the South. Variable definitions: K physical capital stock; H human capital stock; W wage of unskilled labor; MPK marginal product of K net of depreciation; MPH marginal product of H net of depreciation; *Incgap* is per worker income gap of North-South over North; Y/L is average labor productivity; B_n is net foreign assets of the North; K/Y is the physical capital to output ratio; Alpha share of total investment going to S; subscripts s, n and w refer to South, North and Western Hemisphere respectively.

otherwise not occur were efficiency improvements to fall on other factors. The difference in results shows up most clearly in the South's share of total investment. Under the H-O bias, this increases by 11 percentage points, while under the New Trade Theory view it rises by almost 19 percent. The South benefits under a capital bias because it attracts investment, while under the H-O view the productivity of its abundant and immobile factor is raised. Both lead to similar aggregate results, but the mechanism at work is quite different.

A useful summary of the results of this model are given in table 6, which contains the dynamic GDP multipliers for a productivity-induced trade liberalization shock under alternative factor biases, but with slight smaller estimated productivity impacts to trade liberalization: 1 percent in the North and 6 percent in the South. Looking at the table, a couple of general results emerge. First, in the case of both a Heckscher-Ohlin and a Neutral factor bias, the multipliers all exceed one and in the case both the Hemisphere exceed two by the year 2020. In the case of the New Trade Theory bias, the regional multiplier is slightly less than two, at 1.9, and in excess of 2.0 for the South. However for the North, for reasons already discussed, the multiplier is uniformly less than one for all years

Table 6. Dynamic gains multipliers: 1% productivity shock to North; 6% productivity shock to South

	Neutral bias					
G.D.P.	2000	2005	2010	2015	2020	2025
South	1.25	1.54	1.78	1.97	2.14	2.28
North	1.01	1.04	1.10	1.17	1.23	1.29
Hemisphere	1.21	1.47	1.71	1.94	2.15	2.35
	Heckscher-Ohlin Bias					
G.D.P.	2000	2005	2010	2015	2020	2025
South	1.17	1.40	1.59	1.74	1.87	1.98
North	0.99	1.11	1.25	1.40	1.55	1.69
Hemisphere	1.14	1.38	1.61	1.82	2.02	2.20
	New Trade Theory Bias					
G.D.P.	2000	2005	2010	2015	2020	2025
South	1.10	1.41	1.64	1.82	1.98	2.11
North	0.72	0.58	0.47	0.38	0.28	0.17
Hemisphere	1.01	1.23	1.42	1.59	1.75	1.89

and falling over time; by 2025 dynamic gains in the North are less than 20 percent of the static gains.

Sensitivity Results[23]

Parameter sensitivity of these results was investigated for a number of the two key parameters, in particular, the elasticity of investment flows (γ) and the rate of human capital formation (g). As both capital and human capital accumulation are the two driving factors in the growth performance of the model, one might suspect changes in these parameters would have a strong impact on results. However, this turned out not to be the case. Long-run dynamic multipliers barely changed with changes in these parameters. There are some differences in the transition dynamics, however. With a high rate of return elasticity on the investment allocation function, α rises sharply and then falls relative to the base. With a low elasticity, α rises slowly over the entire thirty-year period. The results on output confirm these differences – a high elasticity tends to push the output gains toward the earlier years, while a low elasticity pushes them toward the later years. If one were to conduct welfare analysis and use discounted consumption streams as a welfare indicator these would be parameter sensitive.

[23] Detailed sensitivity tables are available upon request.

7 Conclusion

A two-country dynamic GE model of North and South America is simulated with productivity shocks chosen to mimic the static productivity effects of trade liberalization. Over the course of two to three decades, the long-run impact of policy-induced changes in investment in physical and human capital can lead to results substantially different from models that take factor endowments as given. The presence of strong human capital intensity differences between regions gives rise to long-lived transition dynamics and the slow movement of capital from the rich North to the poor South. Policy changes such as the creation of a free trade area or liberalization of investment flows shift these long-term dynamic paths. This paper examines how a WHFTA would impact on these dynamics. In the calibration, all income differences are attributed to differences in factor endowments and technology is assumed to be identical in both regions. The model gives numbers quite different from calculations that conventional static general equilibrium models would suggest on the effects of the economic integration of North and South America. The estimates suggest the long-run income gains to Latin America could be on the order of 20 percent of GDP. Long-run multipliers on income gains tend to be on the order of 2 to 3 times traditional static gains for the South[24] and small to negligible for the North. While these results are both model and calibration specific, the implication is clear. Moving to a framework in which human and physical capital endowments change endogenously is essential to understanding the longer-term impact of economic policy. The simple model suffers from both a high level of commodity aggregation and reliance on the assumption that technology is internationally identical; in these respects, it fails to incorporate a sufficiently realistic view of the process of trade integration as it interacts with economic growth. The next step is to construct models that simultaneously explain trade patterns, accommodate international differences in technology and retain an emphasis on long-term factor accumulation.

Appendix 1

Steady state and dynamics in a two-country model

Let $k_n = K_N/L_N$, $k_s = K_S/L_S$, $h_n = H_N/L_N$, $h_s = H_S/L_S$. Assume identical savings parameters in both countries, no taxation and equal population growth

---

[24] The GDP multipliers for the South are much smaller than the dynamic welfare multipliers in the Baldwin (1992) framework that utilizes a completely specified set of intertemporal preferences. Within a different theoretical framework, and using a steady state restrictions on the base, Baldwin estimates GDP increases due to additional capital formation induced by the EC 1992 integration shock range from 30 to 130 percent. Results are obviously theory dependent, but his results confirm the general point made here as the importance of induced indirect accumulation effects from policy shocks.

rates of n. Let the rate of technological change equal 0, or alternatively assume it to be Harrod-netural and redefine labor in efficiency units. The dynamics of the physical and human capital stocks in the North are given by

$$\dot{K}_N = \alpha S(Y_N + Y_S) - \delta_K K_N \tag{a.1}$$

$$\dot{H}_N = gY_N - \delta_H H_N \tag{a.2}$$

The equations for the South are similar except α is replaced by $1 - \alpha$. The share function is dependent upon capital stocks and ratios of marginal products of capital. Using the linear homogeneity of $F(K, H, L)$ a.1 and a.2 can be used to derive the dynamics for k_n and h_n. Let $f(K/L, H/L) \equiv F(K, H, L)/L$ be the per capita production function. The factor ratio dynamics are given by

$$\dot{k}_n/k_n = \frac{(1-\alpha)sf(k_n, h_n)}{k_n} + \frac{\alpha sf(k_s, h_s)}{k_s} - (\delta_K + n) \tag{a.3}$$

$$\dot{h}_n/h_n = \frac{gf(k_n, h_n)}{h_n} - (\delta_H + n). \tag{a.4}$$

A similar set of equations can be derived for the South. The steady-state restrictions are derived by setting a.3 and a.4 for North and South both equal to 0. In addition, the requirement of equal rates of return on mobile capital require identical marginal products in both regions; that is

$$f_1(k_n, h_n) = f_1(k_s, h_s) \ . \tag{a.5}$$

In a steady state with equal marginal products of K, the share $1 - \alpha = K_N/(K_{N+}K_S)$. Let $z = L_S/L_N$ which, given identical growth rates of the labor force in both regions, is a constant. The share equation can be expressed as

$$1 - \alpha = \frac{k_n}{k_n + zk_s} \tag{a.6}$$

substituting a.6 into a.3 set equal to 0 gives a steady state restriction on (k_n, h_n, k_s, h_s). a.3 for North and South are functionally dependent so that the fourth equation defining the steady state is (a.5).

One solution to this set of steady-state equations is given by

$$\begin{aligned} k_n &= k = k^* \\ h_n &= h_s = h^* \end{aligned} \tag{a.7}$$

with (k^*, h^*) defined by the equations

$$\begin{aligned} sf(k^*, h^*) &= (\delta_K + n)k^* \\ gf(k^*, h^*) &= (\delta_H + n)h^* \end{aligned} \tag{a.8}$$

This steady-state solution has the property that both countries have identical factor ratios, factor prices and income per worker. It is possible that there are other steady-states in this model, although simulation results all tended toward this solution from the calibrated starting values.

References

Arrow KJ, Chenery HB, Minhas BS, Solow RM (1961) Capital-labor. substitution and economic efficiency. Review of Economics and Statistics. LXIII:225–50

Baldwin R (1992) Measurable dynamic gains from trade. Journal of Political Economy 100/1:162–74

Ballard C, Fullerton D, Shoven JB, Whalley J (1985) A general equilibrium model for tax policy evaluation. U. of Chicago Press, Chicago

Barro RJ, Sali-i-Martin X (1992) Convergence. Journal of Political Economy 100/2:223

Barro RJ (1991) Economic growth in a cross-section of countries. Quarterly Journal of Economics 106:407–443

Barro RJ, Lee JW (1993) International comparisons of educational attainment. Journal of Monetary Economics 32:363–94

Ben-Porath Y (1967) The production of human capital and the life cycle of earnings. Journal of Political Economy 75:352–65

Cohen D (1993) Low investment and large LDC debt in the 1980s. American Economic Review 83/3:437–49

Corden M (1971) The effects of trade on the rate of growth. In: Bhagwati JN (ed) Trades, balance of payments and growth. North Holland, Amsterdam

DeGregorio J (1992) Economic growth in Latin America. Journal of Development Economics 39:59–84

Edwards S (1992) Trade orientation, distortions and growth in developing countries. Journal of Development Economics 39:31–57

Eichengreen B, Goulder LH (1992) Trade liberalization in general equilibrium: intertemporal and interindustry effects. Canadian Journal of Economics XXV/2:253–80

Grossman G, Helpman E (1990) Comparative advantage and long-run growth. American Economic Review 80:796–815

Harris RG (1985) Trade, industrial policy and canadian manufacturing. Toronto Ontario Economic Council

Harris RG, Robertson P (1993) Free trade in the Americas: Estimates of the impact of a Western Hemispheric free trade area. Working paper, Simon Fraser University, Canada

Havrylyshyn O (1990) Trade policy and productivity gains in developing countries. The World Bank Observer 5/1:1–24

Helliwell JF (1994) Trade and technical progress. In: Pasinetti LL, Solow RM (eds) Economic growth and the structure of long-term development. St. Martin's Press, International Economic Association

Hofman AA (1992) Capital accumulation in Latin America: A six country comparison for 1950–89. Review of Income and Wealth 38/4:365–91

Kendrick JW (1976) The formation and stocks of total capital. NBER and Columbia University Press, New York

Kreuger A (1983) Trade and employment in developing countries: Synthesis and conclusions. U of Chicago Press, Chicago

Leamer EE (1984) Sources of international comparative advantage: Theories and evidence. M.I.T. Press, Cambridge Mass

Lucas RE (1990) Why doesn't capital flow from rich to poor countries? American Economic Review 80/2:92

Lucas RE (1988) On the mechanics of economic development. Journal of Monetary Economics 22:2–42

Mankiw NG, Romer D, Weil DN (1992) A contribution to the empirics of economic growth. The Quarterly Journal of Economics CV11:407–38

McMahon WW (1992) Relative returns to human and physical capital in the US and efficient investment strategies. Economics of Education Review 10/4:283

Pack H (1988) Industrialization and trade. Chapter 9 In: Chenery H, Srinivasan TN (eds) Handbook of Development Economics Volume 1. North Holland, New York
Press WH, Flannery BP, Teukolsky SA, Vetterling WT (1990) Numerical recipes: The art of scientific computing. Cambridge University Press, London
Psacharopoulos G (1985) Returns to education: A further international update and implications. Journal of Human Resources 20: 583–604
Rivera-Batiz LA, Romer P (1991) Economic integration and endogenous growth. Quarterly Journal of Economics CVI/2: 531–56
Romer P (1986) Increasing returns and long-run growth. Journal of Political Economy XCIV: 1002–37
Romer P (1990) Endogenous technical change. Journal of Political Economy 98: S71–S102
Schultz TP (1988) Education investments and returns. Chapter 13 In: Chenery H, Srinivasan TN (eds) Handbook of Development Economics Volume 1. North Holland, New York
Summers R, Heston A (1991) The penn world tables (Mark 5): An expanded set of international comparisons, 1950–1968. The Quarterly Journal of Economics 327–365
United Nations (1988) World demographic estimates and projections 1950–2025. United Nations, New York
United Nations (1992) Human development report. Oxford University Press, London
United Nations (1992) Handbook of International Trade and Development Statistics. United Nations Conference on Trade and Development, New York
United States Department of Commerce (1992) Survey of current business
Warner A (1992) Did the debt crisis cause the investment crisis? Quarterly Journal of Economics 107: 1161–1186

First version received: January 1995
Final version received: November 1995

The Engine of Growth or its Handmaiden?
A Time-Series Assessment of Export-Led Growth

RAYMOND G. RIEZMAN AND CHARLES H. WHITEMAN[1]

Department of Economics, University of Iowa, Iowa City IA 52242, USA

PETER M. SUMMERS

Department of Economics and Centre for International Economic Studies, University of Adelaide, Adelaide SA 5005, Australia

Abstract: This paper presents an analysis of time-series data for the countries in the Summers-Heston (1991) data set, in an attempt to ascertain the evidence for or against the export-led growth hypothesis. We find that standard methods of detecting export-led growth using Granger-causality tests may give misleading results if imports are not included in the system being analyzed. For this reason, our main statistical tool is the measure of conditional linear feedback developed by Geweke (1984), which allows us to examine the relationship between export growth and income growth while controlling for the growth of imports. These measures have two additional features which make them attractive for our work. First, they go beyond mere *detection* of evidence for export-led growth, to provide a measurement of its *strength*. Second, they enable us to determine the temporal pattern of the response of income to exports. In some cases export-led growth is a long-run phenomenon, in the sense that export promotion strategies adopted today have their strongest effect after eight to 16 years. In other cases the opposite is true; exports have their greatest influence in the short run (less than four years). We find modest support for the export-led growth hypothesis, if "support" is taken to mean a unidirectional causal ordering. Conditional on import growth, we find a causal ordering from export growth to income growth in 30 of the 126 countries analyzed; 25 have the reverse ordering. Using a weaker notion of "support" – stronger conditional feedback from exports to income than vice versa, 65 of the 126 countries support the export-led growth hypothesis, although the difference in strength is small. Finally, we find that for the "Asian Tiger" countries of the Pacific Rim, the relationship between export growth and output growth becomes clearer when conditioned on human capital and investment growth as well as import growth.

Key Words: Export-led growth, time series, causality

JEL Classification System-Numbers: F14, F43, C32

---

[1] We are grateful to J. David Richardson, Narayana Kocherlakota, Tin Nguyen, two anonymous referees, and seminar participants at the 1992 Midwest International Economics meetings, the University of Adelaide, and the 1994 conference of the Economics Society of Australia, for helpful comments and discussions. The analysis of the Penn-World Table (Mark 5.5) was greatly simplified by the spreadsheet macros and templates developed by Dr. Sailesh K. Tanna of the Coventry Business School. Riezman and Whiteman acknowledge support from the National Science Foundation, under grants SES 90-23056 and SES 89-22419, respectively. Any remaining errors are our own.

1 Introduction

One of the most enduring questions in economics involves how a nation could accelerate the pace of its economic development. One of the most enduring answers to this question is to promote exports – either because doing so directly influences development via encouraging production of goods for export, or because export promotion permits accumulation of foreign exchange which permits importation of high-quality goods and services, which can in turn be used to expand the nation's production possibilities. In either case, growth is said to be *export-led*; the latter case is the so-called "two-gap" hypothesis (McKinnon, 1964; Findlay, 1973).

The early work on export-led growth consisted of static cross-country comparisons (Michaely, 1977; Balassa, 1978; Tyler, 1981; Kormendi and Meguire, 1985). These studies generally concluded that there is strong evidence in favour of export-led growth because export growth and income growth are highly correlated. However, Kravis pointed out in 1970 that the question is an essentially dynamic one: as he put it, are exports the handmaiden or the engine of growth? To make this determination one needs to look at time series to see whether or not exports are driving income. This approach has been taken in a number of papers (Jung and Marshall, 1985; Chow, 1987; Serletis, 1992; Kunst and Marin, 1989; Marin, 1992; Afxentiou and Serletis, 1991), designed to assess whether or not individual countries exhibit statistically significant evidence of export-led growth using Granger causality tests.

We adopt this dynamic approach, but make a number of important modifications. First, we use data from a single source designed to provide a consistent set of comparable cross-country statistics on output – the purchasing power index data of Summers and Heston (1991). This data set avoids the standard difficulty that output valued at official exchange rates may not provide an accurate picture of a nation's stage of economic development. The intertemporal effect of this phenomenon is especially important when one is interested in the pattern of economic development. For example, as a country develops, its traded (i.e., exported) goods sector may grow relative to other sectors. Thus just as output has grown, the official-exchange-rate valuation of output will more accurately measure actual output precisely because exports constitute a larger fraction of output. This will make it appear to be the case that exports lead output regardless of the underlying source of output growth. Use of the purchasing power measure attenuates this confounding measurement error effect, since its valuation of output relies less heavily on a country's traded goods. This paper uses data from Mark 5.5 of the Penn-World Table (Summers and Heston, 1991), which covers the years 1950–1990.[2] Our measure of income growth is total *real*

[2] Although the Summers-Heston (1991) paper includes data only through 1988 (Mark 5), an updated version (Mark 5.5) includes data through 1990. This version is available via anonymous ftp

gross domestic product in *current* international dollars, which is computed by multiplying the CGDP series for each country by its population. Exports and imports are also expressed in current international dollars, and are derived from the Penn-World Table.[3]

Second, this paper strives to provide a consistent set of *measurements* of the importance of exports in leading economic growth. We employ several procedures which, while not new, have not previously been applied to this problem. These measures enable us to go beyond mere *detection* of evidence for export-led growth to the measurement of its strength.

The third modification is that we take account of imports explicitly. Other studies typically focus on the bivariate relationship between income and exports.[4] But as noted above, theory suggests that imports may play a central role in explaining export-led growth. Indeed, we find that omitting imports from the analysis may either mask or overstate the effect of exports on income.

Fourth, for a subset of countries, we also investigate whether other often-omitted variables influence the relationship between income and exports. In particular, we find that conditioning on measures of physical and human capital generally sharpens inferences regarding the relationship between export growth and output growth.

Finally, we are able to determine the temporal pattern of the response of income to exports. In some cases export-led growth is a long-run phenomenon, in the sense that export-promotion strategies adopted today have their strongest effect after eight to 16 years. In other cases the opposite is true; exports have their greatest influence in the short run (less than four years). It may also be the case that a country may exhibit a strong export-led growth effect at particular frequencies (i.e., time horizon), even though there may be little evidence of the effect in the overall measure.

While we feel that these findings are interesting in themselves, they also provide a set of facts that may serve as a guide to theorists who are currently working to develop better theories of economic growth.

---

from the NBER (nber.harvard.edu). Since this paper was written, a further update (Mark 5.6) has been released and is also available via ftp.

[3] The variable OPEN (exports + imports as % of CGDP) is given in the Penn-World Table, and the current net foreign balance (cnfb; as a percentage of CGDP) can be obtained by the formula $100 - cc - ci - cg = cnfb$, where cc, ci, and cg are the percentage shares of consumption, investment and government spending, respectively, in CGDP. Then exports/CGDP = (OPEN + cnfb)/200, and imports/CGDP = (OPEN − cnfb)/200.

[4] Exceptions are Serletis (1992), who includes imports; Ghartey (1993), who includes the terms of trade and the capital stock; and Kunst and Marin (1989), who study the causal relationships between productivity, export growth, the terms of trade and OECD output.

2 The State of the Evidence

2.1 Existing Evidence

Existing tests for the presence of export-led growth generally rely on the concept of Granger causality.[5] That is, it is customary to check whether exports help predict output once historical output has been taken into account. More specifically, let x_t denote exports and y_t denote output. Then estimate the following two equations by ordinary least squares:

$$\begin{aligned} x_t &= \sum_{j=1}^{p} a_j x_{t-j} + \sum_{j=1}^{p} b_j y_{t-j} + u_t \\ y_t &= \sum_{j=1}^{p} c_j x_{t-j} + \sum_{j=1}^{p} d_j y_{t-j} + v_t \end{aligned} \tag{1}$$

and test the null hypotheses

$$\begin{aligned} &H_1\colon c_j = 0\ , \quad j = 1, \ldots, p, \text{ exports fail to Granger-cause (help predict) output;} \\ &H_2\colon b_j = 0\ , \quad j = 1, \ldots, p, \text{ output fail to Granger-cause (help predict) exports}^6. \end{aligned} \tag{2}$$

If neither hypothesis is rejected, then exports and output are causally independent, whereas if both are rejected, there is bi-directional causality between the two.[7]

Table 1 lists several recent time-series studies of export-led growth, together with their methods, data sources and results. It is readily apparent that since the seminal paper of Jung and Marshall (1985), many refinements have been used in assessing the empirical evidence for export-led growth. These refinements include modifications of the standard Granger causality test, including tests for optimal lag length (Chow, 1987; Darrat, 1987; Kunst and Marin, 1989; Ahmad and Kwan, 1991; Bahmani-Oskooee et al, 1991; Serletis, 1992; Marin, 1992; Ghartey, 1993; Oxley, 1993), tests for nonstationarity and/or cointegration between the variables (Afxentiou and Serletis, 1991; Serletis; Oxley), and including

[5] The remainder of the paper focuses exclusively on the time-series approach to export-led growth, as opposed to the cross-sectional approach, or analyses of the determinants of growth along the lines of Barro (1991).

[6] As pointed out by several authors, the testing procedure described in (1) and (2) is valid only if x and y are (covariance) stationary time series.

[7] Many authors (including Granger, 1969) use the term "feedback" to describe the case of rejection of both null hypotheses in (2). Because we measure export-led growth using the "measures of linear feedback" introduced by Geweke (1982, 1984), we use the term "bidirectional causality" here to avoid confusion.

Table 1. Previous time-series studies of export-led growth

Author(s)[a]	Method: Causality	Method: Lag Length	Variables and Sources	Sample	Results[b]
Jung & Marshall (1985)	Granger-causality (GC)	–	Real GDP, real exports *International Financial Statistics* (IFS)	37 Less Developed Countries (LDCs)	$x \rightarrow y$ in Indonesia, Egypt, Costa Rica and Ecuador
Chow (1987)	Sims's version of GC	–	Manufactured exports, manufacturing output; from *Yearbook of International Trade Statistics*, *Yearbook of National Account Statistics*, *Taiwan Statistical Data Book*, *Key Indicators of Developing Member Countries of Asian Development Bank*	Argentina, Brazil, Hong Kong, Israel, Korea, Mexico, Singapore, Taiwan	No causality in Argentina; $x \rightarrow y$ in Mexico; $x \leftrightarrow y$ in all others
Darrat (1987)	White (1980)	No formal tests; up to 4 lags examined	Growth rates of real GDP and real exports, from IFS and *World Development Report*	Korea, Taiwan, Singapore, Hong Kong	$x \rightarrow y$ in Korea
Ram (1987)	Times series regression; aggregate production function specification, incorporating possible export externalities		Real GDP, exports, investment share, population growth; from World Bank's *World Tables* (WT)	88 LDCs	$x \rightarrow y$ in 38 or 37 countries (depending on specific model being estimated); positive but insignificant relationship in another 35 or 40
Kunst & Marin (1989)	GC	2 methods: a) AIC on diag. elements of AR coefficient matrix; off-diag. elements set at 4 b) diag. elements as in a; off-diag. set by backward elimination from maximum 8 lags	Exports, terms of trade and productivity, all in manufacturing, OECD GDP	Austria	OECD GDP → Productivity

Table 1. Continued

Author(s)[a]	Method		Variables and Sources	Sample	Results[b]
	Causality	Lag Length			
Ahmad & Kwan (1991)	GC on pooled sample; AIC for lag length	Akaike Information Criterion (AIC)	Real GDP per capita, level and growth rate; real exports (total and mfd), share of mfd exports in total; from *Economic Indicators of African Development*	47 African countries	no $x \rightarrow y$ in any of several specifications; little causality overall
Bahmani-Oskooee et al (1991)	Standard GC, also measured by FPE reduction	Final Prediction Error (FPE)	Real exports and GDP (1975 prices); from IFS, *Statistical Yearbook of the Republic of China*	20 LDCs	$x \rightarrow y$ in 10 (including those for which tests conflict); unidirectional positive relationship in Nigeria & Taiwan only
Afxentiou & Serletis (1991)	GC on growth rates after unit root (Phillips-Perron) and cointegration (Engle-Yoo) tests	Schwartz Criterion (SC)	Real exports (IFS) and GNP (Summers-Heston 1988)	All countries classified as industrial by IMF (16)	$x \leftrightarrow y$ in U.S.; $y \rightarrow x$ in Norway, Canada, Japan (with 10-yr lag in Canada, Japan)
Kugler (1991)	Tests for presence of exports in cointegrating relationship, using Johansen/Juselius procedure ADF for stationarity	AIC	Real GDP (GNP for US), private consumption, investment and exports; from OECD	US, Germany, Japan, UK, France, Switzerland	Exports enter cointegrating vector only in Germany and France
Marin (1992)	GC	Bayesian Information Criterion (BIC)	As in Kunst & Marin (1989)	Germany, U.K., U.S., Japan	$x \rightarrow y$ for all four, but little impact as measured by sum of AR coefficients
Serletis (1992)	GC after Phillips-Perron tests for unit roots, Engle-Granger tests for cointegration	SC	Exports, imports, GNP; from Urquhart (1988)	Canada	$x \rightarrow y$ except for post-WWII period

Bahmani-Oskooee and Alse (1993)	Regression analysis of error-correction model, after ADF for stationarity, and ADF and CRDW for cointegration		Real exports and income; quarterly data constructed from annual IFS figures	Colombia, Greece, Korea, Malaysia, Pakistan, Philippines, Singapore, South Africa, Thailand	$x \leftrightarrow y$ for all but Malaysia (x and y not cointegrated in Malaysia)
Dodaro (1993)	GC	Set at 2 lags	Real GDP, exports of goods and non-factor services; from WT	87 LDCs	$x \rightarrow y$ (positive effect) in 7; $y \rightarrow x$ (positive effect) in 13
Ghartey (1993)	FPE, Hsiao (1979)	FPE, BIC	Exports, GNP, capital stock, terms of trade; from *Survey of Current Business* (US); *Quarterly National Income Statistics*, *Monthly Statistics of Exports and Imports*, and *Financial Statistics, Taiwan District* (Taiwan); *Dept. of National Accounts, Economic Research Institute*, and *Economic Planning Agency* (Japan)	U.S., Japan, Taiwan	$x \rightarrow y$ in Taiwan, $y \rightarrow x$ in U.S., terms of trade $\rightarrow x$ in Japan
Oxley (1993)	Modified Wald test (Schmidt, 1976) after ADF and Johansen tests for unit roots & cointegration	FPE	Real GDP, exports (1914 prices); from Nunes et al (1989)	Portugal	$y \rightarrow x$
Ukpolo (1994)	Time series regression of output on disaggregated exports		Real GDP; exports of fuel, non-fuel primary products, and manufactures; sizes of public and private sectors, from World Bank	Congo Republic, Kenya, Morrocco, Nigeria, Senegal, Sierra Leone, Tanzania, Togo	$x \rightarrow y$ for non-fuel primary products

[a] See the cited works for specific details regarding methods, years of data sources; etc.

[b] x is the export variable, y is the income variable (both vary across studies); arrows denote directions of causality

other variables besides exports and growth (Kunst and Marin; Serletis; Marin; Ghartey). Rather than present an exhaustive comparison of the results of all of these papers, we summarize some of the major differences below.

In their work on causality and export-led growth, Jung and Marshall (1985) analyze the relationship between the growth rate of real exports and the growth rate of real output, for 37 developing countries. Depending on the outcome of Granger causality tests, as described above, they then characterize the countries in their sample as exhibiting one of four causal patterns: Export Promotion (EP, what we call export-led growth), Internally Generated Exports (IGE), Export-Reducing Growth (ERG), or Growth-Reducing Exports (GRE). This characterization is made on the basis of the sign of the sum of the coefficients on lags of the causal variable in the equation for the dependent variable. Jung and Marshall find evidence for the export-led growth hypothesis in only four of the 37 countries: Indonesia, Egypt, Costa Rica and Ecuador.

Chow (1987) performs a similar analysis on eight of the most successful export-oriented newly industrialized countries (NICs), using the growth rate of manufacturing output as a measure of industrial development. With two exceptions, Chow finds bi-directional causality in each country.[8] Direct comparisons with Jung and Marshall's results are hampered by the fact that Chow does not attempt to determine the sign of the relationship (i.e., whether export growth causes positive or negative output growth), as well as by the use of different variables. However, results for four of the six countries common to the two samples (Brazil, Korea, Mexico and Taiwan) differ across the studies. Jung and Marshall find no significant causality in Brazil or Mexico, and causality only from output to exports in Korea and Taiwan. The two papers draw similar inferences about the existence of causality in Israel, although Jung and Marshall argue that the effect is negative in each direction.

Unlike these two papers, Serletis (1992) also includes the growth of imports in his analysis. In Canadian data from 1870–1985, he finds that export growth causes GNP growth over the full sample and in the pre-WWII subsample. At the same time, he finds no evidence that import growth causes either export growth or income growth.

Marin (1992) presents a vector autoregressive (VAR) analysis of data for Germany, the United Kingdom, the United States and Japan. Using quarterly data for manufactured exports, the terms of trade, OECD output and labor productivity, Marin performs preliminary tests for the cointegration of exports and productivity (i.e., tests of whether the two variables have a long-run equilibrium relationship). Although he finds no conclusive evidence of cointegration between these two variables, he does find evidence of a cointegrating relationship between exports, productivity and the terms of trade, except for the UK.

---

[8] Note that Chow uses Sims's version of the Granger-causality test; 3 *future values* (leads) of each variable are included in the regression equations (1), along with 3 lags.

Marin's Granger-causality tests support the export-led growth hypothesis for the four countries in his study, but he finds that the "quantitative impact of exports on productivity seems to be negligible," (Marin, 1992, p. 685) on the basis of the sum of the autoregressive coefficients on lagged values of exports in the productivity equation.

Other large-scale studies reach divergent conclusions regarding export-led growth. Bahmani-Oskooee et al. (1991) examine 20 less-developed countries (LDCs), all of which are also studied by Jung and Marshall. Although they find evidence of a causal relationship between exports and growth in half of these countries (including cases in which their two test procedures gave different results), they find evidence of a unidirectional positive relationship[9] only in Nigeria and Taiwan. Like Jung and Marshall, they find evidence for export-led growth in Indonesia. However, the two papers reach different conclusions for Korea, Taiwan and Thailand (export-led growth in Bahmani-Oskooee et al; export-reducing growth, causality from growth to exports, and internally generated exports, respectively, in Jung and Marshall).

Afxentiou and Serletis (1991) find no export-led growth in any of the 16 industrial countries in their sample. Although they find unidirectional causality from output growth to export growth in Norway, Canada and Japan, there is a ten-year lag in the effect for the latter two countries. The only other causal relationship they find is bidirectional causality in the U.S.

The clear message from table 1 is that a great variety of techniques, data sets and country groups have been employed in empirical assessments of the export-led growth hypothesis, with an equally wide variety of results. Our main motivation in undertaking the present study was a desire to reconcile these diverse results, or at least to discover why they could not be reconciled. Moreover, our use of the Summers-Heston (1991) data set and Geweke's (1984) measures of linear feedback also illustrates the value of *measuring* any export-led growth effects, as opposed to simply detecting them.

In interpreting the results below, it will prove useful to be precise about how we translate patterns of causality into statements about export-led growth. When used in this paper, "export-led growth" means that there exists a causal ordering (either direct or indirect) from export growth to income growth, with no "return loop" to export growth. For example, the bidirectional causality found by Chow does not meet our definition of export-led growth, since output growth Granger-causes export growth. Clearly, our definition is not unique. However, we feel that it is the best in terms of emphasizing the extent to which export growth *leads* income growth.[10]

Broadly speaking, the results of bivariate Granger causality tests we performed with the Summers-Heston data are consistent with those of other

9 Based on the sign of the sum of the autoregressive coefficients, as in Jung and Marshall (1985) and Marin (1992).

10 Theoretical reasons for exports leading growth are summarized in, *inter alia*, Jung and Marshall (1985, p. 3), or Kunst and Marin (1989, p. 699).

authors, who find little evidence of export-led growth.[11] Of the 126 countries for which results are available, only 16 display evidence of export-led growth (i.e., unidirectional causality from exports to income) at the 10 percent significance level.[12] There is evidence of "growth-led exports" in 14 countries, while only three appear to have bidirectional causality between exports and income. Thus, the majority of the world's countries exhibit no clear causal ordering between exports and income. However, as we argue below, the results of bivariate Granger causality tests do not provide a comprehensive picture of the evidence regarding export-led growth.

In order to conserve space and simplify exposition, the body of this paper presents results only for a subset of countries in the Summers-Heston data set. This subset includes Hong Kong, Indonesia, Japan, (the Republic of) Korea, Malaysia, the Philippines, Singapore, Taiwan and Thailand: results for all countries in the sample are collected in an unpublished appendix.[13] We focus on these countries in particular because they are often cited as instances of the success of export promotion strategies.

Table 2 presents the results of the bivariate Granger causality analysis for our subset of countries. Here, evidence in favour of the export-led growth hypothesis consists of export growth (x) causing income growth (y), by which we mean that the null hypothesis of no causality from x to y is rejected at the 10 percent critical level, but not vice versa, by which we mean the null of no causality from y to x is *not* rejected at the 10 percent level. Columns 3 and 5 present marginal significance levels for the Granger-causality tests, while columns 7 and 8 contain the same information for the tests of no (unconditional) linear feedback in the sense of Geweke (1982). Further discussion of Geweke's linear feedback measures is given below. Causal inferences based on each of these tests are given in the final two columns of the table.

In columns 4 and 6 of table 2, we report the average response of each variable to a unit shock in the other, over a 16-year period.[14] This provides a means of assessing the sign of the relationship between export growth and output

---

[11] An appendix containing a complete set of our results for all 126 countries, as well as the details of the computation of the conditional linear feedback statistics reported below, is available via anonymous ftp from iks.biz.uiowa.edu. The file is called "RSW95.zip" and is in the \pub directory.

[12] The majority of the 24 missing countries have insufficient data for one or more variables to allow estimation. The major oil-exporting countries (e.g., Saudi Arabia, Kuwait, the United Arab Emirates) have been excluded from Mark 5.5 of the data set.

[13] Tables 4 and 7 below include additional countries, in order to illustrate specific points. The appendix is available upon request from the authors. See note 11.

[14] Doing this requires identifying economic shocks (to exports, to income) from statistical residuals. We follow Sims (1980) and use a World-causal chain scheme whereby the export shock is the residual in the export equation and the output shock is that part of the output residual which is orthogonal to (uncorrelated with) the export shock (i.e., exports are ordered "first"). We do not consider alternative identifying restrictions or causal orderings in this paper; for this reason, the results should be taken as suggestive.

Table 2. Measures of export-led growth, 2-variable system

COUNTRY	DATA	$x \rightarrow y$[b] GC	impulse[c]	$y \rightarrow x$[b] GC	impulse[c]	$x \rightarrow y$[b] LF	$y \rightarrow x$[b] LF	OPEN[d]	Inference[e] (GC)	Inference[e] (LF)
HONG KONG	1960–90	0.4590	0.0015	0.2624	0.0002	0.3875	0.1962	268.22	0	0
INDONESIA	1960–90	0.7174	0.0051	0.8582	−0.0032	0.6675	0.8302	50.92		
JAPAN	1950–90	0.8530	0.0001	0.0135	0.0079	0.8240	0.0053	21.58	$y \rightarrow x$	$y \rightarrow x$
REP. OF KOREA	1953–89	0.3200	0.0022	0.1242	−0.0014	0.2470	0.0773	65.72 (89)	0	$y \rightarrow x$
MALAYSIA	1955–90	0.9881	0.0067	0.9896	−0.0003	0.9855	0.9873	156.06		
PHILIPPINES	1950–90	0.7707	0.0011	0.0165	0.0034	0.7283	0.0068	61.16	$y \rightarrow x$	$y \rightarrow x$
SINGAPORE	1960–90	0.6000	0.0055	0.5726	0.0010	0.5369	0.5072	373.83	0	0
TAIWAN	1951–90	0.0110	0.0033	0.1215	−0.0048	0.0041	0.0769	89.43	$x \rightarrow y$	$x \leftrightarrow y$
THAILAND	1950–90	0.2031	0.0022	0.1903	−0.0014	0.1436	0.1327	78.43		

[a] x is the growth rate of exports; y is the growth rate of income (total GDP in current international dollars; see Summers and Heston, 1991).
[b] Marginal significance level for the null hypothesis of no unidirectional causality (Granger causality F-tests in columns 3 and 5, unconditional linear feedback in columns 7 and 8).
[c] Average impulse response over 16 year period.
[d] Exports plus imports as a percentage of CGDP (Summers and Heston, 1991), data for 1990 unless otherwise indicdated.
[e] Inference regarding causal ordering, at 10% level. GC = Granger causality, LF = linear feedback, "→" = unidirectional causality, "↔" = bidirectional causality.

growth.[15] For example, a unit shock to export growth in Korea (i.e., a one-time doubling of exports) leads to an average increase in the rate of income growth of 0.22 percent per year for 16 years. Doubling income leads to a drop in export growth of 0.14 percent per year over the same period.[16] Of all the countries in our study that display evidence of export-led growth, none has a negative response of income to export shocks. Column 9 in the table presents the variable OPEN from the Summers-Heston (1991) data set, which is the share of trade in CGDP. The values reported are for the most recent year available (1990 unless indicated).

2.2 *The Role of Import Growth*

With one exception, previous studies of export-led growth have not addressed the role of import growth in the export-income relationship. Serletis (1992) includes lagged values of import growth in his examination of Canadian data, and finds no Granger causality from import growth to either income growth or export growth. That is, letting m_t denote imports, he estimated equations of the form

$$\begin{aligned} x_t &= \sum_{i=1}^{p} a_j x_{t-j} + \sum_{i=1}^{p} b_j y_{t-j} + \sum_{i=1}^{p} f_j m_{t-j} + u_t \\ y_t &= \sum_{i=1}^{p} c_j x_{t-j} + \sum_{i=1}^{p} d_j y_{t-j} + \sum_{i=1}^{p} g_j m_{t-j} + v_t \end{aligned} \tag{3}$$

and tested the null hypotheses

$$\begin{aligned} &H_1\colon c_j = 0\ ,\quad j = 1, \ldots, p \text{ (exports fail to Granger-cause output in the three-variable universe)} \\ &H_2\colon b_j = 0\ ,\quad j = 1, \ldots, p \text{ (output fail to Granger-cause exports in the three-variable universe),} \end{aligned} \tag{4}$$

as well as similar hypotheses regarding the f_j and g_j. Table 3 reports the results of Granger causality tests in this three-variable system, for the countries listed in table 2.[17]

---

[15] Using the sign of the sum of the autoregressive coefficients, as is done in Jung and Marshall (1985), Marin (1992) and Bahmani-Oskooee et al. (1991), amounts to examining the impulse response at an infinite horizon.

[16] The impulse response analysis discussed here differs from many such applications, in that we do not (necessarily) think of the changes in growth rates as being induced by policy changes. Rather, it is our analogue to summing our estimated autoregressive coefficients (see the previous footnote).

[17] Note that this version of Granger causality tests exclusion restrictions on each equation separately, rather than in a full three-variable VAR. The conditional linear feedback measures reported below are based on such a trivariate system. This difference, combined with sampling error, accounts for the disparity in results between our Granger causality and conditional linear feedback tests.

Table 3. Granger-causality tests, 3-variable system

Country	Data	$x \to y$[a,b]	$y \to x$	$x \to m$	$y \to m$	$m \to x$	$m \to y$
HONG KONG	1960–90	0.1562	0.1557	0.3946	0.0652	0.3108	0.2722
INDONESIA	1960–90	0.1442	0.8001	0.8710	0.7633	0.9159	0.1774
JAPAN	1950–90	0.6564	0.0105	0.0574	0.0823	0.0093	0.7552
REP. OF KOREA	1953–89	0.0406	0.2763	0.0091	0.3866	0.0454	0.0846
MALAYSIA	1955–90	0.3609	0.5146	0.0889	0.3727	0.0588	0.0070
PHILIPPINES	1950–90	0.3136	0.0029	0.0565	0.0001	0.1117	0.1698
SINGAPORE	1960–90	0.9162	0.8546	0.3814	0.6479	0.2972	0.7786
TAIWAN	1951–90	0.0953	0.1527	0.3351	0.7924	0.8939	0.8371
THAILAND	1950–90	0.5530	0.1458	0.1137	0.1776	0.4905	0.6979

[a] x is the growth rate of exports; m is the growth rate of imports; y is the growth rate of income (total GDP in current international dollars; see Summers and Heston, 1991).
[b] Marginal significance level for the null hypothesis of no unidirectional causality.

Table 4 demonstrates the importance of import growth in the causal ordering. Omitting imports can result in both "type I" and "type II" errors – spurious rejection of export-led growth as well as spurious detection of it. In columns 2 through 7 we present the marginal significance levels for the Granger causality F-tests in two systems: the two-variable system of export growth and income growth, and a three-variable system with import growth (m) included. Comparing the two rows for each of the six countries listed, we find that the omission of import growth can mask significant causality between exports and income, or may cause spurious causality.[18] For examples of the former, consider Ghana, South Africa and Korea. In the two-variable system of exports and income, there is no significant causal ordering for these countries. However, the second row for each of these countries shows that there does exist a significant two-stage causal chain, running from exports to imports to income, as well as a direct exports-to-income chain. There is also evidence of bidirectional causality between exports and imports in Korea.

In Japan, the "growth-led exports" phenomenon apparently operates both directly and indirectly through imports. Again, there is evidence of bidirectional causality between exports and imports.

The remaining countries in table 4 provide evidence of the possibility that causal inferences in the two-variable system may be due to omitted variable bias. In each of these countries, significant causality in the first row disappears in the second. The "growth-led exports" inference for Argentina does not change, but it is apparently an indirect causal chain, from income to imports to exports (a "reverse two-gap model"). By contrast, the (bivariate) export-led growth evidence for Peru is reversed completely in the trivariate system, re-

[18] For simplicity's sake, we will use the term "exports" instead of "growth rate of exports," and so on. When we wish to refer to the *level* of any variable we will say so explicitly.

Table 4. Granger-causal orderings, 2-variable vs 3-variable systems

	$x \to y$	$y \to x$	$x \to m$	$y \to m$	$m \to x$	$m \to y$
GHANA	0.2309	0.8141				
	0.0068	0.8096	0.0521	0.3552	0.6667	0.0226
SOUTH AFRICA	0.2249	0.4357				
	0.0177	0.6549	0.0314	0.0258	0.1103	0.0017
ARGENTINA	0.6289	0.0144				
	0.5029	0.3726	0.3530	0.0261	0.0959	0.4956
COLOMBIA	0.0641	0.0340				
	0.0216	0.5229	0.0783	0.5796	0.4980	0.2218
PERU	0.0146	0.9991				
	0.1493	0.2891	0.4988	0.0785	0.0074	0.9612
SWEDEN	0.0079	0.6523				
	0.2723	0.7658	0.0003	0.0220	0.0344	0.4092
JAPAN	0.8530	0.0135				
	0.6564	0.0105	0.0574	0.0823	0.0093	0.7552
REP. OF KOREA	0.3200	0.1242				
	0.0406	0.2763	0.0091	0.3866	0.0454	0.0846

[a] Entries are marginal significance levels for null hypotheses of no Granger causality. Notation parallels that of Table 3.

vealing an indirect link similar to that in Argentina. In Colombia, exports appear to cause both income and imports, while in Sweden there is evidence of bidirectional causality between exports and imports, with imports being caused in turn by income.

As we have seen, imports may play the role of a confounding variable in causal ordering (i.e., imports affect both income and exports). Failure to account for imports can therefore produce misleading results. In the remainder of this paper, all our results explicitly account for imports.

2.3 *Perspective on the Evidence*

There are two major problems with the use of Granger causality tests in searching for export-led growth. The first concerns the difference between statistical significance of the Granger causality F-tests and the strength of the relationship between exports and income. Marginal significance levels (or p-values) cannot be interpreted as indicators of the strength or weakness of any causal relationship. While p-values are certainly of interest, they are arguably of secondary importance to a consistent measurement of the causal relationship itself.

The second major problem is the limited time horizon of Granger causality tests. A finding that exports Granger-cause income means only that the variance in the *one-step-ahead* forecast error, made from predicting income linearly using its own past, is reduced when lags of exports are included. There is no a priori reason to think that any causal relationship between exports and imports must necessarily become apparent in a year.[19]

We present two ways of addressing these problems. The first is the decomposition of forecast error variance, and the second uses the measures of conditional linear feedback developed by Geweke (1984). Both methods provide measurements of the strength of feedback between exports and income, which are comparable across countries. These measures also allow for a flexible time horizon. These techniques have been used for some time in the empirical macroeconomics literature, but to our knowledge have not previously been applied to the study of export-led growth.

3 New Measures of Export-Led Growth

3.1 Forecast Error Variance Decomposition

The forecast error variance decomposition (FEVD) is a way to answer the question, "How much of the variance in forecast errors of future income growth can be attributed to innovations in export growth?" This technique is standard in the VAR approach; for details, the reader is referred to Doan (1992), Sims (1980), etc.

Because the FEVD is based on the decomposition of the covariance matrix of the three-variable vector autoregression (VAR), and because this decomposition is not unique, the fraction of the forecast error in income attributable to exports generally changes depending on the ordering of the variables. In order to set a criterion for export-led growth, we seek countries in which exports explain at least 25 percent of the variance of the five-year-ahead forecast of income, when exports are placed second in the decomposition ordering. In other words, this ordering gives imports the "first shot" at explaining the variance of income forecasts. We chose a five-year horizon based on evidence for a world business cycle of roughly that duration (Riezman and Whiteman, 1991). Countries that meet our criterion are thus the ones in which the role of export growth is particularly strong in explaining income growth.

19 This study, like most others, uses annual data.

Table 5. Five-year forecast error variance decomposition

Country	$x - m - y$[a]	$m - x - y$[a]	% y[b]
HONG KONG	18.97	11.60	67.93
INDONESIA	22.88	44.60	44.53
JAPAN	2.85	2.82	94.37
REP. OF KOREA	17.43	24.38	63.35
MALAYSIA	67.18	19.48	21.29
PHILIPPINES	3.47	3.49	89.61
SINGAPORE	56.61	4.65	42.33
TAIWAN	58.18	17.58	39.16
THAILAND	22.23	13.04	59.08

[a] Entries are the percent of the five-year forecast error in income which is attributable to innovations in exports, for the given ordering.
[b] Percentage of income forecast error variance attributable to income innovations.

Table 5 reports FEVD results for the Wold-causal chain orderings $x - m - y$ and $m - x - y$.[20] The last column of the table reports the fraction of income forecast error variance explained by income innovations. This column gives an indication of the degree to which income growth is exogenous with respect to export growth and import growth.

3.2 *Measures of Linear Feedback*

Unconditional linear feedback: The linear feedback measures developed by Geweke (1982, 1984) provide an alternative to both Granger causality tests and the FEVD. These statistics are designed not just to *detect* a feedback relationship (i.e., a causal ordering) but to provide a measure of its *strength.* While the Granger causality statistics simply reflect whether forecast error variance is reduced by adding another variable, it is useful to consider the extent of this reduction. Let $F_{x \to y}$ denote the measure of linear feedback from exports to income. The reduction in the variance of the (one-step-ahead) mean squared income forecast error, when exports are included in the regression, is given by $-\exp(-F_{x \to y})$. Pierce (1982) notes that $1 - \exp(-F_{x \to y})$ can be interpreted analogously to the coefficient of determination (R^2) in ordinary regression. As noted by Geweke (1982), $F_{x \to y}$ has all the features one expects in a measure – it is positive, monotone, and (in its R^2 form) lies between zero and unity. The absence of Granger causality from x to y is equivalent to $F_{x \to y} = 0$. Furthermore, these measures are invariant under filtering of the time series by (possibly

20 See footnote 10 above.

different) invertible lag operators. Finally, when the data are measured in comparable units (e.g., the growth rates used here) this measure is comparable across countries.

We report the marginal significance levels for the test of (unconditional) linear feedback in Table 2 (columns 7 and 8), along with the bivariate Granger-causality results. These statistics are monotonic transformations of the F statistics computed in Granger causality tests for a system of (possibly vector-valued) time series **u** and **v**. When multiplied by the sample size, these measures have an asymptotic chi-square distribution, with degrees of freedom equal to the number of lags if **u** and **v** are univariate.[21] The two measures of causality are generally consistent. Of the 33 countries that exhibit a significant Granger-causal ordering, 31 have the same ordering as measured by Geweke's linear feedback measures. A causal ordering is somewhat more likely using Geweke's measures; 13 countries have evidence of "Geweke feedback" but no Granger causality. Only two countries exhibit significant Granger causality but no linear feedback.[22] In addition, for the countries that pass one test but not the other, the marginal significance levels are not "off" by very much.

Conditional linear feedback: When income is forecast using lags of itself and imports, adding lagged values of exports reduces forecast error variance by an amount given by the same formula as above, but using $F_{x \to y|m}$, the measure of *conditional* linear feedback from exports to income (Geweke, 1984). Both the conditional and unconditional measures can be decomposed by frequency in order to examine the nature of the causal relationship at various time horizons. This feature is discussed in the next section.

The great attraction of the measures of *conditional* linear feedback is that they allow us to focus on the causal relationship between exports and output, while at the same time controlling for imports. This helps us avoid the "omitted variables" situation described in section 2.2. In contrast to the unconditional linear feedback measures however, there is no tractable asymptotic distribution theory available for the conditional measures. We therefore use Monte Carlo integration to compute Bayesian posterior distributions for these statistics (computational details are given in the Appendix, along with our non-informative prior distribution).

Table 6 presents the conditional linear feedback statistics for our subset of nine countries. (Results for all countries are presented table 9.) The conditional linear feedback measures in table 6 are expressed in their "R^2" version for ease of exposition. Thus, point estimates indicate that for Hong Kong, roughly

---

21 When **u** and **v** are multivariate, the degrees of freedom is equal to (number of lags) $*$ (dimension of **u**) $*$ (dimension of **v**). See Geweke (1982, 1984) for a more complete description of these measures.

22 Actually, these two countries (Syria and Taiwan) show evidence of significant but *different* causal orderings under the two measures: export-led growth under Granger causality, but bidirectional causality under Geweke's measures. Apart from these two, the "Granger causal set" of countries is a proper subset of the "Geweke feedback set."

19 percent of the one-step ahead forecast error variance for income growth is explained by export growth, after the effects of import growth have been accounted for. Conversely, 25 percent of the forecast error variance for export growth is explained by income growth.

There is evidence for export-led growth when the bulk of the $F_{x \to y|m}$ distribution lies to the right of the $F_{y \to x|m}$ distribution. Note that in Taiwan, the 90th percentile of the distribution of $F_{y \to x|m}$ lies below the 10th percentile of the $F_{x \to y|m}$ distribution. We believe this constitutes strong evidence of export-led growth, and use this condition as our preferred criterion for assessing the conditional linear feedback estimates.

This criterion for export-led growth is met in 19 of the countries in our sample.[23] Comparable evidence in favor of "growth-led exports" is present in 10 countries, including Japan and Korea in table 6.[24] It therefore seems that the export-led growth hypothesis is somewhat more likely than its converse.

Expressing the feedback measures in terms of percentage of forecast error variance explained is also useful in cases where no clear causal ordering is present. For example, although a causal ordering is indicated in only three countries in table 6, point estimates of the predictive power of exports in explaining income growth exceed the converse in six of the nine.[25] Moreover, feedback from income growth to export growth is stronger for these nine countries than that for the sample overall: point estimates of the R^2 version of $F_{y \to x|m}$ are 40 percent for the countries in table 6, and 34 percent for all 126 countries. Comparable figures for $F_{x \to y|m}$ are 36 percent in both groups. It would therefore seem that although the conditional feedback measures provide weak support for export-led growth in these countries, the strength of the causal relationship differs little, on average, from the world as a whole.

An interesting pattern emerges when our results are compared with those of Jung and Marshall (1985), Bahmani-Oskooee et al (1991), and Afxentiou and Serletis (1992). First, we tend to find evidence of export-led growth more often than these authors. Using our weaker criterion, we find export-led growth in nine of the 37 countries studied by Jung and Marshall (compared to their four); in five of 20 studied by Bahmani-Oskooee et al (they find three); and in three of 16 studied by Afxentiou and Serletis (who found one). Second, although there are instances where our conclusions match those of these other authors, our results differ in general. For example, we confirm Jung and Marshall's findings in their four "export promotion" countries (Indonesia, Egypt, Costa Rica, Ecua-

---

[23] An alternative criterion would be for $\hat{F}_{x \to y|m} > F^{(90)}_{y \to x|m}$ and $\hat{F}_{y \to x|m} < F^{(10)}_{x \to y|m}$ where $\hat{F}$ and $F^{(j)}$ denote the point estimate and the jth posterior percentile, respectively, of the indicated measure of feedback. This weaker criterion has more of the flavour of a standard one-sided hypothesis test. Measured in this way, 30 countries (24% of the sample) show evidence of export-led growth.

[24] Or 25 (20% of the sample), using the weaker criterion of footnote 18.

[25] "Point estimates" are computed using the posterior mean values of VAR parameters. Also, note that Indonesia, the Philippines and Singapore narrowly miss satisfying our weaker criterion; the required difference in posterior deciles is less than 1% in each case.

Table 6. Linear feedback conditional on imports (R^2 measure)

COUNTRY	DATA	$1-\exp(-F_{x\rightarrow y\mid m})$[a] 10th	50th	90th	pt. est.	$1-\exp(-F_{y\rightarrow x\mid m})$[a] 10th	50th	90th	pt. est.	Inference[b]
HONG KONG	1960–90	0.1475	0.2521	0.4047	0.1858	0.1892	0.2752	0.3803	0.2493	
INDONESIA	1960–90	0.1354	0.2832	0.4809	0.2075	0.0243	0.0850	0.2100	0.0274	
JAPAN	1950–90	0.0417	0.0929	0.2176	0.0319	0.6121	0.7284	0.8070	0.7468	$y \rightarrow x$
REP. OF KOREA	1953–89	0.2134	0.3296	0.4518	0.2737	0.5205	0.6209	0.6980	0.6439	$y \rightarrow x$
MALAYSIA	1955–90	0.4703	0.6033	0.7176	0.6081	0.3922	0.5324	0.6278	0.5308	
PHILIPPINES	1950–90	0.3630	0.4364	0.4961	0.4494	0.3266	0.3815	0.4474	0.3689	
SINGAPORE	1960–90	0.3802	0.5784	0.7207	0.5638	0.1837	0.3589	0.5122	0.3877	
TAIWAN	1951–90	0.5104	0.6487	0.7380	0.6546	0.2030	0.3535	0.4686	0.3838	$x \rightarrow y$
THAILAND	1950–90	0.2187	0.3367	0.4457	0.2948	0.1945	0.2852	0.4250	0.2440	

[a] $F_{x\rightarrow y\mid m}$ is the measure of linear feedback from exports to income, conditional on imports. $F_{y\rightarrow x\mid m}$ is interpreted similarly. Table entries are the point estimate (pt. est.) and the 1st, 5th, and 9th deciles of the posterior distributions of $1-\exp(-F_{x\rightarrow y\mid m})$. This latter quantity is analogous to the coefficient of determination (R^2) or fraction of variation explained.

[b] $x \rightarrow y$ means that the 10th posterior decile of $1-\exp(-F_{x\rightarrow y\mid m})$ lies above the 90th posterior decile of $1-\exp(-F_{y\rightarrow x\mid m})$. $(x \rightarrow y)$ means that the point estimate of $1-\exp(-F_{x\rightarrow y\mid m})$ lies above the 90th posterior decile of $1-\exp(-F_{y\rightarrow x\mid m})$, and the point estimate of $1-\exp(-F_{y\rightarrow x\mid m})$ lies below the 10th posterior decile of $1-\exp(-F_{x\rightarrow y\mid m})$. $y \rightarrow x$ and $(y \rightarrow x)$ are interpreted similarly.

dor),[26] but of the 27 causal inferences made by the others, we reach the same conclusion in only eight (including Ecuador and Indonesia). It could be that this is due to the fact that none of these three papers includes import growth in their analysis, or to differences in data sets, length of sample period or technique.

Additional light can be shed on our results by considering the relationship between a country's openness and the support for the export-led growth hypothesis in that country. Table 7 lists the 10 countries with the "strongest" (conditional) causal inference in each direction (i.e., from exports to income and vice versa). In measuring strength, we computed the difference between the R^2 for exports causing income and the R^2 for income causing exports. We interpret this difference as the relative strength of export-led growth, and report it as the variable RSX in table 7. We also report each country's degree of openness.

Examination of table 7 shows that openness is neither necessary nor sufficient for a causal inference between exports and income. In the 20 countries in table 7, the correlation between openness and the relative strength of exports is just 0.0883.[27] This result suggests that the success or failure of trade policies in stimulating income growth depends on more than merely increasing the *volume* of trade.[28]

3.3 *The Temporal Nature of Export-Led Growth: Conditional Feedback by Frequency*

A key motivation for the use of Geweke's measures of linear feedback is that these statistics may be additively decomposed by frequency. This enables us to examine not only the overall strength of a causal relationship, but also the temporal horizon over which it acts. We may therefore gain new insights into whether export-led growth is a long- or short-term phenomenon, if it is particularly strong at business cycle frequencies, etc. Details of the frequency decomposition are given in the Appendix.[29]

---

[26] Ecuador is another "borderline" case, similar to the countries in footnote 22.

[27] For all 126 countries analyzed, this correlation is 0.0246, while for those for which we make a causal inference, it is 0.0654.

[28] Indeed, the fact that some of the world's most open economies are those of sub-Saharan Africa suggests that the trade-growth relationship is not a simple one.

[29] Note that this decomposition addresses a different issue than that of selecting the appropriate lag length in a standard Granger causality test. The latter is concerned with the appropriate specification of the autoregressive representation of the system; the former is derived from the moving average representation.

Table 7. Relationship between conditional linear feedback (R^2 measure) and openness

COUNTRY	$1 - \exp(-F_{x \to y \mid m})$[a]	$1 - \exp(-F_{y \to x \mid m})$[a]	RSX[b]	OPEN[c]	Inference[d]
EGYPT	0.7498	0.0507	0.6991	65.06	$x \to y$
NEPAL	0.8267	0.2107	0.6159	35.15	$x \to y$
URUGUAY	0.6698	0.1128	0.5570	46.54	$x \to y$
GHANA	0.5052	0.0268	0.4784	48.75	$x \to y$
RWANDA	0.6168	0.1517	0.4651	27.17	$x \to y$
MALI	0.6333	0.1704	0.4629	51.33	$x \to y$
MOROCCO	0.6355	0.2042	0.4313	56.13	$x \to y$
ICELAND	0.6594	0.2368	0.4226	72.02	$x \to y$
IRAN	0.4460	0.0269	0.4191	23.8	$x \to y$
TUNISIA	0.5785	0.1761	0.4024	90.78	$x \to y$
average	0.6321	0.1367	0.4954	51.67	–
SEYCHELLES	0.1845	0.5485	−0.3640	109.77	$y \to x$
REP. OF KOREA	0.2737	0.6439	−0.3702	65.72	$y \to x$
GUINEA-BISSEAU	0.1064	0.4873	−0.3809	78.99	$y \to x$
MALAWI	0.0439	0.4284	−0.3845	58.02	$y \to x$
CAMEROON	0.1046	0.5037	−0.3991	40.34	$(y \to x)$
ZIMABWE	0.0607	0.5213	−0.4607	64.88	$y \to x$
YEMEN	0.0952	0.6081	−0.5128	41.9	$y \to x$
ARGENTINA	0.1463	0.7765	−0.6302	20.79	$y \to x$
BANGLADESH	0.1466	0.8564	−0.7097	26.42	$y \to x$
JAPAN	0.0319	0.7468	−0.7148	21.58	$y \to x$
average	0.1194	0.6121	−0.4927	52.84	–
ρ(RSX, OPEN)[e]				0.0883	

[a] Point estimates of $1 - \exp(-F_{x \to y \mid m})$ and $1 - \exp(-F_{y \to x \mid m})$, as defined in table 6. Countries listed are those with the ten largest and ten smallest values for RSX.

[b] Relative strength of exports, defined as the difference between columns 2 and 3.

[c] As in table 2.

[d] $x \to y$, $(x \to y)$, $y \to x$ and $(y \to x)$ as defined in table 6.

[e] Coefficient of correlation between RSX and OPEN.

Figures 1 and 2 illustrate the usefulness of the frequency decompositions. The figures compare the conditional feedback between exports and income for Japan and Korea, respectively. According to table 6, both countries display strong evidence of growth-led exports. However, the temporal nature of the relationship is quite different, as the figures show. In Japan, feedback from exports to income is virtually nonexistent at all frequencies (figure 1a). Although the posterior medians of the various distributions are around 20 percent for cycles of 5.3 years or less, the corresponding point estimates never exceed 10 percent. Feedback from income to exports (figure 1b) is much stronger at all frequencies; point estimates increase from just under 60 percent in the very short run, to 90 percent in the long run.

In Korea, the pattern of feedback from exports to income is similar to that for Japan in the short run, with point estimates around 20 percent (figure 2a). However, feedback in this direction becomes much stronger in the long run, exceeding 80 percent in the very long run. The pattern of feedback from income to exports (figure 2b) is nearly the mirror image, with point estimates declining from 70 percent at cycles of 4.57 years to just over 10 percent at the longest cycles. Using the criteria introduced in the last section on a frequency-by-frequency basis, we find weak export-led growth (i.e., $(x \rightarrow y)$, in the notation of table 6) for Korea for cycles longer than 10.67 years. In Japan, we find at least weak growth-led exports at all cycles longer than 2.29 years, with our stronger criterion met for cycles of eight years or longer.

Although this decomposition of the conditional linear feedback measures by frequency provides a more detailed analysis of export-led growth within a particular country than was possible before, it leaves unanswered the question of *why* the export growth-income growth relationship differs across countries. The answer to this question requires a level of detailed analysis at the individual country level which is clearly beyond the scope of this paper. However, we believe this type of analysis can be used to direct future research into the appropriate *implementation* of export promotion policies in particular countries.

3.4 The Role of Investment and Human Capital

Given the results presented so far, a natural question arises: How do we know that our three-variable system is free of the "omitted variables" problem discussed above? In particular, what would happen if our analysis used human and/or physical capital accumulation as additional conditioning variables? Table 8 provides a partial answer. There we present values of the feedback between exports and income, conditional on human capital growth and investment growth as well as import growth, for the countries in table 6 (except Taiwan, for which we do not have a sufficiently long series for human

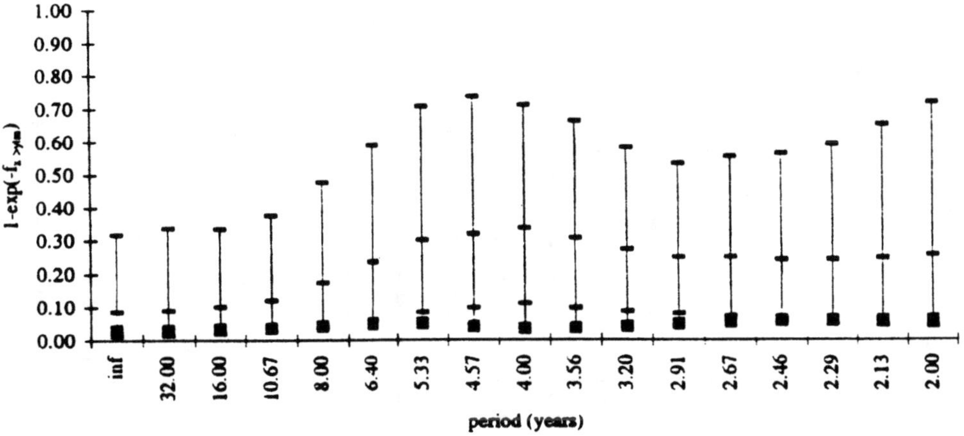

Fig. 1a. Conditional linear feedback from exports to income, Japan. Point estimates (filled squares) and 1st, 5th and 9th deciles (horizontal bars) of the posterior distribution of $1 - \exp(-f_{y>x|m})$, by frequency

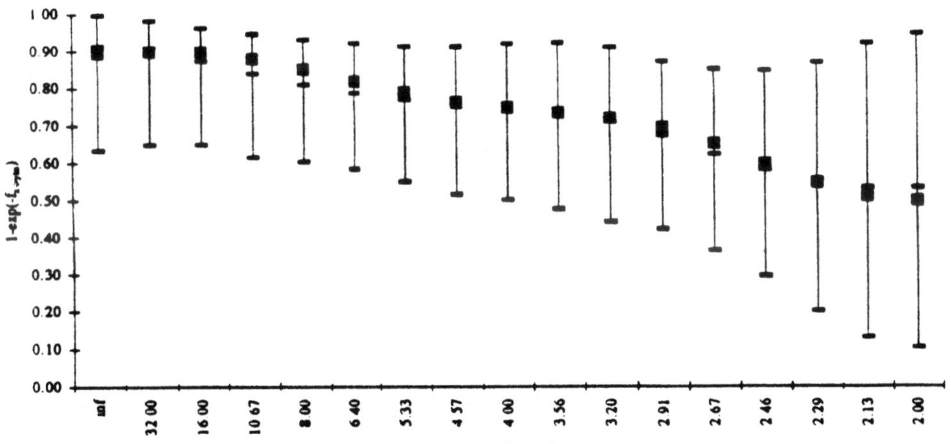

Fig. 1b. Conditional linear feedback from income to exports, Japan. Point estimates (filled squares) and 1st, 5th and 9th deciles (horizontal bars) of the posterior distribution of $1 - \exp(-f_{y>x|m})$, by frequency

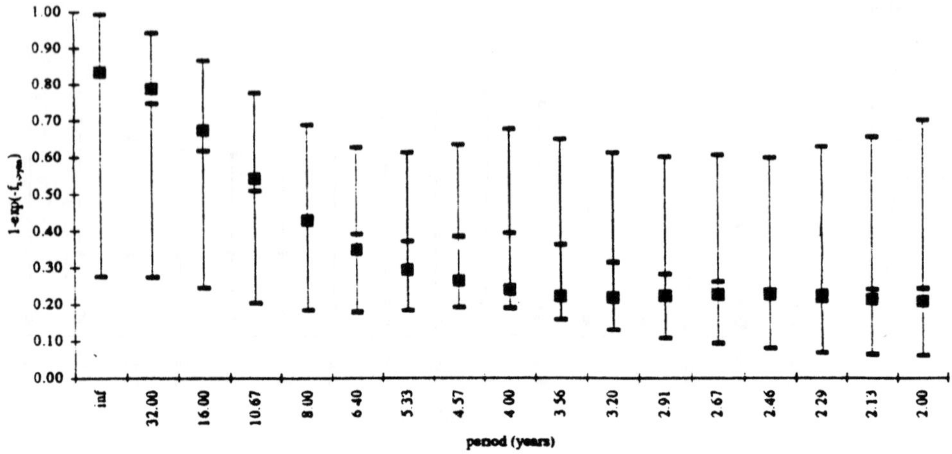

Fig. 2a. Conditional linear feedback from exports to income, Korea. Point estimates (filled squares) and 1st, 5th and 9th deciles (horizontal bars) of the posterior distribution of $1 - \exp(-f_{x>y|m})$, by frequency

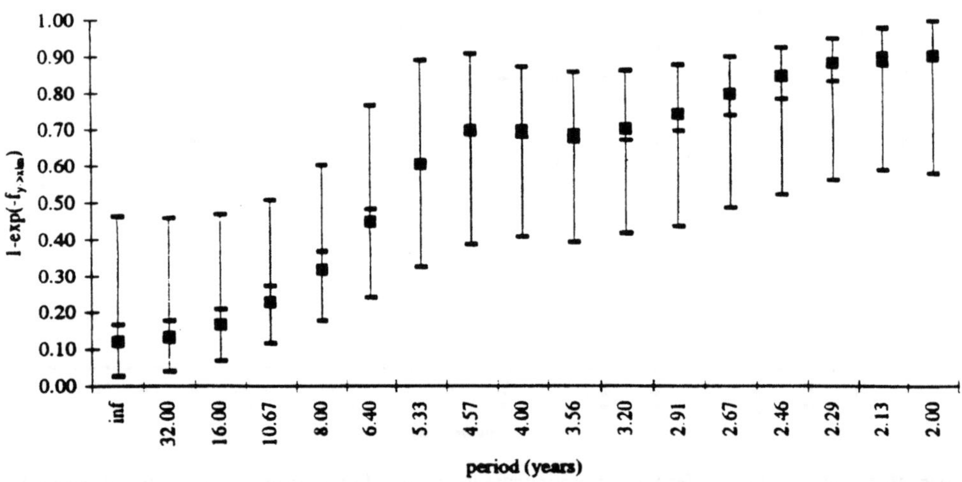

Fig. 2b. Conditional linear feedback from income to exports, Korea. Point estimates (filled squares) and 1st, 5th and 9th deciles (horizontal bars) of the posterior distribution of $1 - \exp(-f_{x>y|m})$, by frequency

capital).[30] A comparison of these two tables shows that the strength of conditional feedback in each direction increases with the addition of variables to the conditioning set. The sole exception is in Korea, where $F_{y\to x|h,i,m}$ is lower than $F_{y\to x|m}$. Evidence for growth-led exports remains strong in Japan, but weakens considerably for Korea. Our weak criterion for causal inference is now met in Indonesia (export-led growth) and Thailand (growth-led exports). Malaysia, Singapore and Thailand now have stronger feedback from income growth to export growth than vice versa; this is the reverse of the results in table 6. Table 8 therefore suggests that our results may be subject to some degree of omitted variable bias.

4 Conclusions

This paper has addressed some of the limitations of existing methods of detecting evidence for the export-led growth hypothesis. In particular, we have shown that failure to account for the role of import growth can produce misleading results in the analysis of the relationship between export growth and income growth. We have presented two alternative methods of measuring the export-income relationship, which allow us to control for the effect of imports. Use of these measures (the FEVD and conditional linear feedback) also permits us to investigate the nature of export-led growth at flexible time horizons, rather than focusing on a one-year horizon.

We believe our analysis points out several facts that need to be considered by theorists developing models of economic growth. First, export-led growth, when interpreted as a unidirectional causal ordering from exports to income, finds modest support in the Summers-Heston data set, seeming slightly more likely than the reverse ordering. Thirty of the countries in our study meet this definition of export-led growth, compared to 25 which have growth-led exports. The particular definition used (especially whether one interprets bidirectional causality as a form of export-led growth) may increase the prevalence of export-led growth still further. For example, the strength of conditional linear feedback from exports to income is stronger than feedback in the opposite direction in 65 of the 126 countries we study. Second, the role of the growth rate of imports cannot be ignored when examining the relationship between export growth

[30] The human capital measure is primary school enrolment as a percentage of primary school age children in each country (UNESCO), through 1990. Because this data is available only every five years from 1960–1985 for most countries, we use linear interpolation to estimate the data for the missing years. Investment is the total investment expenditure in CGDP (Summers and Heston, 1991).

Table 8. Linear feedback conditional on human capital, investment, and imports (R^2 measure)

COUNTRY	DATA	$1-\exp(-F_{x\to y\|h,i,m})$[a] 10th	50th	90th	pt. est.	$1-\exp(-F_{y\to x\|h,i,m})$[a] 10th	50th	90th	pt. est.	Inference[b]
HONG KONG	1960–90	0.3250	0.4841	0.6496	0.3714	0.4491	0.5596	0.6529	0.5324	
INDONESIA	1960–90	0.5472	0.6566	0.7483	0.6946	0.2473	0.4038	0.5600	0.3095	$(x \to y)$
JAPAN	1950–90	0.2080	0.3720	0.5558	0.2316	0.7629	0.8343	0.8815	0.8513	$y \to x$
REP. OF KOREA	1953–89	0.3905	0.5206	0.6588	0.5162	0.5104	0.6070	0.6970	0.6257	
MALAYSIA	1955–90	0.6174	0.7185	0.8035	0.7128	0.6816	0.7892	0.8556	0.7960	
PHILIPPINES	1950–90	0.4848	0.6006	0.7007	0.6146	0.4552	0.5519	0.6477	0.5484	
SINGAPORE	1960–90	0.5758	0.7379	0.8460	0.7535	0.5465	0.6960	0.7917	0.7733	
TAIWAN[c]	1951–90	NA	NA	NA	NA	NA	NA	NA	NA	NA
THAILAND	1950–90	0.4212	0.5443	0.6367	0.5287	0.5912	0.7007	0.7857	0.7160	$(y \to x)$

[a] $F_{x\to y|h,i,m}$ is the measure of linear feedback from exports to income, conditional on human capital, investment and imports. $F_{y\to x|h,i,m}$ is interpreted similarly. Table entries are the point estimate (pt. est.) and the 1st, 5th, and 9th deciles of the posterior distributions of $1-\exp(-F_{x\to y|h,i,m})$. This latter quantity is analogous to the coefficient of determination (R^2) or fraction of variation explained.

[b] $x \to y$, $(x \to y)$, $y \to x$ and $(y \to x)$ are defined analogously to the same type of inference in table 6.

[c] Unavailable due to the lack of a sufficiently long data series for human capital.

and income growth. Third, the effects of export growth on income growth not only vary across countries, they are not uniform over time for the same country. In particular, even in a country such as Korea, which exhibits *overall* evidence of growth-led exports, there may be time horizons at which feedback from exports to income dominates that from income to exports. This suggests that it may prove fruitful to examine the temporal nature of export-led growth more closely, in addition to its geographical occurrence.

Regarding the question raised at the beginning of the paper, "How can a country accelerate the pace of its economic development?" our results provide little in the way of policy prescriptions, nor were they intended to. They do indicate that trade and growth interact in an important and subtle way that merits further research.

Appendix

Table 9. Linear feedback between export growth and income growth, conditional on import growth

COUNTRY	DATA	$1-\exp(-F_{x\to y\mid m})$[a] 10th	50th	90th	pt est	$1-\exp(-F_{y\to x\mid m})$[a] 10th	50th	90th	pt est	Inference[b]
ALGERIA	1960–90	0.1076	0.2480	0.4129	0.2044	0.0658	0.1739	0.3089	0.1582	
ANGOLA	1960–89	0.0978	0.2163	0.3505	0.1934	0.2677	0.3896	0.4962	0.3921	$(y\to x)$
BENIN	1959–89	0.1381	0.3338	0.4964	0.3353	0.2291	0.3077	0.4294	0.3061	
BOTSWANA	1960–89	0.0791	0.1411	0.2455	0.1187	0.1150	0.1976	0.3208	0.1871	
BURKINA FASO	1959–90	0.0693	0.1278	0.2447	0.0704	0.0586	0.1093	0.1887	0.0951	
BURUNDI	1960–90	0.1194	0.2681	0.4184	0.2944	0.1255	0.2860	0.4522	0.2956	
CAMEROON	1960–90	0.0743	0.1803	0.3229	0.1046	0.2959	0.4631	0.5912	0.5037	$(y\to x)$
CAPE VERDE IS.	1960–89	0.2417	0.3407	0.4521	0.3321	0.1382	0.2585	0.4538	0.1595	
CENTRAL AFRICAN REP.	1960–90	0.0996	0.1438	0.2322	0.1141	0.2343	0.3444	0.4543	0.3437	$y\to x$
CHAD	1960–90	0.3175	0.4037	0.5021	0.4247	0.3230	0.4375	0.5397	0.4554	
COMOROS	1960–86	0.1835	0.3227	0.4794	0.3192	0.1084	0.2079	0.3466	0.1886	
CONGO	1960–90	0.1534	0.2699	0.4216	0.2109	0.1188	0.2145	0.3734	0.2043	
DJIBOUTI	1970–87	0.6343	0.7554	0.8560	0.7699	0.4957	0.6928	0.7839	0.6652	
EGYPT	1950–90	0.6509	0.7433	0.8075	0.7498	0.0443	0.0952	0.1978	0.0507	$x\to y$
ETHIOPIA	1960–86	0.1919	0.3949	0.5654	0.4126	0.4117	0.5020	0.6093	0.5004	
GABON	1960–90	0.4199	0.5622	0.6633	0.5746	0.0899	0.1795	0.2766	0.1851	$x\to y$
GAMBIA	1960–90	0.0348	0.1179	0.2656	0.0597	0.2112	0.2993	0.4056	0.2682	$(y\to x)$
GHANA	1955–89	0.3808	0.4858	0.5608	0.5052	0.0341	0.1004	0.2580	0.0268	$x\to y$
GUINEA	1959–89	0.1133	0.2098	0.3614	0.2033	0.2228	0.2735	0.3709	0.2476	
GUINEA-BISSEAU	1960–90	0.0866	0.1352	0.2228	0.1064	0.2839	0.4677	0.6134	0.4873	$y\to x$
IVORY COAST	1960–90	0.5048	0.6248	0.7159	0.6320	0.0983	0.2547	0.3982	0.2436	$x\to y$
KENYA	1950–90	0.0717	0.1460	0.2840	0.1303	0.1553	0.2340	0.3826	0.1530	
LESOTHO	1960–90	0.6106	0.7616	0.8441	0.8212	0.5621	0.6699	0.7457	0.7065	
LIBERIA	1960–86	0.3262	0.4508	0.5715	0.4580	0.2408	0.3513	0.4589	0.2956	
MADAGASCAR	1960–90	0.2550	0.4033	0.5327	0.4286	0.1636	0.2815	0.4085	0.2564	
MALAWI	1954–90	0.0433	0.1061	0.2275	0.0439	0.3076	0.4209	0.5269	0.4284	$y\to x$
MALI	1960–90	0.4787	0.6089	0.7194	0.6333	0.0869	0.1868	0.3277	0.1704	$x\to y$

MAURITANIA	1960–90	0.3281	0.4873	0.6357	0.5071	0.0706	0.1959	0.3516	0.1466	$(x \to y)$
MAURITIUS	1950–90	0.0613	0.1640	0.3058	0.0902	0.1923	0.3402	0.4765	0.3412	$(y \to x)$
MOROCCO	1950–90	0.4717	0.6038	0.7053	0.6355	0.0880	0.2084	0.3711	0.2042	$x \to y$
MOZAMBIQUE	1960–90	0.1489	0.2794	0.4277	0.2678	0.2874	0.3980	0.5111	0.3992	
NAMIBIA	1960–89	0.2309	0.3506	0.4484	0.3669	0.3562	0.4850	0.6157	0.4856	
NIGER	1960–89	0.2424	0.4024	0.5559	0.4241	0.3834	0.5328	0.6432	0.5696	
NIGERIA	1950–90	0.1264	0.2239	0.3704	0.1913	0.0187	0.0753	0.2047	0.0505	
REUNION	1960–88	0.2045	0.3324	0.4574	0.3409	0.0518	0.1399	0.2830	0.0893	$(x \to y)$
RWANDA	1960–90	0.4413	0.6187	0.7505	0.6168	0.1057	0.1786	0.3033	0.1517	$x \to y$
SENEGAL	1960–90	0.2749	0.4047	0.5203	0.4440	0.4011	0.5535	0.6917	0.5774	
SEYCHELLES	1960–89	0.1275	0.2240	0.3590	0.1845	0.4023	0.5162	0.6121	0.5485	$y \to x$
SIERRA LEONE	1961–90	0.0697	0.1663	0.3090	0.1167	0.1903	0.3379	0.4398	0.3261	$(y \to x)$
SOMALIA	1960–89	0.2129	0.3992	0.5901	0.3968	0.3556	0.4878	0.6024	0.4958	
SOUTH AFRICA	1950–90	0.5854	0.6788	0.7603	0.6842	0.3077	0.4857	0.6254	0.4937	$(x \to y)$
SUDAN	1971–90	0.5188	0.6857	0.8268	0.7555	0.3811	0.5246	0.6399	0.5391	
SWAZILAND	1960–89	0.1354	0.2405	0.4010	0.2064	0.2669	0.4086	0.5383	0.4259	$(y \to x)$
TANZANIA	1950–88	0.0613	0.1388	0.2596	0.0832	0.0857	0.2090	0.3757	0.1962	
TOGO	1960–90	0.2593	0.3949	0.5293	0.3715	0.0765	0.1823	0.3464	0.1518	$(x \to y)$
TUNISIA	1960–90	0.4596	0.5687	0.6583	0.5785	0.1580	0.2306	0.3238	0.1761	$x \to y$
UGANDA	1950–89	0.4567	0.5688	0.6731	0.5677	0.3036	0.4673	0.5951	0.4773	
ZAIRE	1950–89	0.3217	0.4257	0.5105	0.3989	0.2265	0.2969	0.4182	0.3011	
ZAMBIA	1955–90	0.1663	0.3271	0.4598	0.3414	0.0553	0.1045	0.1830	0.0578	$(x \to y)$
ZIMBABWE	1954–90	0.0400	0.1021	0.2126	0.0607	0.3446	0.4807	0.5886	0.5213	$y \to x$
BAHAMAS	1977–87	NA	NA	NA	NA	NA	NA	NA	NA	NA
BARBADOS	1960–89	0.2433	0.3803	0.4988	0.3698	0.3621	0.4988	0.6225	0.5223	
BELIZE	1985–85	NA	NA	NA	NA	NA	NA	NA	NA	NA
CANADA	1950–90	0.1031	0.1929	0.3410	0.1046	0.0527	0.1365	0.2814	0.0726	
COSTA RICA	1950–90	0.2759	0.4376	0.5661	0.4458	0.1527	0.2353	0.3691	0.2153	$(x \to y)$
DOMINICA	1985–85	NA	NA	NA	NA	NA	NA	NA	NA	NA
DOMINICAN REP.	1950–90	0.0330	0.0990	0.2399	0.0459	0.0290	0.1184	0.2603	0.0931	
EL SALVADOR	1950–90	0.1843	0.3774	0.5481	0.3609	0.4285	0.5530	0.6544	0.5611	$(y \to x)$
GRENADA	1984–90	NA	NA	NA	NA	NA	NA	NA	NA	NA
GUATEMALA	1950–90	0.1289	0.2624	0.4106	0.1804	0.0969	0.2045	0.3774	0.1558	
HAITI	1960–89	0.4229	0.5454	0.6426	0.5609	0.0835	0.2003	0.3674	0.2006	$x \to y$

Table 9. Continued

HONDURAS	1950–90	0.3157	0.4311	0.5275	0.4381	0.1782	0.3075	0.4245	0.2776	$(x \rightarrow y)$
JAMAICA	1953–89	0.2812	0.4561	0.5896	0.4407	0.3221	0.4166	0.5447	0.4212	
MEXICO	1950–90	0.3828	0.5021	0.6143	0.5203	0.3157	0.4078	0.5124	0.3977	
NICARAGUA	1960–87	NA	NA	NA	NA	NA	NA	NA	NA	NA
PANAMA	1950–90	0.1616	0.3319	0.4867	0.3222	0.1308	0.2457	0.3870	0.2390	
PUERTO RICO	1955–89	0.2970	0.5409	0.7117	0.5608	0.4970	0.5773	0.6631	0.5883	
ST. LUCIA	1985–85	NA	NA	NA	NA	NA	NA	NA	NA	NA
ST. VINCENT & GRENADA	1985–85	NA	NA	NA	NA	NA	NA	NA	NA	NA
TRINIDAD & TOBAGO	1950–90	0.2274	0.3540	0.4844	0.3710	0.3006	0.4297	0.5440	0.4472	
U.S.A.	1950–90	0.0426	0.1473	0.3163	0.1061	0.1122	0.2642	0.4387	0.2572	
ARGENTINA	1950–90	0.0753	0.1725	0.3429	0.1463	0.6437	0.7339	0.7961	0.7765	$y \rightarrow x$
BOLIVIA	1950–90	0.1344	0.2685	0.4350	0.2473	0.3213	0.4843	0.6162	0.4860	$(y \rightarrow x)$
BRAZIL	1950–90	0.0685	0.1827	0.3431	0.1521	0.2178	0.4024	0.5388	0.4089	$(y \rightarrow x)$
CHILE	1950–90	0.0729	0.1649	0.3039	0.1498	0.1816	0.3195	0.4588	0.3525	$(y \rightarrow x)$
COLOMBIA	1950–90	0.4629	0.6008	0.7366	0.5877	0.4471	0.5659	0.6518	0.5808	
ECUADOR	1950–90	0.4484	0.5716	0.6857	0.5571	0.2791	0.4302	0.5572	0.4488	
GUYANA	1950–90	NA	NA	NA	NA	NA	NA	NA	NA	NA
PARAGUAY	1950–90	0.1160	0.1891	0.3058	0.1439	0.1670	0.2801	0.4101	0.2583	
PERU	1950–90	0.4100	0.5398	0.6426	0.5501	0.4110	0.5402	0.6617	0.5591	
SURINAME	1960–89	0.4076	0.5566	0.6678	0.6036	0.1969	0.3249	0.4926	0.3216	$(x \rightarrow y)$
URUGUAY	1950–90	0.4647	0.6229	0.7371	0.6698	0.1012	0.1675	0.2936	0.1128	$x \rightarrow y$
VENEZUELA	1950–90	0.0678	0.1878	0.3612	0.1433	0.1348	0.2853	0.4399	0.2614	
BAHRAIN	1985–88	NA	NA	NA	NA	NA	NA	NA	NA	NA
BANGLADESH	1959–90	0.0702	0.1702	0.3176	0.1466	0.7999	0.8636	0.9143	0.8564	$y \rightarrow x$
BHUTAN	1985–85	NA	NA	NA	NA	NA	NA	NA	NA	NA
CHINA	1968–90	0.2694	0.4125	0.5536	0.4056	0.0334	0.0891	0.1763	0.0659	$x \rightarrow y$
HONG KONG	1960–90	0.1475	0.2521	0.4047	0.1858	0.1892	0.2752	0.3803	0.2493	
INDIA	1950–90	0.2618	0.3749	0.4873	0.3537	0.1812	0.2952	0.4174	0.3135	

INDONESIA	1960–90	0.1354	0.2832	0.4809	0.2075	0.0243	0.0850	0.2100	0.0274	
IRAN	1955–89	0.2789	0.4429	0.5960	0.4460	0.0265	0.0835	0.2139	0.0269	$x \rightarrow y$
IRAQ	1953–87	0.3038	0.4682	0.5959	0.4954	0.1365	0.2870	0.4414	0.2708	$(x \rightarrow y)$
ISRAEL	1953–90	0.4039	0.5394	0.6693	0.5624	0.0649	0.1806	0.3464	0.1805	$x \rightarrow y$
JAPAN	1950–90	0.0417	0.0929	0.2176	0.0319	0.6121	0.7284	0.8070	0.7468	$y \rightarrow x$
JORDAN	1954–90	0.2271	0.4240	0.5763	0.4326	0.4162	0.5558	0.6693	0.5926	
REP. OF KOREA	1953–89	0.2134	0.3296	0.4518	0.2737	0.5205	0.6209	0.6980	0.6439	$y \rightarrow x$
KUWAIT	1985–89	NA	NA	NA	NA	NA	NA	NA	NA	NA
LAOS	1984–90	NA	NA	NA	NA	NA	NA	NA	NA	NA
MALAYSIA	1955–90	0.4703	0.6033	0.7176	0.6081	0.3922	0.5324	0.6278	0.5308	
MONGOLIA	1984–90	NA	NA	NA	NA	NA	NA	NA	NA	NA
MYANMAR	1950–89	0.3091	0.4030	0.5150	0.3824	0.1000	0.2262	0.4186	0.2272	
NEPAL	1951–86	0.7522	0.8168	0.8619	0.8267	0.1376	0.2434	0.4133	0.2107	$x \rightarrow y$
OMAN	1985–89	NA	NA	NA	NA	NA	NA	NA	NA	NA
PAKISTAN	1950–90	0.1419	0.2614	0.3814	0.2381	0.2593	0.3934	0.5234	0.3966	$(y \rightarrow x)$
PHILIPPINES	1950–90	0.3630	0.4364	0.4961	0.4494	0.3266	0.3815	0.4474	0.3689	
QATAR	1985–89	NA	NA	NA	NA	NA	NA	NA	NA	NA
SAUDI ARABIA	1985–89	NA	NA	NA	NA	NA	NA	NA	NA	NA
SINGAPORE	1960–90	0.3802	0.5784	0.7207	0.5638	0.1837	0.3589	0.5122	0.3877	
SRI LANKA	1950–89	0.3573	0.5201	0.6551	0.4761	0.2513	0.4328	0.6093	0.4235	
SYRIA	1960–90	0.4872	0.6182	0.7135	0.6486	0.1692	0.2880	0.3897	0.2672	$x \rightarrow y$
TAIWAN	1951–90	0.5104	0.6487	0.7380	0.6546	0.2030	0.3535	0.4686	0.3838	$x \rightarrow y$
THAILAND	1950–90	0.2187	0.3367	0.4457	0.2948	0.1945	0.2852	0.4250	0.2440	
UNITED ARAB EMIRATES	1985–89	NA	NA	NA	NA	NA	NA	NA	NA	NA
YEMEN	1969–89	0.0426	0.1303	0.3005	0.0952	0.4047	0.5773	0.6827	0.6081	$y \rightarrow x$
AUSTRIA	1950–90	0.2499	0.3868	0.5659	0.3143	0.2721	0.3442	0.4105	0.3490	
BELGIUM	1950–90	0.3543	0.5215	0.6470	0.5131	0.1526	0.2371	0.3686	0.2289	$(x \rightarrow y)$
BULGARIA	1980–90	NA	NA	NA	NA	NA	NA	NA	NA	NA
CYPRUS	1950–90	0.4553	0.5452	0.6235	0.5504	0.3237	0.4437	0.5650	0.4327	
CZECHOSLOVAKIA	1960–90	0.1164	0.2343	0.3975	0.1980	0.2796	0.3990	0.5318	0.4199	$(y \rightarrow x)$
DENMARK	1950–90	0.2949	0.4708	0.6292	0.4911	0.2968	0.4123	0.6020	0.4894	
FINLAND	1950–90	0.3737	0.4506	0.5457	0.4357	0.3863	0.5268	0.6378	0.5408	
FRANCE	1950–90	0.1232	0.2602	0.4301	0.2368	0.2889	0.3768	0.4831	0.3589	

Table 9. Continued

FED. REP. GERMANY	1950–90	0.0413	0.1052	0.2170	0.0512	0.0671	0.1468	0.2525	0.1340	
GREECE	1950–90	0.2552	0.4187	0.5750	0.4560	0.3727	0.4785	0.5758	0.4918	
HUNGARY	1970–90	0.4804	0.7365	0.8747	0.7958	0.7758	0.8459	0.9023	0.8463	
ICELAND	1950–90	0.5593	0.6551	0.7300	0.6594	0.1601	0.2418	0.3441	0.2368	$x \rightarrow y$
IRELAND	1950–90	0.0304	0.0933	0.2132	0.0383	0.1102	0.2224	0.3817	0.1980	
ITALY	1950–90	0.2794	0.3446	0.4343	0.3451	0.0261	0.1192	0.2806	0.0575	$(x \rightarrow y)$
LUXEMBOURG	1950–90	0.0458	0.1012	0.2490	0.0463	0.0865	0.1686	0.2877	0.1421	
MALTA	1954–89	0.7142	0.7724	0.8149	0.7720	0.2938	0.4452	0.5775	0.4587	$x \rightarrow y$
NETHERLANDS	1950–90	0.2272	0.4475	0.6190	0.4218	0.1794	0.2504	0.3277	0.2447	
NORWAY	1950–90	0.2387	0.3720	0.5059	0.3156	0.3919	0.5142	0.6241	0.4843	
POLAND	1970–90	NA	NA	NA	NA	NA	NA	NA	NA	NA
PORTUGAL	1950–90	0.1646	0.3163	0.4727	0.3082	0.3795	0.5128	0.6195	0.5312	$(y \rightarrow x)$
ROMANIA	1985–85	NA	NA	NA	NA	NA	NA	NA	NA	NA
SPAIN	1950–90	0.1211	0.2571	0.3994	0.2206	0.1763	0.2853	0.4243	0.2699	
SWEDEN	1950–90	0.4790	0.5776	0.6613	0.5687	0.5153	0.6613	0.7780	0.6983	
SWITZERLAND	1950–90	0.2759	0.4054	0.5356	0.4002	0.0562	0.1170	0.2090	0.0971	$x \rightarrow y$
TURKEY	1950–90	0.0937	0.2327	0.4390	0.2749	0.0927	0.2388	0.4039	0.2222	
U.K.	1950–90	0.1149	0.2008	0.3295	0.1472	0.1918	0.3245	0.4774	0.3313	$(y \rightarrow x)$

[a] $F_{x \rightarrow y|m}$ is the measure of linear feedback from exports to income, conditional on imports. $F_{y \rightarrow x|m}$ is interpreted similarly. Table entries are the point estimate (pt. est.) and the 1st, 5th, and 9th deciles of the posterior distributions of $1 - \exp(-F_{x \rightarrow y|m})$. This latter quantity is analogous to the coefficient of determination (R^2) or fraction of variation explained.

[b] $x \rightarrow y$ means that the 10th posterior decile of $1 - \exp(-F_{x \rightarrow y|m})$ lies above the 90th posterior decile of $1 - \exp(-F_{y \rightarrow x|m})$. $(x \rightarrow y)$ means that the point estimate of $1 - \exp(-F_{x \rightarrow y|m})$ lies above the 90th posterior decile of $1 - \exp(-F_{y \rightarrow x|m})$, and the point estimate of $1 - \exp(-F_{y \rightarrow x|m})$ lies below the 10th posterior decile of $1 - \exp(-F_{x \rightarrow y|m})$. $y \rightarrow x$ and $(y \rightarrow x)$ are interpreted similarly.

References

Afxentiou PC, Serletis A (1991) Exports and GNP cuasality in the industrial countries 1950–1985. Kyklos 44/2:167–179

Ahmad J, Kwan ACC (1991) Causality between exports and economic growth. Economics Letters 37:243–248

Bahmani-Oskooee M, Mohtadi H, Shabsigh G (1991) Exports, growth and causality in LDCs: A re-examination. Journal of Development Economics 36:405–415

Bahmani-Oskooee M, Alse J (1993) Export growth and economic growth: An application of cointegration and error-correction modeling. Journal of Developing Areas 27(4)

Balassa BA (1978) Policy reform in developing countries. Oxford, New York, Pergamon Press

Barro RJ (1991) Economic growth in a cross-section of countries. Quarterly Journal of Economics 106:407–501

Chow PCY (1987) Causality between export growth and industrial development: Empirical evidence from the NICs. Journal of Development Economics 26:55–63

Darrat AF (1987) Are exports an engine of growth? Another look at the evidence. Applied Economics 19:277–283

Doan T (1992) RATS users' manual, Version 4.0. Evanston, Estima

Dodaro S (1993) Exports and growth: A reconsideration of causality. Journal of Development Areas 27:227–244

Findlay R (1973) International trade and development theory. New York, Columbia University Press

Ghartey EE (1993) Causal relationship between exports and economic growth: Some empirical evidence in Taiwan, Japan and the U.S. Applied Economics 25:1145–1152

Geweke J (1982) Measurement of linear dependence and feedback between multiple time series (with discussion and rejoinder). Journal of the American Statistical Association 77/378:304–324

Geweke J (1984) Measures of conditional linear dependence and feedback between time series. Journal of the American Statistical Association 79/388:907–915

Hsiao C (1979) Autoregressive modelling of Canadian money and income data. Journal of the American Statistical Association 74:553–560

Jung WS, Marshall PJ (1985) Exports, growth and causality in developing countries. Journal of Development Economics 18:1–12

Kormendi RC, Meguire PG (1985) Macroeconomic determinants of growth: Cross-country evidence. Journal of Monetary Economics 16/2:141–163

Kravis IB (1970) Trade as a handmaiden of growth: Similarities between the 19th and 20th centuries. Economic Journal 80:850–872

Kugler P (1991) Growth exports and cointegration: An empirical investigation. Weltwirtschaftliches Archiv 127(2):73–81

Kunst RM, Marin D (1989) On exports and productivity: A causal analysis. Review of Economics and Statistics 699–703

Marin D (1992) Is the export-led growth hypothesis valid for industrialized countries? Review of Economics and Statistics 678–688

McKinnon RI (1964) Foreign exchange constraints in economic development and efficient aid allocation. Economic Journal 74:388–409

Michaely M (1977) Exports and growth: An empirical investigation. Journal of Development Economics 4/1:49–53

Nunes A, Mata E, Valerio N (1989) Portuguese economic growth, 1833–1985. Journal of European Economic History 18:291–330

Oxley L (1993) Cointegration, causality and export-led growth in Portugal, 1865–1985. Economics Letters 43:163–166

Pierce DA (1982) Comment on geweke, Measurement of Linear Dependence and Feedback Between Multiple Time Series. Journal of the American Statistical Association 77/378:315–316

Ram R (1987) Exports and economic growth in developing countries: Evidence from time-series and cross-section data. Economic Development and Cultural Change 36(1): 51–72

Riezman R, Whiteman CH (1991) World business cycles. University of Iowa Department of Economics Working Paper 91-26

Sengupta JK, España JR (1994) Exports and economic growth in Asian NICs: An econometric analysis for Korea. Applied Economics 26: 41–51

Serletis A (1992) Export growth and Canadian economic development. Journal of Development Economics 38: 133–145

Sims CA (1980) Macroeconomics and reality. Econometrica 48/1: 1–48

Summers R, Heston A (1988) A new set of international comparisons of real product and price level estimates for 130 countries, 1950–1985. Review of Income and Wealth 34: 1–25

Summers R, Heston A (1991) The penn-world table (Mark 5): An expanded set of international comparisons, 1950–1988. Quarterly Journal of Economics 106: 327–368

Tyler WG (1981) Growth and export expansion in developing countries: Some empirical evidence. Journal of Development Economics 9/1: 121–130

Ukpolo V (1994) Export composition and growth of selected low-income African countries: Evidence from time-series data. Applied Economics 26: 445–449

UNESCO Yearbook of Statistics, various years

Urquhart MC (1988) Canadian economic growth, 1870–1985. Institute for Economic Research, Discussion paper 734, Queen's University, Kingston, Ontario

White H (1980) A heteroskedasticity-consistent covariance matrix estimator and a direct test for heteroskedasticity. Econometrica 48: 817–838

First version received: January 1995
Final version received: November 1995

III Analysis of Co-Movements and Convergence at Regional Level of Incomes

Productivity and Convergence Across U.S. States and Industries

ANDREW B. BERNARD[1]

Department of Economics, M.I.T., Cambridge, MA 02139, USA

CHARLES I. JONES[1]

Department of Economics, Stanford University, Stanford, CA 94305, USA

Abstract: We examine the sources of aggregate labor productivity movements and convergence in the U.S. states from 1963 to 1989. Productivity levels vary widely across sectors and across states, as do sectoral output and employment shares. The main finding is the diverse performance of sectors regarding convergence. Using both cross-section and time series methods, we find convergence in labor productivity for both manufacturing and mining. However, we find that convergence does not hold for all sectors over the period. Decomposing aggregate convergence into industry productivity gains and changing sectoral shares of output, we find the manufacturing sector to be responsible for the bulk of cross-state convergence.

Key Words: Economic growth, labor productivity, convergence, industry composition, panel unit roots

JEL Classification: O47, O51, C33

1 Introduction

In recent years, a large body of empirical work has developed on the question of whether regions, particularly countries, are becoming more similar in terms of their aggregate income and productivity. This research, stimulated largely by the resurgence of work on growth theory, has dealt almost exclusively with the yes-or-no question of whether countries are converging. While the debate continues, the sources of these aggregate productivity movements at the sectoral level remain largely unstudied.

In this paper, we explore the sources of aggregate labor productivity convergence in U.S. states during the period 1963–1989.[2] Using data on sectors in U.S.

1 We thank Kevin Hetherington and Sevin Yeltekin for excellent research assistance, and the World Economy Laboratory at M.I.T. and the Center for Economic Policy Research at Stanford for financial assistance.

2 The fact of state convergence during the period is remarkably uncontroversial relative to other samples of countries and regions. See Barro and Sala-i-Martin (1991, 1992) for cross-section analyses, Carlino and Mills (1993) and Quah (1994) for time series approaches.

states, we examine productivity levels and growth rates across states.[3] Additionally, we ask whether individual sectors exhibit convergence and therefore contribute to aggregate convergence, and whether the changing mix of industries is an important factor.

While most work on productivity movements and convergence has concentrated on aggregate cross-country comparisons, some research has studied movements within countries, in particular across the U.S. states. In several papers, Barro and Sala-i-Martin (1991, 1992) document convergence across U.S. states in terms of income per capita and gross state product per capita. They find that convergence holds in aggregate across U.S. states using cross-section techniques with speeds of convergence to steady state around 2 percent per year. Considering productivity growth by sector from 1963–1989, Barro and Sala-i-Martin (1991) conclude that convergence was occurring in all sectors, although more rapidly in manufacturing than in other sectors. They also conclude that a lack of aggregate convergence after the early 1970s was due primarily to relative price movements in oil-related industries. In separate work, Keil and Vohra (1993) also emphasize the importance of oil and mining, arguing that convergence across states disappears once the influence of oil and other extractive industries is taken into account. In contrast, our results do not point towards mining or mining-intensive states as critical in the overall convergence, or lack thereof, of labor productivity from 1963–1989.

This paper is divided into two main sections. The first section, Section 2, discusses the state productivity data that underlies our results. We highlight interesting variation in productivity levels, employment shares, and growth rates across states and sectors. Examples include the tremendous differences in labor productivity across sectors and the enormous variation across states in manufacturing employment shares. Then we discuss the sources of state productivity growth. Here, our primary findings are twofold: productivity growth in the manufacturing sector accounts for the bulk of private non-farm productivity growth, and the shift away from highly productive sectors to sectors with lower productivity reduced productivity growth for the average state by 0.23 percentage points, or 28 percent of productivity growth.

The second main part of the paper, Section 3, documents the evidence on sectoral convergence across the U.S. states. Employing both cross-section and time series methodologies, we consider the evidence for convergence in labor productivity across states for total private output and for individual sectors. As in other studies, we find evidence for convergence in gross state product per worker over the period 1963–1989; catch-up for total labor productivity is occuring at a rate of over 4 percent per year. However, unlike previous work, our results for individual sectors show substantial variation. There is strong evidence of convergence for manufacturing and mining using both cross-section

[3] Throughout the paper, the term "productivity" will often be used without a modifier to refer to labor productivity.

and time series techniques. On the other hand, the construction and wholesale/retail trade sectors show no evidence of convergence over the period, while the results are mixed to negative for transportation and other services. The disparity of outcomes suggests that sectoral composition plays an important role in convergence of aggregate labor productivity. Decomposing convergence in total labor productivity, we find that increases in within-sector productivity account for 73 percent of the total, with changing sectoral composition making up the balance. Manufacturing productivity increases were the most important industry contribution. A final section contrasts these results to those from work on sectoral convergence in the OECD and concludes.

2 State Productivity

2.1 *Productivity Levels and Growth Rates*

This paper is fundamentally concerned with the movements of labor productivity across states and industries over the last thirty years. Labor productivity is constructed as the ratio of gross state product (GSP) to state employment for the period 1963 to 1989.[4] The industries analyzed here are mining; construction; manufacturing; transportation and public utilities; wholesale and retail trade; finance, insurance, and real estate (F.I.R.E.); and other services.[5] Our "total" sector reflects the sum of these sectors, i.e. it represents the total private non-farm part of the economy.

Table 1 summarizes our data by reporting productivity levels and variation averaged across the fifty states and the District of Columbia.[6] Several interest-

---

[4] Gross state product data is obtained from the Bureau of Economic Analysis for the fifty states plus the District of Columbia. Data was provided for 1963–1977 and for 1977–1989 in constant 1982 prices. The two sets of data were merged using the 1977 data in each data set. State employment data represents annual averages and is from the Bureau of Labor Statistics for the period 1950–1993, although only the 1963–1989 data is used in this project. Our results differ from those in Barro and Sala-i-Martin (1991) in part because we employ more recent revisions of Gross State Product data covering a longer time span. These revisions shift as much as 0.6 percent of U.S. GDP between regions over a 10-year period (see Trott, Dunbar and Friedenberg, 1991).

[5] Because of missing data early in the sample (typically employment data), a few states are omitted from our calculations for certain sectors. The following states are omitted from the mining sector and the other services sector for this reason: Delaware, Hawaii, Maine, Maryland, Massachusetts, Michigan, and Rhode Island. Connecticut is also dropped from the mining and construction sectors because of missing data.

[6] Averaging across states gives each state equal weight, while the U.S. level effectively weights states by their size. With the exception of the mining sector (where the U.S. productivity level is much higher than the productivity level for the average state), the results are very similar for these two summary measures.

Table 1. Productivity levels and variation across states

Sector	Average 1963	Coefficient of Variation 1963	Average 1989	Coefficient of Variation 1989
Mining	124274	104.6	130029	110.1
Construction	56230	24.2	38122	49.9
Manufacturing	23393	25.9	46459	16.3
Trans/PubUtilities	37129	8.8	71718	12.1
Wholesale/Retail	20577	12.6	25897	12.6
F.I.R.E.	91094	22.8	92047	19.9
Other Services	26739	14.6	22398	15.3
Total	34023	30.7	40146	29.3

Note: Numbers are calculated by averaging (or computing standard deviation) across states.

ing results are apparent. First, there is remarkably wide variation in productivity levels, both across sectors and across states. The mining sector is by far the most productive sector according to the labor productivity measure, at $130,029 per worker in 1989 as compared to $40,146 per worker for our private non-farm total. In 1989, the manufacturing sector ranks in the middle in terms of productivity at $46,459 per worker, exceeding construction ($38,122), wholesale/retail trade ($25,897) and the other services ($22,398) sectors. Interestingly, the notion that manufacturing is an especially productive sector is not readily apparent in the table, particularly at the beginning of the sample. In 1963, the manufacturing sector was second from the bottom in terms of productivity, exceeding only the wholesale/retail trade sector but below the other services sector.

This observation leads one immediately to wonder about measurement error, and there is ample evidence in Table 1 of the kind of problems in measuring productivity that have been documented by Baily and Gordon (1988), Griliches (1994), and others. As one striking example, notice that according to this data, average productivity in the construction sector has fallen by 32 percent percent, from $56,230 in 1963 to $38,122 in 1989. Labor productivity also appears to fall in the other services sector and to remain relatively unchanged in the finance, insurance, and real estate (F.I.R.E.) sector.

The variation in productivity levels across sectors is matched by a large amount of variation in productivity levels across states. The standard deviation of productivity levels for the total private non-farm sector is 30.7 percent of the average productivity level in 1963 and falls only slightly to 29.3 percent by 1989, as shown by the coefficients of variation in Table 1. The coefficient of variation in the manufacturing sector displays a standard pattern of convergence, beginning at 25.9 percent in 1963 and falling to 16.3 percent in 1989, while other sectors show very different behavior. The mining sector shows extremely large variation, with a coefficient of variation of 104.6 percent in 1963 and 110.1 percent in 1989. On the other hand, the transportation/public utilities sector

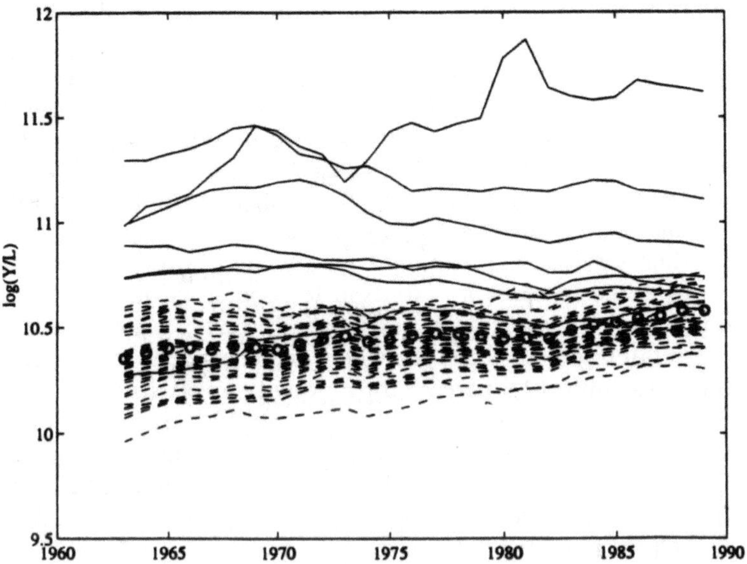

Fig. 1. Private non-farm productivity. The U.S. is indicated by circles. Mining states are solid, and non-mining states are dashed

shows relatively little variation across states, at 8.8 percent in 1963 and 12.1 percent in 1989.

Figure 1 displays labor productivity data for the total private non-farm sector. In the figure, the "mining" states are displayed with solid lines, while the remaining states are displayed with broken lines.[7] Labor productivity for the U.S. is indicated by circles. Perhaps the most striking result in the figure is the difference between the mining and non-mining states. The mining states are much more productive in aggregate than the remaining states. In part, this results from the large labor productivity in the mining sector, combined with the large share of mining in non-farm private output for these states. However, it turns out that the mining states are typically the most productive states in the other sectors as well. For example, Alaska is the most productive state in construction, wholesale/retail trade, F.I.R.E., and other services in 1963. Although we find it plausible that the mining states are the most productive states in mining, it is much more difficult to believe this productivity advantage carries over into other sectors of the economy. In fact, much of this apparent higher productivity may reflect problems in adjusting for relative

[7] The "mining" states are defined as those that average more than 20 percent of output in the mining sector. These states, together with their average mining shares, are Alaska (30.7%), Louisiana (39.8%), New Mexico (29.3%), Oklahoma (25.6%), Texas (23.9%), and Wyoming (46.1%).

prices. For this reason, we will often exclude the mining states from our analysis.[8]

Productivity levels by sector for the non-mining states are displayed graphically in Figure 2. In this and subsequent figures, the data for the United States is plotted with circles, while the data for California is highlighted as a thick solid line. This figure reinforces the results discussed in Table 1. Productivity in manufacturing, transportation, wholesale/retail trade, and in the private non-farm sector as a whole shows substantial growth. Measurement problems in construction and other services are apparent in the declining productivity levels and in the substantial increase in variation for construction in the late 1970s. In general, productivity levels differ substantially across states within a sector. In wholesale/retail trade, for example, where the coefficient of variation in 1989 from Table 1 was only 12.6 percent, productivity levels still vary substantially, from $34,026 per worker in Connecticut to only $20,661 in Montana. As a prelude to the results on convergence, one sees distinct evidence of convergence in manufacturing and mining, some evidence for the total, and little or no evidence of a narrowing in cross-section dispersion for the other sectors. This evidence will be considered more formally in the next section.

Growth rates for both the full sample and the non-mining sample are displayed in Table 2 for comparison.[9] Labor productivity grew at an annual rate of 0.53 percent for the average state in our full sample during 1963–1989, and slightly faster at 0.62 percent for the non-mining sample. However, this summary statistic masks substantial variation across sectors and states. Measured

Table 2. Growth rates – percent

				Nonmining		
Sector	U.S.	Average	StdDev	U.S.	Average	StdDev
Mining	−1.79	0.28	3.15	−0.28	0.65	2.95
Construction	−1.99	−1.83	1.65	−2.16	−2.17	1.20
Manufacturing	2.37	2.51	0.95	2.32	2.48	0.95
Trans/PubUtilities	2.30	2.24	0.46	2.27	2.19	0.46
Wholesale/Retail	0.93	0.78	0.40	0.89	0.77	0.36
F.I.R.E.	0.11	0.03	0.79	0.05	−0.08	0.74
Other Services	−0.59	−0.76	0.40	−0.64	−0.76	0.33
Total	0.61	0.53	0.67	0.69	0.62	0.48

[8] The District of Columbia, in which the government sector accounts for 45.3 percent of gross state product and in which productivity in the construction sector in 1989 at $135,901 was more than twice its closest rival, will also be excluded whenever the mining states are excluded. The next mining state in line to be excluded was West Virginia, with 18.5 percent of its output in mining. However, it did not seem to be an outlier in terms of productivity in the other sectors.

[9] The growth rates are constructed by regressing the natural log of productivity on a constant and a time trend. The coefficient on the time trend is reported as the average growth rate.

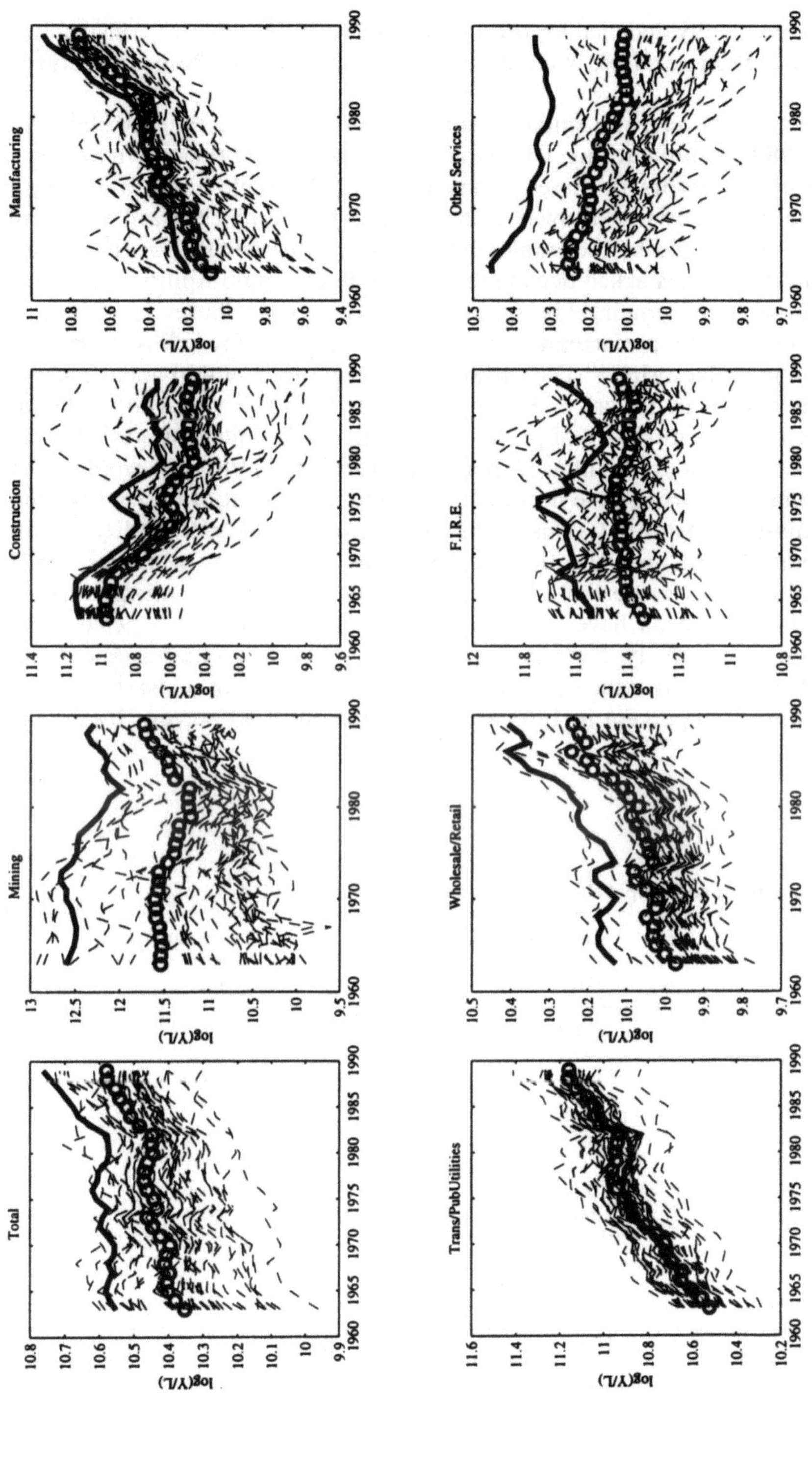

Fig. 2. Productivity levels by state (non-mining sample). The U.S. is indicated by circles and California is indicated by a solid line

productivity actually declined for the average non-mining state for construction, F.I.R.E., and other services, while it rose at 2.48 percent in the manufacturing sector.

Table 3 reports average employment and output shares across states for 1963 and 1989. Manufacturing, wholesale/retail trade, and other services are the most important sectors in the economy in terms of employment and output shares. The well-known shift away from manufacturing and toward trade and services is documented by the employment shares. Interestingly, for the average state we do not see a marked decline in the manufacturing output share despite the decline in employment. The maintenance of output shares is a mark of the relatively strong performance in terms of productivity growth that has occurred in manufacturing.[10] The variation across states in employment shares is marked, as shown in Figure 3. For example, in 1963 the variation in manufacturing employment shares of private non-farm employment ranges from less than 10 percent to more than 50 percent. Moreover, although employment shares in manufacturing have declined over time, the variation in employment shares remains substantial. This wide variation is consistent with a theory that emphasizes the specialization across states in different activities. Much of the Midwest has more than 40 percent of its employment in manufacturing; Florida and Texas have manufacturing shares of only 16.3 percent and 21.8 percent, respectively. Nevada specializes in producing entertainment, and this is reflected in our data by an employment share in "other services" that begins at about 30 percent in 1963 and rises to around 50 percent by the late 1980s.

Table 3. Employment and output shares for average state (percent)

Sector	Employment shares		Output shares	
	1963	1989	1963	1989
Mining	2.8	1.4	8.9	5.7
Construction	7.5	5.7	12.4	5.3
Manufacturing	31.2	20.2	22.6	24.2
Trans/PubUtilities	9.0	6.7	9.9	12.0
Wholesale/Retail	26.4	29.1	16.6	19.4
F.I.R.E.	5.7	6.9	15.4	15.8
Other Services	17.9	30.0	14.7	17.5
Total	100.0	100.0	100.0	100.0

[10] For manufacturing, the output shares for the average state differ somewhat from the output shares for the United States. The manufacturing employment share in the U.S. declined from 36.0 percent in 1963 to 21.6 percent in 1989, while the output share was relatively steady at 26.5 percent in 1963 and 25.7 percent in 1989.

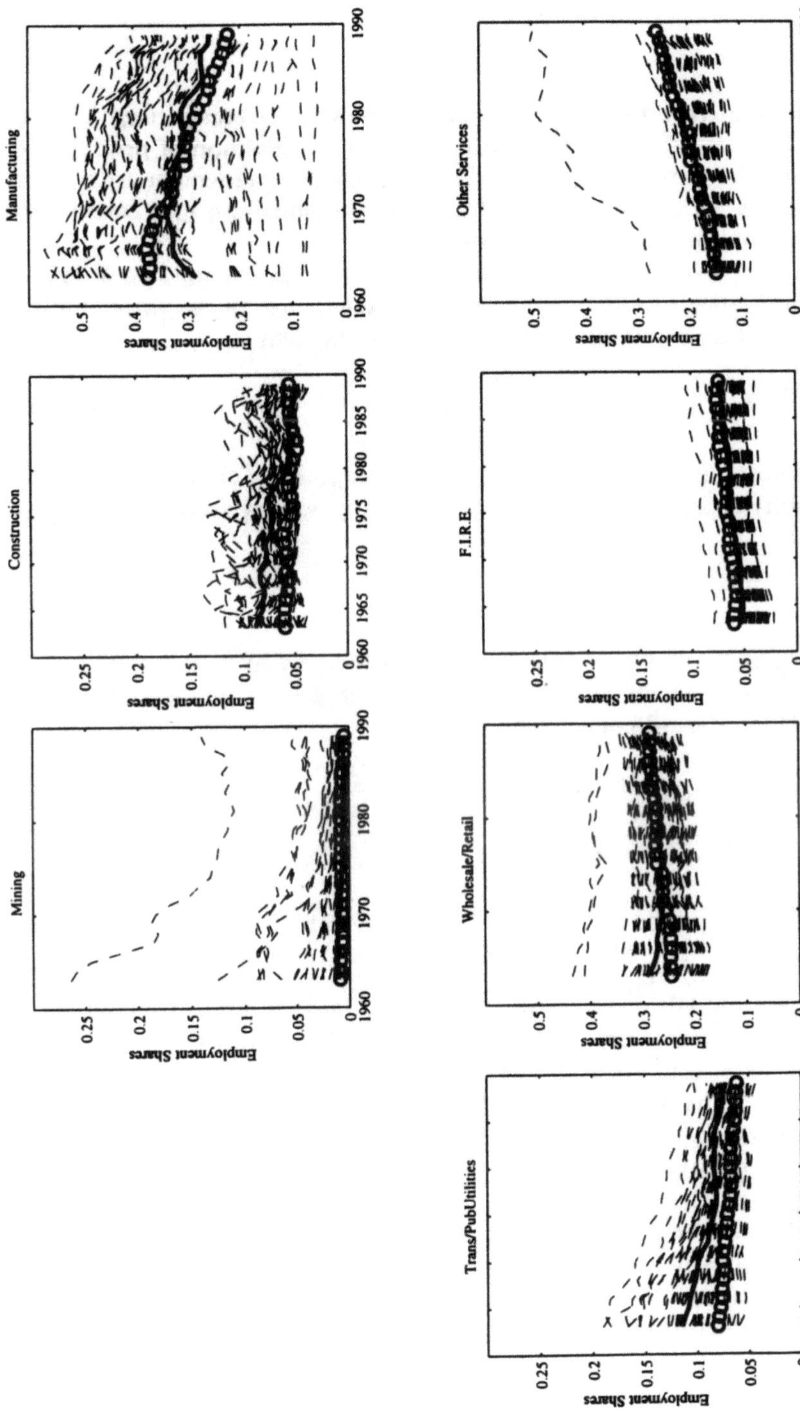

Fig. 3. Employment shares by state. The U.S. is indicated by circles

2.2 Sources of State Productivity Growth

Where does the growth in private non-farm productivity come from? The answer certainly varies across states and involves a combination of productivity growth within the various sectors and a shifting of employment from some sectors to others. In this section, we formalize this intuition and construct a decomposition of state productivity growth.

We can write private non-farm labor productivity in a state as a weighted sum of sectoral labor productivity, where the weights are the sectoral employment shares. Letting $y \equiv Y/L$ represent labor productivity,

$$y = \sum_i \frac{Y_i}{L_i} \cdot \frac{L_i}{L} \equiv \sum_i y_i \cdot w_i \ . \tag{1}$$

Using this accounting framework, we can decompose the change in aggregate labor productivity in each state into between and within sector components as follows:

$$\Delta y = \sum_j \Delta y_j \cdot \overline{w_j} + \sum_j \Delta w_j \cdot \overline{y_j} \ . \tag{2}$$

Here, the change is calculated between two periods, 0 and T, and $\bar{x}$ represents the average value of x across the two periods. Rewriting this decomposition in terms of percentage changes we get

$$\% \Delta y = \sum_j \underbrace{\% \Delta(y_j) \left(\frac{y_{j,0}}{y_0}\right) \overline{(w_j)}}_{\text{Productivity Growth Effect (PGE)}} + \sum_j \underbrace{\Delta(w_j) \frac{\overline{(y_j)}}{y_0}}_{\text{Share Effect (SE)}} \ . \tag{3}$$

Finally, these percentage changes can be annualized by dividing by T.

The first component, which we call the productivity growth effect, captures the contribution of within sector labor productivity growth for the state, using the average sectoral labor shares over the period in question as weights. If the employment shares had remained constant over the period in question, this would be the only term present. The second term, the share effect, shows the contribution of changing sectoral composition to aggregate labor productivity growth, where the share changes are weighted by average relative labor productivity for the sector over the period. Sectors with declining employment shares will have negative share effects.

Table 4 reports the average of the productivity growth effects and share effects for the states in our sample.[11] The average annual percentage change in labor productivity for this sample was 0.82 percent. The most important sector in generating this productivity growth was the manufacturing sector: had

[11] Our sample includes the non-mining states with complete data for 1963–1989.

Table 4. Sources of productivity growth

Sector	Growth effect	%	Share effect	%	Total effect	%
Mining	0.04	5	−0.10	−12	−0.06	−7
Construction	−0.17	−21	−0.08	−10	−0.25	−31
Manufacturing	0.81	99	−0.47	−57	0.34	41
Trans/PubUtilities	0.31	38	−0.14	−17	0.17	21
Wholesale/Retail	0.18	22	0.09	11	0.27	33
F.I.R.E.	0.00	0	0.13	16	0.13	16
Other Services	−0.12	−15	0.34	41	0.22	26
Total	1.05	128	−0.23	−28	0.82	100

Note: This table reports the average of the productivity growth decompositions for the non-mining states. Several other states are excluded because of missing data. See text for discussion. Rows and columns may not sum exactly because of rounding.

productivity not grown in that sector, aggregate productivity growth would (on average) have been lower by 0.81 percentage points, or 99 percent of the total. In other words, without productivity growth in the manufacturing sector, private non-farm productivity would essentially have been unchanged between 1963 and 1989. Share effects, though, were also important. The shift in employment for the average state was away from manufacturing, mining, construction, and transportation/public utilities, and toward the various service sectors, which on average had lower productivity. Shifting sectoral decomposition reduced productivity growth by 0.23 percentage points, or 28 percent of total productivity growth.

In this section, we have documented the substantial heterogeneity in productivity levels and growth rates over both industries and states. We now turn to an analysis of convergence in labor productivity across states and sectors.

3 Convergence in Labor Productivity

To understand the roles of sectors in the convergence of total labor productivity across states, we outline a simple model of catch-up and test its cross-section and time series implications. In addition we decompose catch-up in the average state into its within- and between-sector components.

3.1 A Basic Model of Productivity Convergence

The neoclassical growth model without technology predicts convergence in output per worker for similar, closed economies based on the accumulation of capital. However, even in the absence of catch-up due to capital accumulation, the narrowing of technology differentials can contribute to the convergence in labor productivity. To capture these effects, we construct a simple model of productivity catch-up.

We assume that labor productivity, y_{ijt}, evolves according to

$$\ln y_{ijt} = \gamma_{ij} + \lambda \ln D_{ijt} + \ln y_{ijt-1} + \ln \varepsilon_{ijt} \tag{4}$$

with γ_{ij} being the asymptotic rate of growth of sector j in state i, λ parameterizing the speed of catch-up denoted by D_{ijt}, and ε_{ijt} representing an industry and state-specific productivity shock. We allow D_{ijt}, the catch-up variable, to be a function of the productivity differential within sector j in state i from that in state 1, the most productive state,

$$\ln D_{ijt} = -\ln \hat{y}_{ijt-1} \tag{5}$$

where a hat indicates a ratio of a variable in state i to the same variable in state 1, i.e.

$$\hat{y}_{ijt} = \frac{y_{ijt}}{y_{1jt}} . \tag{6}$$

This formulation of productivity catch-up implies that productivity gaps between states are a function of the lagged gap in the same productivity measure.[12] For example, if labor productivity is the measure of productivity, then lagged gaps in labor productivity determine the degree of catch-up.

This formulation of output leads to a natural path for productivity:

$$\ln \hat{y}_{ijt} = (\gamma_{ij} - \gamma_{1j}) + (1 - \lambda) \ln \hat{y}_{ijt-1} + \ln \hat{\varepsilon}_{ijt} . \tag{7}$$

In this framework, values of $\lambda > 0$ provide an impetus for "catch up": productivity differentials between two states increase the relative growth rate of the state with lower productivity. However, only if $\lambda > 0$ and if $\gamma_i = \gamma_1$ (i.e. if the asymptotic growth rates of productivity are the same) will states exhibit a tendency to converge. Alternatively, if $\lambda = 0$, productivity levels will grow at different rates permanently and show no tendency to converge asymptotically.[13] Considering the relationship between long-run growth rates across states, we can rewrite the difference equation in equation (7) to yield

$$\bar{g}_i = -\frac{(1 - (1 - \lambda)^T)}{T} \ln \hat{y}_{io} + \frac{1}{T} \sum_{j=0}^{T} (1 - \lambda)^{T-j} (\gamma_i - \gamma_1 + \ln \hat{\varepsilon}_{ij}) \tag{8}$$

[12] This specification can be easily derived from a log linear approximation to a continuous time growth model with a Cobb-Douglas production technology: see Barro and Sala-i-Martin (1992) and Mankiw, Romer, and Weil (1992). Dowrick and Nguyen (1989) use a similar specification to test for catch-up in TFP in OECD countries.

[13] Of course, if the state with the lower initial level has a higher long run growth rate, γ_i, the states may appear to be converging in small samples.

where $\bar{g}_i$ denotes the average growth rate relative to state 1 between time 0 and time T. This is the familiar regression of long-run average growth rates on the initial level, where catch-up is denoted by a negative coefficient on the level.[14]

Another testing approach is to estimate equation (7) directly. If $\lambda > 0$, then the difference between the technology levels in the two states will be stationary. If there is no catch-up ($\lambda = 0$), then the difference of productivity in state i from that in state 1 will contain a unit root. The drift term $\gamma_i - \gamma_1$ will typically be small but nonzero if the states' technologies are driven by different processes (i.e. under the hypothesis of no convergence). Under the hypothesis of convergence, $\gamma_i = \gamma_1$ is plausible.

Unlike most previous empirical work on convergence, which has used either cross-section or time series techniques, we employ both methodologies for testing convergence in this paper. The definitions of convergence implied by the two econometric approaches are distinct. Cross-section analyses focus on the transition to equilibrium growth paths. Convergence is taken to be a narrowing of initial differences in productivity levels over some time horizon, less productive states growing faster than more productive ones (β-convergence), or the reduction in cross-region variance of productivity (σ-convergence), although one does not necessarily imply the other. This distinction between β-convergence and σ-convergence is particularly important for work on sectoral productivity convergence. If, for a given sector, states are in steady state, then we should expect to find no evidence of σ-convergence. We may, however, find a negative and significant coefficient in the growth rate regression.[15]

To reconcile any inconsistencies in the cross-section evidence and to provide another testable definition of convergence, we also employ a time series testing methodology. Time series studies generally define convergence as transitory deviations from identical long-run trends, either deterministic or stochastic. Tests in this framework look for permanent deviations in relative income paths using cointegration or unit root techniques. Due to the relatively short time period for our sample, we employ recent advances in panel unit root analysis to test the convergence hypothesis.

First, we consider evidence on the time paths of cross-section variance of sectoral labor productivity levels as well as regressions of long run productivity growth rates on initial levels. Sectors display widely varying behavior; some show no reduction in variance, others substantial reductions. To complement this analysis, we look for convergence within the time series framework, testing for transitory versus permanent differences in productivity levels. Finally, to reconcile these varying patterns across industries with aggregate convergence for total industry, we calculate contributions of shifting share and sectoral productivity growth to aggregate convergence.

---

[14] For potential problems with this type of regression, see Bernard and Durlauf (1996) and Quah (1993).

[15] See Quah (1993) for a detailed discussion of this version of Galton's fallacy.

3.2 *Cross-Section Evidence: σ and β Convergence*

As in other studies, we find substantial evidence of catch-up and convergence in aggregate labor productivity across the U.S. states from 1963–1989. The first panel of Figure 4 shows the cross-section standard deviation for the log of aggregate labor productivity for all states (dashed line) and for non-mining states (solid line). Both series show substantial drops in the variance of cross-state productivity throughout the period, providing evidence of convergence in total labor productivity. The inclusion of the mining states dramatically increases the overall dispersion of productivity and is the source of substantional year-to-year variation as well.[16]

The remaining panels of Figure 4 show the movements in the cross-section standard deviations for the seven aggregate sectors, again for all states and non-mining states separately. While dispersion in aggregate labor productivity declined steadily over the period, the individual sectors differ dramatically from one another. Most sectors show no evidence of declining cross-section dispersion; in particular, there is significant evidence for σ-convergence only in mining and manufacturing. In mining, the cross-section standard deviation drops by half over the period, whether or not mining states are included in the sample. Similarly in manufacturing, there is a dramatic reduction in the variance of labor productivity through the early 1980s and only a slight rise thereafter. Except for the dramatic rise in the standard deviation for the construction sector, most other sectors show little trend in the dispersion of labor productivity across states over the period.

The inclusion of the mining states substantially raises the variation in labor productivity across states without affecting the movements in the standard deviation over time. Work on state convergence by Keil and Vohra (1993) suggested that convergence results for U.S. states were driven by the mining sector, while Barro and Sala-i-Martin argued that oil-related industries were the source of divergence in the 1970s. While we find that mining productivity is substantially different from that of other sectors, there is no evidence that the exclusion of the mining states affects the conclusions on catch-up and convergence.

Table 5 contains the results from cross-section regressions of long-run labor productivity growth on log labor productivity levels in 1963 of the form

$$\Delta \ln y_i = \alpha + \beta \ln y_{i,1963} + \varepsilon_{it} .$$

---

[16] These results differ from those in Barro and Sala-i-Martin (1991) who find increases in dispersion after 1973 which they attribute to large impacts of relative oil price movements in mining states. Our results suggest that the inclusion of mining states does not affect the overall downward trend in cross-state variation.

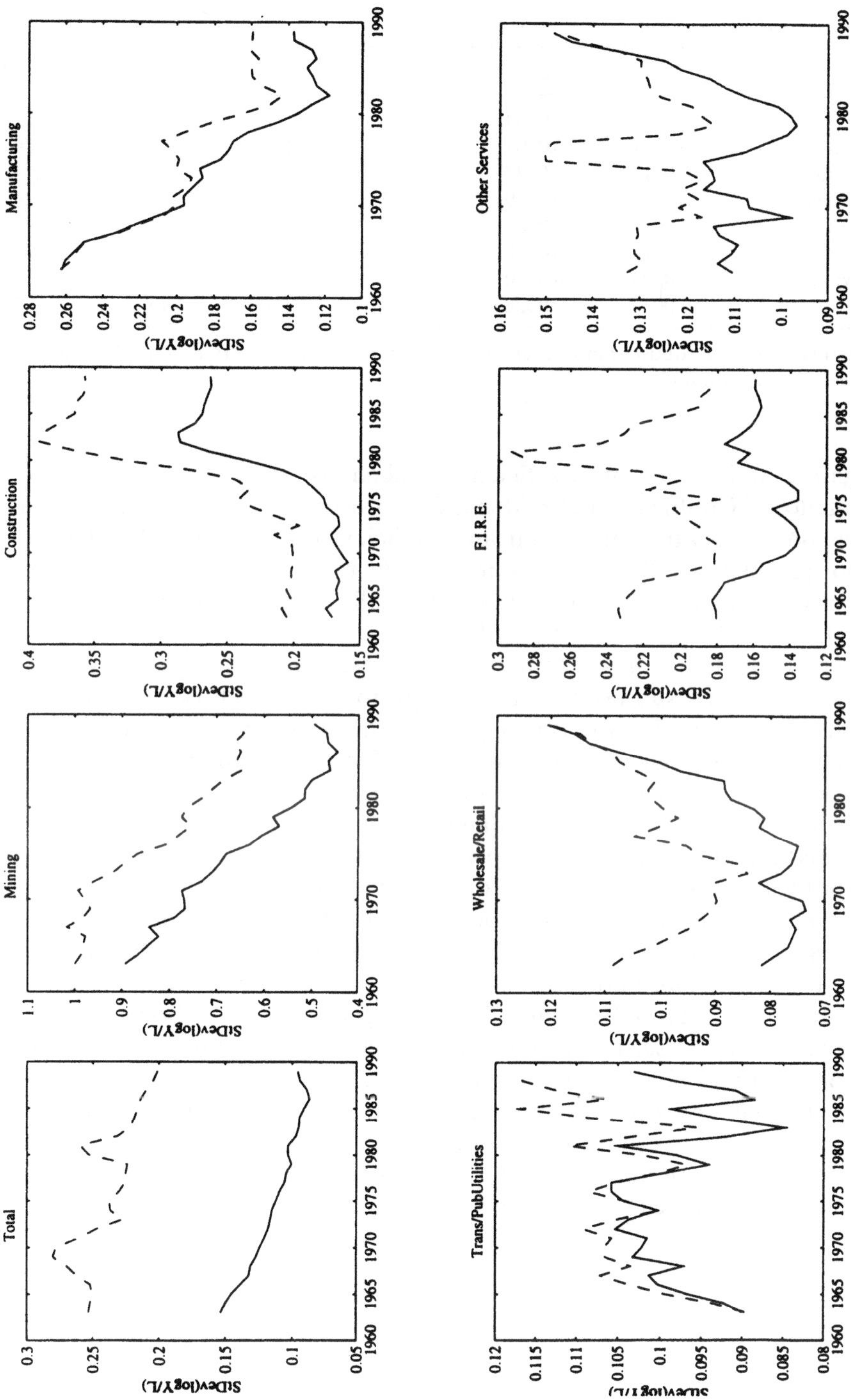

Fig. 4. Cross-section standard deviations by state. Solid is the non-mining sample. Dashed is full sample

Table 5. Convergence regressions

Sector	β	SE	t-stat	λ	t-stat	$\bar{R}^2$
Mining	−0.0281	0.0034	−8.19	0.0512	3.81	.72
Construction	−0.0111	0.0107	−1.04	0.0131	0.87	.00
Manufacturing	−0.0310	0.0032	−9.62	0.0649	3.52	.73
Trans/Utilities	−0.0216	0.0089	−2.43	0.0318	1.55	.16
Wholesale/Retail	−0.0043	0.0065	−0.66	0.0045	0.62	−.01
F.I.R.E.	−0.0215	0.0050	−4.28	0.0317	2.73	.25
Other Services	−0.0029	0.0050	−0.59	0.0030	0.56	−.02
Total	−0.0253	0.0028	−9.08	0.0418	4.94	.65

Note: Heteroskedasticity robust standard errors and t-statistics are reported. λ is the speed of convergence, as in equation (8).

A negative and significant coefficient is taken to be evidence in favor of β-convergence.[17] Confirming the evidence from the cross-section standard deviations, we find a negative and significant coefficient on the initial (log) level of total labor productivity. The point estimate of the rate of catch-up in total labor productivity is 4.18 percent per year, substantially higher than that found by Barro and Sala-i-Martin (1992). Also, 65 percent of the variation in growth rates across states is explained by differences in the initial level of productivity.

Sectors again show substantial variation, although all sectors have negative coefficients. Mining and manufacturing show the strongest evidence for convergence, with highly significant, negative coefficients. Estimates of the rate of catch-up for these sectors are 5.12 percent per year for mining and an astounding 6.49 percent per year for manufacturing. In addition, differences in initial levels explain more than 70 percent of the variation in productivity growth for these two sectors. While no other sectors showed systematic evidence for σ-convergence, both transportation and F.I.R.E. have estimated convergence rates of just over 3 percent per year, though the rate is not precisely estimated for the transportation sector.

While there is substantial evidence for convergence in total labor productivity, both sets of cross-section results suggest that sectors differ dramatically in their productivity characteristics over the period. Only mining and manufacturing are converging in both measures, while construction, wholesale/retail trade, and other services show no evidence of convergence. Moreover, for these sectors, the variation in initial levels explains virtually none of the variation in growth rates, as indicated by the adjusted R^2s.

[17] See Bernard and Durlauf (1996) and Quah (1993) for discussions of problems associated with this measure.

3.3 *Time Series Evidence*

In this section, we continue the study of sectoral convergence by examining time series evidence. We apply an extension of a recent advance in panel unit root econometrics to test for convergence within sectors across states. The sectoral data we employ is available for a relatively short time horizon of 27 years. With such a limited number of years, unit root testing would appear to be questionable due to known power problems in univariate tests. However, work by Levin and Lin (1992) and an extension by Bernard and Jones (1996) present an appropriate technique to test for unit roots in panel data. The basic findings are twofold: (1) that as both N and T go to infinity, the limiting distribution of the unit root estimator is centered and normal,[18] and (2) that the panel setting permits relatively large power improvements.

We consider the following general model with state-specific intercepts:

$$x_{it} = \mu_i + \rho x_{it-1} + \varepsilon_{it} \tag{9}$$

where the $\varepsilon_{it} \sim iid(0, \sigma_\varepsilon^2)$ and $\mu_i \sim iid(\bar{\mu}, \sigma_\mu^2)$. We also assume ε_{it} has $2 + \delta$ moments for some $\delta > 0$ and that $E\mu_i\varepsilon_{it} = 0$ for all i and t. Other standard regularity conditions are assumed to hold.

Let $\hat{\rho}$ and t_ρ be the OLS parameter estimate and t-statistic respectively. Under the null hypothesis of a unit root with nonzero drifts ($\mu_i \neq 0$), Bernard and Jones (1996) prove that asymptotic normality of $\hat{\rho}$ occurs as T goes to infinity.[19]

To examine the convergence hypothesis while taking advantage of the time series aspect of the data, we focus on cross state deviations in labor productivity levels. Letting state 1 denote the benchmark state, our tests will be based on

$$x_{ijt} \equiv D \ln y_{ij}(t) \equiv \ln y_{1j}(t) - \ln y_{ij}(t) \ , \qquad i = 2, \ldots, N \ . \tag{10}$$

Following Bernard and Durlauf (1995), we will say that state i is converging to state 1 if $D \ln y_{ij}(t)$ is stationary. We do not necessarily require $\ln y_{ij}(t)$ to exhibit a unit root with drift, although pretesting indicated that this null hypothesis could generally not be rejected.

The cost of the short time horizon is that we cannot examine the hypothesis that only a subset of the fifty states are converging. The panel test focuses on the

---

[18] Quah (1990) first noted this asymptotic normality result using a random fields data structure and rejected convergence of per capita output for a large cross-section of countries from 1960–1985. His estimator does not permit country-specific intercepts.

[19] The asymptotic normality results are driven by the time trends in x_{it}. This is a multivariate extension of the results in West (1988).

When state-effects are included in the specification, a small-sample bias enters the distribution but disappears as T goes to infinity. This bias is independent of N and is analogous to the bias in standard panel data analysis described by Nickell (1981). As a result, t-statistics require a correction in order to be centered at zero: the uncorrected t-statistics are biased in the negative direction.

extremes: we test the null hypothesis that all fifty states are converging against the alternative that as a group they are not converging. With the difficulty of constructing longer time series for labor productivity by sector, we are unlikely to be able to test convergence in smaller groups of states.

A related issue is how to choose the benchmark state. Asymptotically, of course, this choice should not matter, but in small samples it will be important. We report results when state 1 is chosen in four different ways: first, we choose California as the reference state due to its prominence in the aggregate economy and because it is a productivity leader in many sectors; second, we pick the most productive state in each sector in 1963; third, we use U.S. productivity levels over the period; and finally, we select the median state in terms of sectoral productivity in 1963. The results of our time series tests for convergence are reported in Table 6.

Columns 1 and 2 report the point estimates and t-statistics of the panel unit root tests when California is the benchmark state. The reported estimates of ρ have been bias-adjusted using Monte Carlo simulations and therefore should be centered at their true values. It should be noted that the point estimates may be biased upward if there are deterministic trends in the deviations. The point estimates for total industry, mining, and manufacturing are all significantly less than unity, providing evidence against the unit root null in these sectors and confirming the results from both the cross-section measures. Convergence is occurring in aggregate and in the mining and manufacturing

Table 6. Time series tests of sectoral convergence

Sector	Deviations form:							
	CA		Most		U.S.		Median	
	ρ	t-stat	ρ	t-stat	ρ	t-stat	ρ	t-stat
Mining	0.957	−8.73**	0.961	−7.81**	0.961	−8.28**	0.736	−14.21**
Constr.	1.020	−4.50	0.998	−6.27	1.024	−3.91	1.019	−5.21
Manuf.	0.962	−8.52**	0.985	−4.72*	0.989	−5.80	0.965	−7.81*
Trans/Util.	0.963	−8.38	1.020	−4.83	0.987	−7.07	0.969	−8.07
Wh/Re Trade	1.014	−5.17	0.949	−7.57*	1.036	−1.71	1.020	−3.18
F.I.R.E.	0.997	−4.94	0.917	−9.41**	0.962	−7.95	0.951	−8.59*
Services	1.025	−4.36	1.052	−1.49	0.986	−5.36	0.930	−8.62**
Total	0.968	−6.47**	0.993	−4.61	1.005	−3.53	0.988	−7.05

Note: Asterisks are used to indicate rejection of the null hypothesis of no convergence at the following significance levels: 10 percent (*) and 5 percent (**). This table reports results from panel unit root regressions, as discussed in the paper. All regressions include state-specific intercepts. Lag length was chosen according to the Schwarz information criterion. The bias-adjusted estimate of ρ and the critical values for the t-statistics are taken from Monte Carlo simulations with 2500 iterations. For the Monte Carlo simulation for each sector, log productivity deviations were differenced, and then the means and the standard deviations of these first differences were used to generate the data for the appropriate sample size.

sectors. In contrast, the results for all other sectors fail to reject the null of no convergence with point estimates close to unity.

The alternative specifications for the benchmark state produce variation in the results. Mining shows significant evidence of convergence for all specifications while manufacturing rejects the no convergence null at the 10 percent level in two of the three remaining cases; the point estimate for manufacturing is below one for all variants. Surprisingly, total industry does not reject in any other case and the point estimates remain near one. Construction and transportation/public utilities do not reject in any cases.[20] Other sectors show varying results: other services and wholesale/retail trade reject in only one and typically show large point estimates.

An interesting exception is F.I.R.E. which rejects in two of four specifications and has low point estimates of ρ. F.I.R.E. showed no evidence of σ-convergence in Figure 4 but had a negative and significant estimate of λ in the β-convergence regression. Looking at the log levels of labor productivity for the sector in Figure 2, we see substantial churning in the distribution across states. This may represent a sector that has largely reached steady state, i.e. has already converged.

The time series results broadly confirm the σ-convergence and β-convergence results.[21] Mining and manufacturing show the strongest evidence of convergence. There is some evidence of convergence in F.I.R.E. and less so in total industry, wholesale/retail trade, and other services.

3.4 Sectoral Contributions to Convergence

The cross-section and time series results highlight significant variation across sectors in terms of convergence. A key question remaining is how convergence within sectors and the changing sectoral composition combine to generate the aggregate convergence result. To answer this question, we construct a measure of productivity growth for each state relative to a benchmark as follows:

$$\%\Delta y_{follower} - \%\Delta y_{leader} \tag{11}$$

which is decomposed into productivity growth and share effects:

$$\underbrace{\sum_j [PGE_{follower} - PGE_{leader}]}_{\text{Productivity Growth Effect}} + \underbrace{\sum_j [SE_{follower} - SE_{leader}]}_{\text{Share Effect}} \; . \tag{12}$$

---

20 These results corroborate the faster convergence observed in the cross-section results for mining and manufacturing and the lack of convergence in construction and transportation/public utilities.

21 This is in contrast to much previous work on convergence. Typically, cross-section results and time series results conflict for a given data set. See Bernard and Durlauf (1996) for a theoretical explanation. Exceptions are the studies of sectoral convergence in OECD countries in Bernard and Jones (1994, 1996).

For this exercise, one would ideally like to choose the state with the highest initial private non-farm productivity level and then consider convergence relative to that state. Unfortunately, this means that idiosyncrasies associated with that particular state will drive the results.[22] Because of the difficulty in picking a lead state in aggregate productivity, we consider convergence to productivity levels of the U.S. as a whole. In this case, the U.S. will be considered the "leader" relative to states that begin with a productivity level below that of the U.S. and a "follower" relative to states that begin with a productivity level above the U.S. Convergence for a state with high initial productivity requires slower than average growth while convergence for a state with low initial productivity requires faster than average growth.

To understand the importance of within-sector growth and changing sectoral composition to convergence, we construct relative productivity growth and share effects for each state for each sector. The effects are then averaged across states and the percentage contributions of each effect calculated. If sectoral labor shares remained unchanged, then all convergence would be due to within-sector productivity improvements. Since the actual composition of employment changed differentially across states, some convergence might arise from high productivity states shifting out of high productivity sectors such as manufacturing.

The results for the sectoral decomposition of convergence are given in Table 7. As with the sectoral contributions to labor productivity growth, manufacturing plays the dominant role in state labor productivity convergence. Almost two-thirds of the total convergence for the average state comes from changes in manufacturing productivity. Interestingly, manufacturing's contribution to the rate of convergence would have been even higher except for the negative share effect over the period. This negative share effect represents the fact that, on average, high initial total productivity states shifted out of manufacturing less quickly than the U.S.

Mining, construction, and F.I.R.E. all had negative productivity effect contributions to convergence; high productivity states had relatively high productivity growth in those sectors. All three of these sectors had positive share effects. Tranportation/utilities, wholesale/retail trade, and other services had small positive contributions to convergence from both within sector productivity growth and changing employment shares.

Looking at the relative importance of within sector growth and changing sectoral shares, the overall results from Table 7 are twofold. First, we find that if sectoral shares had been constant, i.e. the share effect had been zero, the average state would have converged more slowly to the U.S. Share effects

---

[22] For example, we might think to use California as our benchmark state. However there is relatively little convergence to California during 1963–1989, especially in the manufacturing sector. This contrasts with research on cross-country convergence where the U.S. is typically the clear productivity leader.

Table 7. Sources of convergence

Sector	Growth effect	%	Share effect	%	Total effect	%
Mining	−0.03	−9	0.07	23	0.04	14
Contruction	−0.03	−11	0.02	6	−0.02	−5
Manufacturing	0.25	83	−0.06	−19	0.19	64
Trans/PubUtilities	0.02	6	0.01	2	0.02	8
Wholesale/Retail	0.02	7	0.01	4	0.03	10
F.I.R.E.	−0.01	−3	0.02	6	0.01	3
Other Services	−0.00	−0	0.02	6	0.02	6
Total	0.22	73	0.08	27	0.30	100

Note: This table reports the average of the convergence decompositions for the non-mining states. Several other states are excluded because of missing data. See text for discussion.

account for about one-quarter of aggregate convergence. Second, without the share changes, growth of productivity within manufacturing would have accounted for all total labor productivity convergence over the period. Within sector growth for the other sectors is relatively unimportant as an explanation of aggregate convergence.[23]

4 Conclusion

This paper explores the large heterogeneity in productivity levels and movements across industries and states in the U.S. Using gross state product per worker as a measure of labor productivity, we document the large and persistent variation of sectoral productivity levels and output shares across states. Rapid growth in manufacturing productivity provided the main source of total state productivity growth; however, the shift of employment out of highly productive sectors such as manufacturing into less productive service sectors reduced annual aggregate productivity growth by 28 percent from 1963 to 1989.

In addition to the variation in productivity levels across sectors, we find substantial heterogeneity in convergence outcomes at the industry level. Using standard cross-section and recent time series techniques, we find the strongest evidence for convergence in the manufacturing and mining sectors. Sectors such as construction, wholesale/retail trade, and other services have almost no evidence of convergence by any measure. Decomposing convergence into within

[23] In work on sectoral convergence in OECD countries, Bernard and Jones (1994, 1996) find comparable net contributions of growth and share effects. However, in those studies, services played a strong role in aggregate convergence, while there was little convergence in manufacturing.

and across sector components reveals that manufacturing contributed almost two-thirds of total catch-up across states.

These sectoral convergence results are in stark contrast to work on OECD industry productivity movements. Analyses of aggregate productivity catch-up from 1970–87 for a sample of 14 OECD countries shows little evidence for convergence in manufacturing and a substantial role for the service sector.[24] The contradiction between these sets of results remains to be explored in future work.

References

Baily MN, Gordon R (1988) The productivity slowdown, measurement issues, and the explosion of computer power. Brookings Papers on Economic Activity 2:347–431

Barro R, Sala-i-Martin X (1991) Convergence across states and regions. Brookings Papers on Economic Activity 107–58

Barro R, Sala-i-Martin X (1992) Convergence. Journal of Political Economy 100:223–51

Bernard A, Durlauf S (1995) Convergence in international output. Journal of Applied Econometrics 10:97–108

Bernard A, Durlauf S (1996) Interpreting tests of the convergence hypothesis. Journal of Econometrics 71:forthcoming

Bernard A, Jones C (1994) Comparing apples to oranges: productivity convergence and measurement across industries and countries. MIT Economics Working Paper 94-12

Bernard A, Jones C (1996) Productivity across industries and countries: time series theory and evidence. Review of Economics and Statistics: forthcoming

Carlino GM, Mills LO (1993) Are US regional incomes converging? A time series analysis. Journal of Monetary Economics 32:335–46

Dowrick S, Nguyen D (1989) OECD comparative economic growth 1950–85: catch-up and convergence. American Economic Review 79:1010–30

Griliches Z (1994) Productivity R&D and the data constraint. American Economic Review 84: 1–23

Keil M, Vohra R (1993) What's Wyoming got that we don't? Mimeo, Northeastern University

Levin A, Lin C (1992) Unit root tests in panel data: asymptotic and finite-sample properties. Discussion Paper 92-23, Department of Economics, University of California San Diego

Mankiw NG, Romer D, Weil D (1992) A contribution to the empirics of economic growth. Quarterly Journal of Economics 107:407–38

Nickell S (1981) Biases in dynamic models with fixed effects. Econometrica 49:1417–26

Quah D (1990) International patterns of growth: I persistence in cross-country disparities. Working Paper, MIT Department of Economics, January

Quah D (1993) Galton's fallacy and tests of the convergence hypothesis. Scandinavian Journal of Economics 95:427–43

Quah D (1994) Convergence empirics across economies with (some) capital mobility. Suntory-Toyota International Centre, LSE Discussion Paper No EM/94/275

---

[24] See Bernard and Jones (1994, 1996).

Trott EA, Dunbar A, Friedenberg H (1991) Gross state product by industry 1977–89. Survey of Current Business 71:43–59
West K (1988) Asymptotic normality when regressors have a unit root. Econometrica 56:1397–1418

First version received: January 1995
Final version received: November 1995

Aggregate and Regional Disaggregate Fluctuations

Danny T. Quah[1]

LSE-Department of Economics, Houghton Street, London WC2A 2AE, Great Britain

Abstract: This paper models fluctuations in regional disaggregates as a nonstationary, dynamically evolving distribution. Doing so enables study of the dynamics of aggregate fluctuations jointly with those of the rich cross-section of regional disaggregates. For the US, the leading state – regardless of which it happens to be – contains strong predictive power for aggregate fluctuations. This effect is difficult to understand if only aggregate disturbances affect aggregate business cycles through aggregate propagation mechanisms. Instead, a better picture might be one of a "wave" of regional dynamics, rippling across the national economy.

Key Words: Aggregate disturbance, business cycle, distribution dynamics, regional fluctuation, stochastic kernel

JEL Classification System-Numbers: C32, C33, E32

1 Introduction

Macroeconomics, by definition, concerns aggregate economic variables. And, traditionally, macro empirics hews to this same discipline. In whichever mainstream version – real business cycle, aggregate demand and aggregate supply or new Keynesian – theoretical and empirical macroeconomics studies the dynamic response of aggregate variables to hypothesized aggregate disturbances.

Departures from this focus exist, but are for the most part minor. In one instance, disaggregates are analyzed only to provide an aggregation theory, i.e., only to understand the macro implications of modelling the underlying micro units. The disaggregates themselves bear but auxiliary interest. In a second instance, the researcher might study empirically the behavior of consumers and firms, say in cross-section or panel data modelling, to understand their responses to changes in their environment. Often, the parameters of those

[1] I thank IIES in Stockholm for its hospitality. I am grateful also to seminar participants at IIES, the LSE Macro Breakfast Group, and the University of Edinburgh, as well as Fischer Black, David Canning, Fabio Canova, and Costas Meghir for helpful suggestions. I owe special thanks to an anonymous referee who carefully read and helpfully criticized an earlier version of the paper. All calculations were performed using the author's econometrics shell t_{SrF}.

disaggregates are then just presented as if immediately having implications for macroeconomic behavior. Such work views disaggregates as providing only *more* data (beyond aggregate time series), not *different* data. The latter, by contrast, is the view that this paper adopts.

There are, of course, counter-examples to the crude characterization just given. Interactions between individual income distributions and macroeconomic dynamics (e.g., Galor and Zeira (1993) and Persson and Tabellini (1994)), between relative prices and aggregate inflation (e.g., Lach and Tsiddon (1992)), and between sectoral imbalance and aggregate unemployment (e.g., Evans (1993) and Lilien (1982)) are instances where disaggregate analysis has contributed insights for understanding macroeconomic fluctuations. In the same vein are the ideas that cross-sectional spillovers can cumulate for aggregate growth and fluctuations (e.g., Durlauf (1993) and Long and Plosser (1983)) and that gross labor flows – rather than just net ones – are informative for macroeconomic business cycles (e.g., Davis and Haltiwanger (1992)).

All these counter-examples share an important distinctive feature. This is that there is significant *two-way* interaction between aggregate and disaggregate behavior: aggregates affect disaggregates, and disaggregates in turn affect aggregates. Because the interaction is two-way, it contradicts the standard assumption, for instance, in panel data work where aggregate variables might affect disaggregates, but not vice versa. Moreover, as the income distribution and relative price examples make clear, the operative economic mechanism sometimes involves a relation between different parts of the disaggregates distribution: interaction between rich and poor, or tradeoffs between high- and low-priced commodities. Then, summary statistics of the distribution – say a conditional mean or cross-sectional variance – will be inappropriate for understanding the relation between disaggregates and aggregates.[2] What is needed, instead, is a way to analyze flexibly the dynamics of an entire distribution (or rich cross-section) of disaggregates.

Few econometric tools extant are appropriate for this. This paper seeks to add to those tools. It explores theoretical and empirical modelling of the joint dynamics of aggregate and regional disaggregate output. The regional disaggregates studied below – the states in the US – are large enough compared to aggregate US output that one cannot casually dismiss the potential effects of disaggregate dynamics on the aggregate. At the same time, there are many enough regional disaggregates to make apparent the modelling difficulties: standard vector time-series methods, for instance, will not do for modelling

---

[2] The easiest way to see this is through an example. Suppose that it is income inequality that matters for aggregate fluctuations and growth, as, e.g., in Galor and Zeira (1993) and Persson and Tabellini (1994). Which income inequality measure should one use in empirical analysis? Theory doesn't always provide an answer since the simplified distributions that appear in a theoretical model are only suggestive of more general economic forces at work. Atkinson's classic paper (1970) shows how alternative inequality measures imply substantively different – and potentially contradictory – views on the inequality actually extant.

the dynamics of a 50 by 1 random vector.[3] If one were to turn then to the joint dynamics of European Union regional disaggregates – as in discussions of regional cohesion – one faces an 800 by 1 vector. Standard methods will be ill-suited for such analyses. This paper studies instead a technique to model the dynamics of a cross-section *distribution*. This technique, therefore, works regardless of how numerous the cross section units get.[4]

The empirical model of distribution dynamics developed below allows quantifying intra-distribution mobility, i.e., measuring how rapidly disaggregates traverse the cross-section distribution. Such measures provide natural calibrations of the speed of adjustment in a cross-section distribution to disaggregate perturbations. Seeing how those measures relate to movements in an aggregate (like GNP) reveals potential connections between aggregate fluctuations and gradual adjustments in disaggregates.[5]

The remainder of this paper is organized as follows. The next section sets down a simple, abstract theoretical framework for understanding the econometric calculations that follow. Section 3 presents some stylized facts; Section 4 gives more detailed analysis. Sections 3 and 4 are not, by any means, intended as formal statistical tests of the predictions in Section 2, only as groundwork for later, more complete study.

The key results from Section 4 are as follows. Mobility, while present, has little to do with aggregate fluctuations. However, leading states – which differ over time – have strong predictive power for aggregate output.[6]

Finally, Section 5 briefly concludes.

2 A Simple Model

This section develops a simple theoretical model to analyze aggregate and regional disaggregate dynamics. The model is stylized to a degree where many

---

[3] Post-War quarterly time-series now contain 200 observations. But a VAR model for a 50 by 1 vector already has 2500 free parameters in the first-order lag matrix coefficient; the variance-covariance matrix for the innovation contributes another 1275. Quah and Sargent (1993) attempt to control this parameter proliferation, using dynamic index representations, but for certain issues – identified below – those will be inappropriate.

[4] Nevertheless, because the cross-section disaggregates are studied in the form of their distribution dynamics, the framework necessarily cannot address every interesting question on disaggregate dynamics. For instance, spatial interaction is altogether ignored in the current work, although Quah (1996c) has used related techniques precisely to investigate such concerns.

[5] See, among others, Davis and Haltiwanger (1992), Evans (1993), Lilien (1982), and Pissarides and McMaster (1990).

[6] A referee has emphasized that the "leading states" findings are not special to the new dynamic-distribution methodology developed in this paper. I agree, but have kept them in the paper nonetheless: those results do relate to the dynamic behavior of distributions, and they do serve to highlight how certain features of distribution dynamics are empirically important, and others not.

interesting effects are absent, but in return it is explicit about the dynamics of the aggregate jointly with those of the entire disaggregate cross-section.[7]

One by-product of the reasoning below is to show the danger in interpreting as causal certain estimated relationships between aggregates and disaggregates. That, however, is not the main point of this section. Instead, the primary goal is to provide a theoretical framework for interpreting models of distribution dynamics.

To interpret variation along the time dimension, Sargent (1981) has emphasized an optimizing, Euler equation characterization. Below, I do the same with variation over the cross section. Then, informally, I put the two together.

To focus on aggregate business cycles, assume that a single good is produced and consumed. To make different regions different, introduce a function $z(x)$, which maps location x to (productivity) characteristics z; the latter could be multidimensional, but is required to be non-negative in each entry. The analysis takes function z fixed, but eventually one would like to allow z to vary over time. Examples of z might include the work ethos on the Microsoft campus, Massachusetts's human capital in technology, and automotive engineering skills around Heathrow Airport: these all change through time in response to economic incentives.

Physical geography is a probability space $(\mathbb{X}, \mathscr{X}, \phi_x)$ that allows for possibly mixed discrete-continuous locations, nonuniform mountains, valleys, and plains, and so on. For different models, one might take $\mathbb{X}$ to be alternately a set comprising two points, a straight line, a circle, or a plane (finite or infinite). Then $\mathscr{X}$ comprises the collection of interesting subsets of $\mathbb{X}$, and the probability measure ϕ_x is a function from elements in $\mathscr{X}$ to $[0, 1]$; it evaluates members of $\mathscr{X}$ to measure their proportions out of total locations $\mathbb{X}$.

With this structure, z can also include measures of distance or accessibility of particular locations x. Physical distance, of course, doesn't change over time, but accessibility might, when roads and electronic highways are built. Therefore, function z can be viewed to have some components time-invariant and observable, others time-varying and unobservable, as well as combinations in between.

Denote employment at location x by $l(x)$; output is given by a standard neoclassical technology:

$$y(x) = f(l(x), z(x)) \ , \tag{2.1}$$

[7] In its focus on aggregate business cycles, the analysis here differs from economic geography work on location and agglomeration dynamics (e.g., Krugman and Venables (1993)). In its focus on many, many regional disaggregates, it differs from that macro time series work (e.g., Engle and Kozicki (1993), Sargent and Sims (1977)) which might seem pertinent and directly applicable; they are not, for reasons already given in the introduction. Work such as Barro and Sala-i-Martin (1991), Blanchard and Katz (1992), and Carlino and Mills (1993) – which either average across the cross-section, or model regional disaggregates separately – are examples where one gets no information about the relation between different parts of the cross section of regions. Likely most directly relevant is work such as Ciccone and Hall (1993), although the analyses there and in this paper differ substantially.

assumed identical across locations. Assume that for any fixed z (including zero), the partial derivative $f_l = \partial f/\partial l$ diverges to infinity as l tends towards zero. In other words, the first input of labor is always highly productive: for z unobservable, specifying f_l at zero z is only a normalization. A measure ϕ_x on locations, together with technology (2.1), a characteristics profile z, and an employment profile l, induces a measure each for characteristics ϕ_z, employment ϕ_l, and output ϕ_y.

The output profile y across locations, in turn, implies observed total output:

$$\bar{y} = \int y(x)\phi_x(dx) = \int f(l(x), z(x))\phi_x(dx) \ .$$

Aggregate output $\bar{y}$ can always be calculated as above, mechanically, regardless of whether z and l are "good" or "bad" allocation profiles. Similarly, one can always find the distribution of wages across locations by calculating:

$$w(x) = f_l(l(x), z(x)) = \frac{\partial f}{\partial l}(l(x), z(x)) \ ,$$

again, mechanically.

More interesting is to ask whether particular allocations z and l, and their evolution over time, can be supported by some economic process. A useful starting point is to allow labor to move freely across locations. In that case, in equilibrium the labor allocation l adjusts so that wages equalize across x, and the labor market clears. Normalizing total labor supply to 1, this is:

$$\begin{aligned} &f_l(l(x), z(x)) = w(x) = \bar{w} \ , \\ &\int l(x)\phi_x(dx) = 1 \ . \end{aligned} \qquad (2.2)$$

A nonnegative function l solving (2.2) is a static (i.e., point-in-time) efficient labor allocation. Assuming f_l unbounded rules out corner solutions where some location might have zero employment. Given any distribution of characteristics ϕ_z, an allocation l satisfying (2.2) for some positive $\bar{w}$ is not just economically sensible; it turns out also to maximize aggregate output $\bar{y}$:

Proposition: Denote by $\mathbb{M}_+$ the class of non-negative measurable functions on $(\mathbb{X}, \mathscr{X})$. Suppose that for x in $\mathbb{X}$ (a.e. $-\ \phi_x$), the function $f(\cdot, z(x))$ has derivative $f_l = \partial f/\partial l > 0$, decreasing in l. Then the program

$$\sup_{l \in \mathbb{M}_+} \int f(l(x), z(x))\phi_x(dx)$$
$$\text{s.t.} \quad \int l(x)\phi_x(dx) \leq 1$$

is solved by any l^* in $\mathbb{M}_+$ such that there exists a positive number ψ for which simultaneously:

(i) $f_l(l^*(x), z(x)) - \psi \leq 0$ *(a.e. $-\ \phi_x$), with equality whenever $l^*(x) > 0$; and*
(ii) $\int l^*(x)\phi_x(dx) = 1$.

(The proof of this result is in the technical appendix.)

Equation (2.2) implies that when $z(x)$ varies over x then so too will efficient employment levels. Stated this way, the result in the proposition seems trivial and obvious. However, the characterization also asserts that nothing about the cross-section standard deviation (or any other moment) of the observed distribution ϕ_l says anything about the behavior of total output about its maximum. There is a precise and natural economic relation embedded in (2.2), but it does not translate simply to, say, using dispersion as a measure of "imbalance" or "disequilibrium." To see this explicitly, it is useful to work through an explicit example.

Suppose z is scalar, and assume the technology:

$$f(l, z) = l^{\alpha} z^{\beta} , \qquad \text{for constants } \alpha \text{ in } (0, 1) \text{ and } \beta > 0 ,$$

so that labor's marginal product is $w = f_l = \alpha l^{\alpha-1} z^{\beta}$. This implies local labor demand

$$l = (\alpha/w)^{1/(1-\alpha)} z^{\beta/(1-\alpha)} .$$

Labor market clearing then is

$$(\alpha/w)^{1/(1-\alpha)} \int z^{\beta/(1-\alpha)} \phi_z(dz) = 1 . \tag{2.3}$$

Define an artificial random variable Z having the distribution given by ϕ_z. Using this notation the integral in the market-clearing condition (2.3) can be rewritten as the expectation $E(Z^{\beta/(1-\alpha)})$ Then (2.3) implies the market clearing wage

$$\overline{w} = \alpha(EZ^{\beta/(1-\alpha)})^{1-\alpha} . \tag{2.4}$$

Define $p(\alpha) = (1 - \alpha)^{-1}$, and recall the definition of p-norm for a random variable,

$$\|Z\|_p = E(|Z|^p)^{1/p} \qquad \text{for } p \geq 1 .$$

The market clearing wage (2.4) thus can also be written:

$$\overline{w} = \alpha \|Z^{\beta}\|_{p(\alpha)} .$$

Using this in the local labor demand function (2.3) we see that the equilibrium employment profile across regions is:

$$l(x) = (\alpha/\overline{w})^{p(\alpha)} z(x)^{\beta p(\alpha)} . \tag{2.5}$$

In characteristics z, employment is increasing, and either convex or concave depending on whether β is greater or less than $p(\alpha)^{-1} = 1 - \alpha$.

When all locations x have the same value of z, the measure ϕ_z places point mass on that value of z. The distribution of employment is then also degenerate at the value given by (2.5). In this special case, employment is equal across regions, and its being so happens to maximize aggregate output $\bar{y}$. In general, however, when z varies over x, then so too will l: equation (2.5) allows calculating ϕ_l from knowledge of ϕ_z. Aggregate output $\bar{y}$ in this more general case is no longer maximized by a degenerate distribution in l, or equivalently, by having zero (small) variance in employment across locations.

Regional output is given by substituting equilibrium employment into the technology:

$$y(x) = (\alpha/\overline{w})^{\alpha p(\alpha)} z(x)^{\alpha\beta p(\alpha)} z(x)^{\beta}$$
$$= (\alpha/\overline{w})^{\alpha p(\alpha)} z(x)^{\beta p(\alpha)} \tag{2.6}$$

and therefore has the same shape in z as does employment. Despite curvature in the technology f, output y and employment l are, roughly speaking, collinear in equilibrium. But then the statements above on employment's distribution and its relation to aggregate output $\overline{y}$ apply immediately to the distribution ϕ_y of regional outputs and its relation to $\overline{y}$.

Integrating $y(x)$ across locations gives aggregate output. In our random variable notation, we can write this as:

$$\overline{y} = (\alpha/\overline{w})^{\alpha p(\alpha)} E(Z^{\beta p(\alpha)})$$
$$= \|Z^{\beta}\|_{p(\alpha)}^{-\alpha p(\alpha)} \cdot \|Z^{\beta}\|_{p(\alpha)}^{p(\alpha)}$$
$$= \|Z^{\beta}\|_{p(\alpha)} = \overline{w}/\alpha \ .$$

Aggregate output therefore behaves as a particular absolute moment of the cross-section distribution of Z. In equilibrium, aggregate output will also be observed to move as does the real wage $\overline{w}$, only more so, since $|\alpha|$ is less than 1. Thus, when wages and output fluctuate over time, wages will be less variable than output.

Substituting this last relation between $\overline{w}$ and $\overline{y}$ into (2.6), we get:

$$y(x) = (\overline{y})^{-\alpha p(\alpha)} \cdot z(x)^{\beta p(\alpha)}$$

or

$$\log y(x) = (-\alpha p(\alpha)) \log \overline{y} + \beta p(\alpha) \log z(x) \ . \tag{2.7}$$

Equation (2.7) looks like an (observable) index model representation for regional outputs: regional dynamics can be viewed as made up of a region-specific disturbance, $\beta p(\alpha) \times \log z(x)$, on top of some multiplier of aggregate output, $(-\alpha p(\alpha)) \times \log \overline{y}$. The development above, however, says that such a representation does *not* imply that aggregate output fluctuations "affect" regions with multiplier $-\alpha p(\alpha)$. Moreover, while the multiplier $-\alpha p(\alpha)$ depends only on parameters of the production technology (and is thus certainly policy-invariant and structural), there is no sense in which it describes the effect on regional outputs of aggregate output movements. Instead, regional and aggregate outputs are jointly determined: neither one causes the other.

Returning now to the general case, it is easy to see that much the same conclusions from the special case (except of course the precise functional form solutions) apply directly. Aggregate and local dynamics can be simply described: If the entire function z is perturbed, then a previously optimal employment profile l need no longer imply a uniform wage across regions, and labor will wish to reallocate towards a new profile. If we maintain the perfect mobility assumption, no new difficulties arise in the general case. We can take a random field – a doubly indexed stochastic process – $z(x, t)$, where the t index denotes time, to drive the dynamics of the system. In each time period t, given $z(\cdot, t)$, the equilibrium employment profile $l(\cdot, t)$ again implies (i) a wage $\overline{w}(t)$ uniform across locations and (ii) maximized aggregate output $\bar{y}(t)$. There is also a resulting equilibrium profile of incomes across regions $y(\cdot, t)$: all the random fields, z, l, and y, indexed by x and t fluctuate across both space and time. Thus, embedded in the equilibrium is a sequence of evolving regional income distributions given by $\phi_y(t)$ fluctuating jointly with $\bar{y}$.

This discussion motivates a new view of aggregate and disaggregate disturbances. In the framework above, a natural definition of an aggregate disturbance is a perturbation that keeps the function z invariant in particular ways – for instance, aggregate disturbances might be associated with perturbations where z is simply shifted vertically. Disaggregate disturbances are then those perturbations that twist z's profile but maintain its vertical location. Put another way, disaggregate disturbances are a "wave" rippling through the surface comprising regional quantities.[8]

The model illustrates why certain kinds of empirical calculations are uninformative. For instance, from equation (2.7), stable relations between aggregates and measures of cross-section dispersion should not be viewed as movements in one implying movements in the other. Both the aggregate and the cross-section distribution are jointly determined. Except in special cases, even the simplest theory gives neither a determinate sign on this relation nor the appropriate statistic of the cross-section distributions to look at.

The aggregate and disaggregate dynamics described thus far are simple and naive. Because I have assumed perfect mobility for labor, calculating the dynamic equilibrium path is easy: just string together in time the static equilibria across the cross-section distribution. Such analysis is interesting, however, for at least three reasons. First, it is convenient to calculate and easy to understand, and thus serves as a benchmark for more difficult calculations. Second, it makes explicit the limits on what we can hope to infer from data on disaggregate fluctuations: examining point-in-time statistics (like means, variances, modes and so on) of the cross-section distributions is unlikely to be fruitful. Third, it suggests where further theoretical and empirical investigation can advance understanding.

To make progress beyond the simple model, some conjecture is needed on the economic mechanism underlying regional adjustments. One way to begin might be to make explicit the pattern of labor mobility, how readily one l profile translates into another. A useful story of regional fluctuations and aggregate business cycles, therefore, will likely embed within it the solution to the follow-

---

[8] Contrast this with a representation like that used in Quah and Sargent (1993) where no similarly simple characterization is available. There, aggregate disturbances are characterized by an extensive set of dynamic orthogonality conditions.

ing abstract problem. How does a distribution of economic activity $\phi_{y,t}$ evolve – form the sequence of measures $\{\phi_{y,t+s}, s = 1, 2, \ldots\}$ – response to an ongoing series of aggregate and idiosyncratic disturbances?[9]

What is needed, therefore, is a model that produces an equilibrium in the form of a vector stochastic difference equation in $\phi_{y,t}$, together with relevant aggregates: such an equation can then be estimated and simulated to give a characterization of steady states $\lim_{t\to\infty} \phi_{y,t}$. Tracing out the transition dynamics implied by that equation then gives some insight into the interplay of fluctuations in aggregates and in the disaggregates dispersed over x.

3 Cross-Section Dynamics Over One Business Cycle

We turn next to empirical application of the preceding ideas. To appreciate the issues to follow, begin by recording some facts on what happened over one complete NBER US business cycle upturn.[10]

Between 1982 and 1990 – a complete NBER trough to peak span – average US per capita nominal personal income rose by 48 percent, an annual growth rate of 7 percent. Over this time, experiences across US states differed. Before looking at these, we establish preliminary intuition by considering some theoretical possibilities.

If the cross-section distribution about the average were stationary, then the relative positions of states might always remain unchanged: the richest states always remain richest; the poorest, poorest. Or, maintaining the hypothesis of an invariant cross-section distribution, some regional disaggregates might rise above the average from below, and others fall below the average from above. Stationary steady state, by itself, places no restriction on intra-distribution mobility.

If individual states were independent and identically distributed both in time and across each other, and the invariant cross-section distribution were symmetric, then any subset of states at the beginning of any time sample would have

[9] One reasonable guess is that in a model without externalities of the kinds in, e.g., Krugman and Venables (1993), $\phi_{y,t}$ will, in response to a one-time disturbance, converge to a distribution as characterized in the Proposition above. But, even if so, such "punctuated equilibrium dynamics" will never be observed in real world data since disturbances are ongoing through time.

[10] The US states series here are constructed from Barro and Sala-i-Martin (1991) and the Data Appendix in Blanchard and Katz (1992). As there, *state* refers to the 50 US states and the District of Columbia. I use nominal personal incomes throughout this section, rather than real. When there is a common general price index – because of the common national currency – the statements here carry over qualitatively unchanged to real personal incomes, as I am comparing behavior across states; similarly, if one studies personal incomes relative to *any* aggregate. The more formal analysis in the next section will use state incomes relative to per capita GDP.

half end up below average and half above, by the end of the time sample. Since this holds for *any* subset of states, it must hold for those states beginning above average, as well as for those beginning below.

There is thus a range of possibilities, all consistent with well-behaved stationary fluctuations about an average (itself possibly varying through time).

We can take the "extreme-case" discussion further. Suppose only aggregate disturbances were important, and the propagation mechanism were an aggregate one. Then up to minimal variation, one should not expect significant asymmetries across states *over business cycles.* Different parts of the cross-section distribution should have roughly the same dynamic behavior relative to the aggregate and to each other. (The discussion in the rest of this section will not speak directly to this point, but we return to it in Section 4 below.)

What, in the event, transpired? The answer is none of the above. In 1982, at the beginning of the upturn, 20 states had per capita personal incomes above the US average. Over the upturn, one half of these – already relatively rich – saw their lead on the US average *increase.* Over the same upturn, again one half of the 31 states initially below average saw their relative incomes fall even further. Thus, the realized event differed from the hypothetical cases previously described: the cross-section spread apart over the upturn, and did so by systematically pulling out even further those parts of the distribution that were already at the extremes.

Details reinforce this conclusion. Of the 20 states that began above average in 1982, only three (Kansas, Texas, and Wyoming) transited below average by 1990; of the 31 initially below average, only one (Rhode Island) transited above average by 1990. Over this upturn the two fastest growers among states already richer than average were New Hampshire and New Jersey, whose leads on the average increased from 0.5% and 19% to 11% and 29% respectively. By contrast, the two worst growers among those already relatively poor were Louisiana and Oklahoma, whose income disparities from the average worsened from −12% and −1% to −26% and −19%, respectively.[11]

What do these facts mean? Is it that as aggregate output grows over the business cycle, those states already rich gain most from the rise in aggregate activity? Or is it instead that rich states are the first ones affected by disturbances, and they then pull the nation out of recession? Whichever the reality is, these regional and state fluctuations are *large.* To see this, recall that most detrending techniques give business cycle fluctuations in US GNP of 3–4 percent about trend (see, among many others, Blanchard and Quah (1989) and Prescott (1986)).[12] If an average business cycle lasts six years, then the measured aggregate growth rate over an upturn is 4 percent over 18 months or 2.7 percent

[11] Overall, the fastest grower was Maine (11% increase over 1982–90, from −19% to −8% about the US average); the worst, Alaska (−25% change over 1982–90), Wyoming, and Oklahoma (both −18%).

[12] I take these numbers as a reasoned consensus although such numbers can, in theory, be dramatically altered by varying the detrending method (Quah (1992)).

per year. From above, New Hampshire and New Jersey's fluctuations, about the national average, are close to 2 percent per year; those of Wyoming and Oklahoma, 3 percent per year. State fluctuations are thus large, compared to aggregate business cycles.

These stylized facts carry a meta-message, reinforcing statements made in the introduction. Intra-distribution dynamics contain regularities. However, the interesting regularities here will not be easily found using standard econometric techniques. To see this, recall what those techniques do. Estimating a panel data model on states or regions takes an average across the cross section (even when allowing for heterogeneities like "individual effects"). The differing behavior of states in the upper and lower parts of the cross-section distribution – if not averaged out exactly – will not be observable as starkly as described above. Certainly how the top 10 percent of the distribution behaves relative to the bottom 10 percent is, in principle, available from panel data estimation (e.g., Lillard and Willis (1978)); it is just that that kind of intra-distribution behavior is not obviously displayed there. Nor will intra-distribution dynamics be conveniently modelled.

By contrast, estimating individual time series models – one for each state, say, to permit differences across Maine and Oklahoma (e.g., Carlino and Mills (1993)) – leaves undetected the co-movements across states. The researcher then cannot tell if rich states vary positively or negatively with poor ones. Attempting to model all those cross-sectional correlations leads, of course, to the (conceptual) degree-of-freedom problems already described in the introduction.

4 Distribution Dynamics

This section develops an empirical model of aggregate and disaggregate fluctuations. The model is designed to take into account the issues previously described: it flexibly permits interactions between aggregates and disaggregates; it allows potentially many, many disaggregates; it captures how one part of the cross-section distribution behaves relative to another. In brief, the model provides the law of motion for a sequence of dynamically evolving distributions.

Take the basic data to be the log of annual state personal income per capita relative to the national average each period.[13] Figure 4.1 is their three-dimen-

[13] This choice is not inconsequential. If, at one extreme, the disaggregates were taken as the (fitted) idiosyncratic components from a dynamic observable index model, then by construction they would be everywhere orthogonal to the aggregate. If, at the other extreme, the disaggregates were unchanged from the original data, then purely mechanically some of their fluctuations would be the same as their aggregate's. The choice made in the text was for two reasons: first, convenience in interpretation; second, following, loosely, Section 2's discussion on "twists" of the cross-section distribution to define disaggregates.

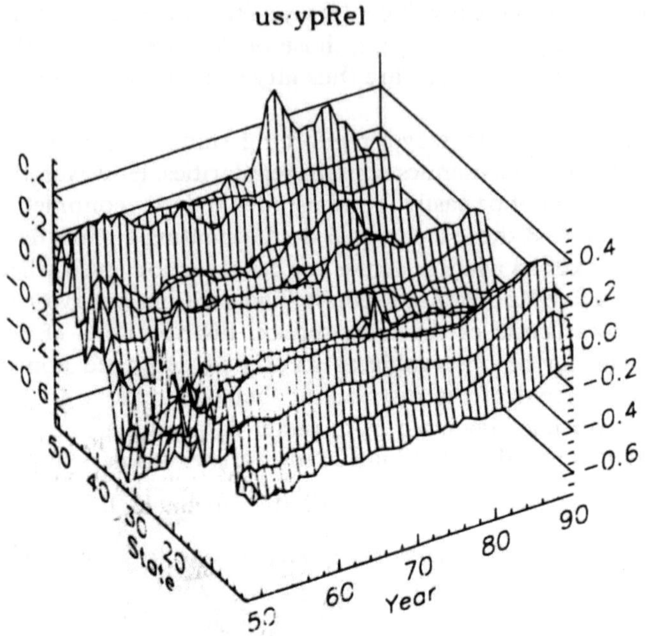

Fig. 4.1. Relative per capita personal incomes (Log), 1948–1990

sional plot; the states in this figure are arrayed in US Census ordering, i.e., beginning with Maine and Massachusetts, and ending with California, Alaska, and Hawaii. Such a graph emphasizes the data's rich variation across both time series and cross-section dimensions. It clarifies why standard multiple time series modelling would be inappropriate here. The cross-section dimension in figure 4.1 has the same order of magnitude as does the time series: an investigator could not even estimate a full-rank variance-covariance matrix from these data, much less the dynamics in a multiple time series model of the 51-variate vector of state incomes.

Establish notation for the subsequent discussion: Let ζ be a fixed, finite-dimensional vector of aggregates – GNP growth rates, national unemployment and so on – and y be a rich cross section of disaggregates. The researcher seeks to characterize the dynamic evolution of the pair (ζ, y). The proposal here is simple: transform the system from (ζ, y) to (ζ, ϕ_y). (Recall from Section 2 that ϕ_y denotes the measure describing the cross-section distribution of y.) Then, the researcher models a system as depicted conceptually in figure 4.2.

The top panel of figure 4.2 contains the standard time-series plot of a scalar economic variable. The bottom panel plots the sequence of evolving distributions (implied by) $\{\phi_{y,t}\colon \text{integer } t \geq 1\}$. It highlights two different characteristics in that sequence: (i) the changing shape of the distribution, and (ii) the intra-distribution dynamics, how a given part of the distribution at time t transits to another part of the distribution by time $t + s$. Call (i) and (ii) *shape* and *mobility*

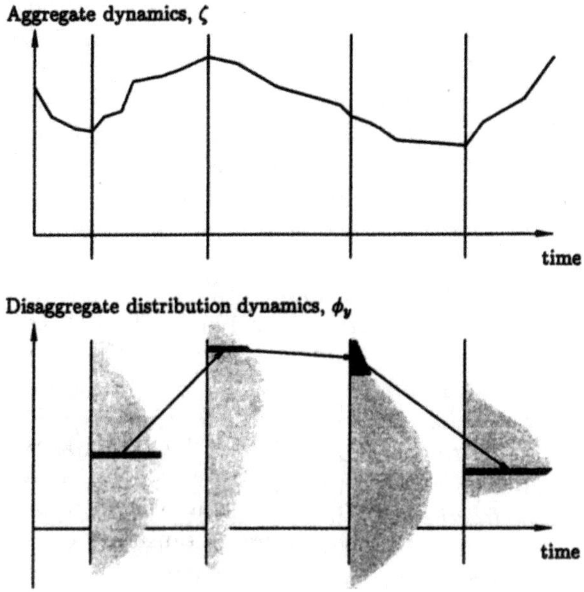

Fig. 4.2. Aggregate and disaggregate distribution fluctuations

dynamics.[14] Subsequent analysis will decompose distribution dynamics into these two components.

To see how the decomposition works, recall that dynamically evolving probability measures $\{\phi_{y,t}\text{: integer } t \geq 1\}$ can be written as a stochastic kernel equation:

$$\forall \text{ measurable } \mathscr{A}: \qquad \phi_{y,t+1}(\mathscr{A}) = \int \mathscr{M}_t(y, \mathscr{A})\phi_{y,t}(dy) \ ; \tag{4.1}$$

(see, for instance, Stokey and Lucas [1989, Ch. 8]). In general, ϕ_y might show more than first-order dependence. As with standard time-series state-space models, however, equation (4.1) is easily modified to permit that.

Each stochastic kernel $\mathscr{M}_t$ encodes information on both type (i) and (ii) dynamics in ϕ_y. When ϕ_y is discrete, then $\{\mathscr{M}_t\text{: integer } t\}$ is just a sequence of stochastic matrices (i.e., square arrays of non-negative numbers with row sums equal to 1). If, further, that sequence is time-invariant then (the observable) ϕ_y

[14] Distinguish intra-distribution mobility (ii) from geographical mobility. The mobility here refers to moving about within the cross-section distribution of per capita incomes, not to moving about across physical space. In this scheme, if three states happen to have the same per capita income, they are not differentiated, even though two of them might be adjacent (like New York and New Jersey) and the third geographically distant (like California). Physical separation has little significance for the measures of economic activity studied here. For instance, when UPS relocated from Greenwich, Connecticut to Atlanta, Georgia, what mattered were the two locations' characteristics, *not* how far apart physically they happened to be (*Financial Times*, 28 October 1993). This idea on the irrelevance of physical separation is studied further in Quah (1996c).

can be viewed as corresponding to the marginal distributions of an artificial (unobserved) Markov chain.[15] Then $\mathcal{M}_0 = \mathcal{M}_t$ (all $t \geq 1$) can be estimated directly from frequency counts.

When ϕ_y is continuous (or mixed discrete-continuous) then $\mathcal{M}_0$ can no longer be represented by a matrix, although it can still be analyzed using related methods (Quah (1996a)). If, however, $\mathcal{M}_t$ varies over time – as we wish to allow here – such analysis is no longer possible. Then, one way to proceed builds on the non-stationarities available in Markov-renewal structures; this is done in Quah (1995b), exploiting insights from Singer and Spilerman (1976). A second possibility is to decompose $\mathcal{M}$ explicitly into shape and mobility components – as suggested in figure 4.2 – and then to parameterize their dynamics separately. We follow this approach here.

Fix a positive integer n: this will be the number of cells in a discretization of the basic data. Then, represent each stochastic kernel $\mathcal{M}_t$ by the pair $(M(t), q(t))$ where $M(t)$ is an $n \times n$ *fractile transition probability matrix* and $q(t)$ is an *n-element quantile set*, i.e., a collection of n disjoint random intervals. (A transition probability matrix is said to be *fractile* when it describes transitions out of cells containing equal fractions of the entire distribution.) To see that this gives a decomposition with the desired properties, it is easiest to provide constructive definitions for M and q.

Denote the basic data by

$$\{y_j(t): j = 1, 2, \ldots, N; t = 0, 1, \ldots, T\}$$

where j denotes cross-sectional units and t indexes time. The sequence ϕ_y relates to the basic data by

$$\forall r \in \mathbb{R}: \qquad \phi_{y,t}((-\infty, r]) = \#\{j: y_j(t) \leq r\} \times N^{-1} .$$

Every fixed positive integer n implies a unique set of equally-spaced probabilities

$$\{m/n: m = 0, 1, \ldots, n\} .$$

Define at time t the quantiles

$$(quant)_m(t) = \inf\{r \in \mathbb{R} \mid \phi_{y,t}((-\infty, r]) > m/n\} , \qquad m = 1, 2, \ldots, n ;$$

and take

$$(quant)_0(t) = -\infty .$$

These give the consecutive disjoint random intervals

$$q_m(t) = ((quant)_{m-1}(t), (quant)_m(t)] , \qquad m = 1, 2, \ldots, n ,$$

[15] This reverses the usual reasoning where one observes the Markov chain, and then infers its unobserved associated probability distributions. Here, it is the cross-section distributions that are observed, and the Markov chain unobservable. Of course, the mathematics works the same either way.

which, in turn, comprise the quantile set

$$q(t) = \{q_m(t): m = 1, 2, \ldots, n\} \ .$$

By construction, $\phi_{y,t}(q_1(t)) = \phi_{y,t}(q_m(t))$ for all m, i.e., the elements of every quantile set have equal measure.

The sequence of quantile sets together with the basic data define the transition probabilities M: let matrix $M(t)$ have (l, m) entry

$$M_{lm}(t) = \frac{\#\{j: y_j(t+1) \in q_m(t+1) \text{ and } y_j(t) \in q_l(t)\}}{\phi_{y,t}(q_l(t))} \ , \qquad l, m = 1, 2, \ldots, n \ .$$

Clearly, $M(t)$ comprises all non-negative entries and has row sums equal to 1. Also immediate, by construction, is that each $M(t)$ is fractile, i.e.,

$$\left(\sum_{m=1}^{n} M_{lm}(t)\right)\phi_{y,t}(q_l(t)) = \phi_{y,t}(q_l(t)) = \phi_{y,t}(q_1(t))$$

is the same for all l.

To summarize, M encodes information on mobility while q encodes information on shape. We can further clarify M's role by using a *mobility index* (Geweke, Marshall, and Zarkin (1986) or Shorrocks (1978)). Analogous to measures of income inequality – summarizing the information in an entire distribution into a single scalar – a mobility index collapses into one number the mobility information in a transition probability. However, as already emphasized above for inequality measures, no single mobility index need be completely satisfactory. Thus we consider four such indexes (three from Geweke, Marshall, and Zarkin (1986) and Shorrocks (1978), and one new). The stochastic kernel representation $(M(t), q(t))$ – a pair for each time period – will imply time series on each of these indexes.

First, take Shorrocks's index μ_1 defined by:

$$\mu_1(M) = \frac{n - \mathrm{tr}(M)}{n-1}$$
$$= \left(\frac{n}{n-1}\right)\left\{n^{-1}\sum_j (1 - M_{jj})\right\} ,$$

where M_{jj} denotes the j-th diagonal entry of the matrix M. Since $1 - M_{jj}$ is the probability of exiting state j, Shorrocks's μ_1 is the inverse of the harmonic mean of expected durations of remaining in a given part of the cross-section distribution. It thus provides one natural index of mobility: the higher is $\mu_1(M)$, the less "persistence" is there in M.

Since the trace of a matrix equals the sum of its eigenvalues, Shorrocks's index can also be written as:

$$\mu_1(M) = \frac{n - \sum_j \lambda_j}{n-1} ,$$

where λ_j are the eigenvalues of M. Thus when M's eigenvalues are all real and nonnegative, Shorrocks's μ_1 is identical to the second index we consider:

$$\mu_2(M) = \frac{n - \sum_j |\lambda_j|}{n-1} \ ;$$

in general. however, μ_1 and μ_2 will differ.

To see the motivation behind μ_2 recall that every stochastic matrix M always has one eigenvalue equal to unity, and all its other eigenvalues bounded from above by 1 in modulus. In the most regular case, when M implies a unique ergodic distribution, the sequence $\{M^k: k \geq 1\}$ converges to that distinguished matrix having all rows equal to the ergodic distribution.[16] Convergence occurs at a geometric rate, given by powers of (Jordan blocks in) the eigenvalues λ_j. Thus the smaller is the modulus of an eigenvalue – the larger is $1 - |\lambda_j|$ – the faster does the corresponding component in M^k converge. Putting these facts together, we see that μ_2 sensibly indexes mobility; it relates positively to the average rate of convergence of the cross-section distribution towards the ergodic limit.

When all eigenvalues except the unit one are strictly less than 1 in modulus, then as horizon k grows, the dominant convergence term is given by $|\lambda_2|$, the modulus of the second largest eigenvalue. Thus, for the same reason that μ_2 is sensible, one might consider our third mobility index:

$$\mu_3(M) = 1 - |\lambda_2| \ .$$

This, like μ_2, indexes the speed of convergence. But whereas μ_2 incorporates *all* the different rates of convergence, μ_3 captures only the asymptotic rate. The two, μ_2 and μ_3, would be identical – up to a scaling involving only n – when evaluated at an M whose smallest eigenvalues, beyond the largest two, turn out to be zero.

Mobility indexes μ_1, μ_2, and μ_3 have previously appeared (Geweke, Marshall, and Zarkin (1986) and Shorrocks (1978)). The discussion above gives conditions under which they coincide, but in general they are not directly related to each other. These mobility indexes – like all others I know in the literature – use only transition probability M information. But the quantile sets also contain relevant information. It means one thing to transit from the poorest 10 percent to the richest 10 percent when the poor and rich differ by only a small amount; it means something else when the poor and rich are orders of magnitude apart. Thus for the last mobility index considered here, I bring in information on the quantile sets.[17]

---

[16] When M is fractile – as here – the uniform distribution is always an ergodic limit.

[17] Yet another mobility index that might be considered measures the speed of transition across the support of the evolving distributions. In its simplest form, it could be the mean first-passage time from the bottom to top 10 percent of the distribution (as used for different purposes in Durlauf and Johnson (1994) and Quah (1996a)). However, experimentation showed such indexes uninformative here; I thus omit the results using them.

To motivate this new index, denoted μ_{AR}, note that the evolution of $\phi_{y,t}$ (and thus of the stochastic kernel $\mathcal{M}_t$) implies an unobservable *scalar* stochastic process $\{\tilde{y}_t\colon \text{integer } t\}$. If for each t, the artificial variable $\tilde{y}_t$ has finite variance, then – even though $\tilde{y}$ is *never* observed – one can calculate the projection $P[\tilde{y}_{t+1} \mid \tilde{y}_t]$ from knowledge of just ϕ_y and $\mathcal{M}$.

(I say that $\tilde{y}$ is artificial because it is not observed directly but only hypothesized by the researcher. In standard time-series analysis, a researcher uses observations on a scalar (or vector) time series Y and then hypothesizes a distribution for that random variable (this is particularly apparent in, say, ARCH models). Here, the opposite happens: the researcher observes the empirical (cross-section) distribution and then hypothesizes a random variable to go along with that distribution. As Quah (1995a, 1996a) has observed, this is usefully viewed as the dual to standard practice in time-series analysis. To compute the projection $P[\tilde{y}_{t+1} \mid \tilde{y}_t]$, one never needs to observe $\tilde{y}$; only the sequence of dynamic cross-moments is needed, and ϕ_y and $\mathcal{M}$ together readily allow calculating that.)

Call ρ_t the coefficient on $\tilde{y}_t$ in this projection, and define the mobility index

$$\mu_{AR,t} = \mu_{AR}(M(t), q(t), q(t+1)) = 1 - \rho_t \ .$$

Call this our fourth mobility index. Why does it measure mobility? Some special cases help answer this. When M is the identity matrix, there is extreme persistence. All parts of the cross-section distribution remain exactly where they begin. When, further, $\phi_{y,t} = \phi_{y,t+1}$, then μ_{AR} is easily shown to be 0. Maintaining this assumption for ϕ_y, suppose now that M only has 1's on the main anti-diagonal: the richest become the poorest; conversely the poorest, richest. A simple calculation then gives μ_{AR} equal to 2 for this case of "extreme mobility" (unlike μ_1, μ_2, and μ_3 the new index μ_{AR} is not restricted to lie between 0 and 1; a simple transformation can, of course, enforce that restriction although nothing relevant hinges on it).

Keeping the skew-symmetric M, now let $\phi_{y,t+1}$ be a mean-preserving spread on $\phi_{y,t}$. The richest now become even poorer than the originally poorest, and vice versa. There is thus greater mobility than before. The value of μ_{AR} increases above 2; by contrast, any mobility index defined only on M would remain unchanged.

Using the same reasoning, when $\phi_{y,t+1}$ is a mean-preserving spread on $\phi_{y,t}$, but M is the identity matrix, the index μ_{AR} decreases below 0. Again, any mobility index ignoring q would remain invariant – concealing that in this example the rich have become richer and the poor poorer.[18] Thus, μ_{AR} correctly captures our intuition on intra-distribution mobility.

Figure 4.3 plots, in its first panel, aggregate GNP annual growth rates, and in subsequent panels μ_1, μ_2, μ_3, and μ_{AR}, respectively. The mobility indexes

---

[18] There are, of course, situations where ignoring ϕ_y is appropriate. If M has all rows identical (and thus equal to the ergodic distribution), the index μ_{AR} equals 1, independent of ϕ_y. In this case, the artificial $\tilde{y}$ is independent (but not necessarily identically distributed) in time. It is appropriate that this case is intermediate between those discussed in the text.

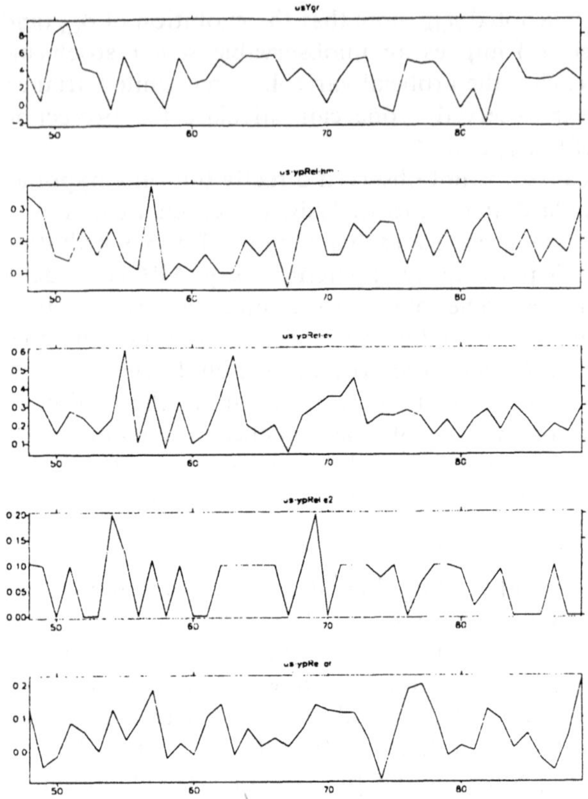

Fig. 4.3. Aggregate fluctuations and intra-distribution mobility. In order, GNP growth rates, μ_1, μ_2, μ_3, and μ_{AR} (See text for definitions.)

fluctuate; they are neither extremely persistent nor serially independent. There are periods – for instance the mid-50s – when all the indexes are large together, but also periods – for instance the 80s – where they show little co-movement.

Over the entire sample the mobility indexes all correlate positively with each other. Thus, even if no single index is perfect, at least all show the same tendencies. The largest correlation is 0.41 for μ_2 with μ_3, suggesting that even for short-run dynamics higher-order mobility and distribution convergence rates are negligible. The smallest correlation is 0.15 for μ_3 with μ_{AR}, suggesting that the location content in μ_{AR} does contain potentially important, independent information.

However, that independent information in μ_{AR} turns out not to be important for aggregate fluctuations. The contemporaneous correlation of μ_{AR} with aggregate growth rates is just 0.06, compared with 0.15 for $\mu_2$with aggregate growth rates, and -0.24 for μ_1 (for μ_3 it is 0.02). Thus, the evidence is weak that intra-distribution mobility has much to do with aggregate GNP movements.

The suggestive evidence over a single upturn, previously discussed in Section 3, turns out to be no more than suggestive. The conjectured links there have no firm basis over the entire sample.[19]

Turn now to shape dynamics. Quah (1994) provides Granger-causality calculations suggesting that it is median and the maximum of the distribution of US states' relative incomes that are most strongly dynamically correlated with aggregate growth rates. Roughly speaking, the maximum Granger-causes aggregate output (but not vice versa), while aggregate output Granger-causes the median (again, but not vice versa). Here, I report results from extending that analysis.

The table gives a compact description of tests of (Granger-causality) exclusion restrictions in trivariate VARs in aggregate growth, the median of the cross-section income distribution (in levels), and the maximum (again of the distribution in levels). Results are presented here for 2- and 5-lag VARs, extremes in the range I tried: larger systems have too few degrees of freedom to say anything precise; systems in between have results intermediate between the extremes given. In the table each cell entry is a pair of numbers giving marginal significance levels for excluding that right-hand-side bloc from the named left-hand-side variable. The first number in each cell is the marginal significance level in the 2-lag VAR; the second, the 5-lag.

The maximum's strong predictive content for aggregate growth rates manifests once again. The marginal significance level for excluding the maximum in the equation for aggregate growth is between 3 percent and 4 percent, and is the smallest of the table's off-diagonal entries. As pointed out in Quah (1994) it is *not* that any single state or region is responsible for this predictive power. Five different states, at different times, were at this point of the distribution. Connecticut was there the longest (17 non-consecutive years out of 43), but using it in the

Table. Exclusion restriction (Granger causality) tests[1] marginal significance levels

Left-hand-side Variable	Right hand side bloc GNP growth	median	maximum
GNP growth	(0.07, 0.33)	(0.95, 0.47)	(0.03, 0.04)
median	(0.23, 0.40)	(0.00, 0.00)	(0.50, 0.44)
maximum	(0.06, 0.17)	(0.02, 0.28)	(0.00, 0.00)

[1] The first number in each cell entry is the marginal significance level for excluding a right hand side bloc in a 2-lag VAR; the second, in a 5-lag VAR. Systems with lag lengths 3 and 4, as expected, give something in between. All VARs include a constant, and were estimated using annual data from 1948 through 1990.

[19] Might dynamic correlations overturn this conclusion? The answer is no. Computing bivariate vector autoregressions in aggregates and mobility indexes showed no interesting significant patterns of Granger causality. Quah (1994, 1996b) discusses other properties of the transition probabilities M.

VAR in place of the maximum loses all predictive content: marginal significance levels increased to over 75 percent in all cases.

The maximum, however, does not help to predict the median: marginal significance levels here exceed 40 percent. In shorter-lag systems, the median appears to help predict the maximum; however, that predictive power is unstable, and vanishes once longer-lag systems are considered. Unlike in bivariate systems the aggregate no longer helps to predict the median – again, marginal significance levels for excluding aggregates from the median's equation exceed 20 percent.

To conclude, the maximum of the distribution – the leading state – contains important predictive information for the aggregate. Little else is stable and significant. These conclusions are difficult to understand if one views aggregate fluctuations as aggregate disturbances moving through an aggregate propagation mechanism. Under that scenario, all parts of the distribution should behave symmetrically with the aggregate; there is no reason why different disaggregates should behave systematically differently in relation to aggregate fluctuations.

Instead, the results here suggest a different picture. Asymmetry is important across different portions of the cross section distribution. Fluctuations appear to constitute a "wave" rippling across regions; the initial impulse for that wave varies, but, on average, locates in the highest-income states.

5 Conclusions and Extensions

This paper has provided a framework for analyzing co-movements in aggregate and regional disaggregate fluctuations. It has developed new tools for modelling dynamically evolving, nonstationary distributions, and applied them to a study of US business cycles.

Section 2 presented a simplistic, naive model. The aim here was to provide a framework for relating distribution dynamics to an explicit economic model. That model served a further concrete role: it highlighted where the investigator needed more empirical facts before proceeding to further theoretical reasoning. As a by-product, however, the model also showed why certain apparently natural point-in-time statistics of cross-section distributions need not be related to aggregate fluctuations, sectoral adjustment, or regional mobility.

The distance between Section 2's theoretical analysis and the empirics in subsequent sections is large but, given available econometric tools, inevitable. The empirical analysis above cannot be interpreted as a test of any assertion from Section 2. Rather, it simply filled in groundwork – future analysis should take the investigation further.

What, however, are the substantive empirical findings at this preliminary stage? Disaggregate dynamics show interesting properties – the mobility indexes and quantile sets are not trivially constant series – but only very particular parts of those disaggregate dynamics are strongly related to aggregate fluctuations. The leading state, varying in identity over time, contains strong predictive power for aggregate fluctuations. By contrast, no single state does so. Why this should be is unclear, but is difficult to understand in models where only aggregate disturbances affect aggregate business cycles through aggregate propagation mechanisms. Instead a better picture might be one of a "wave" of regional dynamics, rippling across the national economy; its initial source varies, depending on which state is the leading one.

Theoretical work to formalize this, and sharpen the empirical analysis, is the next step in this research. One potential way forward is to build on the insights on spillovers and dynamics in Durlauf (1993).

Technical Appendix

This technical appendix contains the proof of Section 2's Proposition.

Proof of Proposition: Suppose that for some positive number ψ *there is a function* $\hat{l}$ *in* $\mathbb{M}_+$ *giving simultaneously:*

(a) *For* x *in* $\mathbb{X}$ *(a.e.* $-\ \phi_x$*),* $\hat{l}(x)$ *in* $\arg\sup_{\lambda \geq 0}\{f(\lambda, z(x)) - \psi\lambda\}$; *and*
(b) $\int \hat{l}(x)\phi_x(dx) = 1$.

Let l *be any other element of* $\mathbb{M}_+$ *such that* $\int l(x)\phi_x(dx) \leq 1$. *By* (a) *we have for* x *in* $\mathbb{X}$ *(a.e.* $-\ \phi_x$*):*

$$f(\hat{l}(x), z(x)) - \psi\hat{l}(x) \geq f(l(x), z(x)) - \psi l(x)$$

or

$$f(\hat{l}(x), z(x)) - f(l(x), z(x)) \geq \psi[\hat{l}(x) - l(x)] \ .$$

Integrating with respect to ϕ_x *on both sides gives:*

$$\begin{aligned}\int (f(\hat{l}(x), z(x)) - f(l(x), z(x)))\phi_x(dx) &\geq \psi[\int (\hat{l}(x) - l(x))\phi_x(dx)] \\ &\geq 0 \ ,\end{aligned}$$

so that

$$\int f(\hat{l}(x), z(x))\phi_x(dx) \geq \int f(l(x), z(x))\phi_x(dx) \ .$$

Thus, (a) *and* (b) *suffice for* $\hat{l}$ *to solve the maximization program. But under the hypotheses of the Proposition,* (a) *and* (i) *are equivalent.* Q.E.D.

References

Atkinson AB (1970) On the measurement of inequality. Journal of Economic Theory 2(3): 244–263
Barro RJ, Sala-i-Martin X (1991) Convergence across states and regions. Brookings Papers on Economic Activity 1: 107–182
Blanchard OJ, Katz LF (1992) Regional evolutions. Brookings Papers on Economic Activity 1: 1–75
Blanchard OJ, Quah D (1989) The dynamic effects of aggregate demand and supply disturbances. American Economic Review 79(4): 655–673
Carlino GA, Mills L (1993) Are US regional incomes converging? A time series analysis. Journal of Monetary Economics 32(2): 335–346
Ciccone A, Hall RE (1993) Productivity and the density of economic activity. Working Paper E-93-6, Hoover Institution, California 94305
Davis SJ, Haltiwanger J (1992) Gross job creation, gross job destruction, and employment reallocation. Quarterly Journal of Economics 107(3): 819–863
Durlauf SN (1993) Nonergodic economic growth. Review of Economic Studies 60(2): 349–366
Durlauf SN, Johnson P (1994) Nonlinearities in integenerational income mobility. Working paper, University of Wisconsin, Economics Department, Madison WI 53706
Engle RF, Kozicki S (1993) Testing for common features. Journal of Business and Economic Statistics 11(4): 369–380
Evans GW (1993) Sectoral imbalance and unemployment in the United Kingdom 1963–84. Oxford Economic Papers 45: 440–456
Galor O, Zeira J (1993) Income distribution and macroeconomics. Review of Economic Studies 60(1): 35–52
Geweke J, Marshall RC, Zarkin GA (1986) Mobility indices in continuous time markov chains. Econometrica 54(6): 1407–1423
Krugman P, Venables AJ (1993) Integration, specialization, and adjustment. Working paper, LSE
Lach S, Tsiddon D (1992) The behavior of prices and inflation: An empirical analysis of disaggregated price data. Journal of Political Economy 100(2): 349–389
Lilien DM (1982) Sectoral shifts and cyclical unemployment. Journal of Political Economy 90(4): 777–793
Lillard LA, Willis RJ (1978) Dynamic aspects of earning mobility. Econometrica 46(5): 985–1012
Long JB, Plosser CI (1983) Real business cycles. Journal of Political Economy 91(1): 39–69
Persson T, Tabellini G (1994) Is inequality harmful for growth? American Economic Review 84(3): 600–621
Pissarides CA, McMaster I (1990) Regional migration, wages, and unemployment: Empirical evidence and implications for policy. Oxford Economic Papers 42: 812–831
Prescott EC (1986) Theory ahead of business cycle measurement. Federal Reserve Bank of Minneapolis Quarterly Review 10(4): 9–22
Quah D (1992) The relative importance of permanent and transitory components: Identification and some theoretical bounds. Econometrica 60(1): 107–118
Quah D (1994) One business cycle and one trend from (many,) many disaggregates. European Economic Review 38(3/4): 605–613
Quah D (1995a) Coarse distribution dynamics for convergence, divergence, and polarization. Working paper, Economics Department, LSE
Quah D (1995b) International patterns of growth: II. Persistence, path dependence, and sustained take-off in growth transition. Working paper, Economics Department, LSE
Quah D (1996a) Convergence empirics across economies with (some) capital mobility. Journal of Economic Growth 1(1) forthcoming
Quah D (1996b) Empirics for economic growth and convergence. European Economic Review 40 forthcoming

Quah D (1996c) Regional convergence clusters across europe. European Economic Review 40 forthcoming
Quah D, Sargent TJ (1993) A dynamic index model for large cross sections. In: Stock J, Watson M (eds) Business Cycles, Indicators, and Forecasting, volume 28, chapter 7, 285–306. University of Chicago Press and NBER, Chicago IL
Sargent TJ (1981) Interpreting economic time series. Journal of Political Economy 89(2):213–248
Sargent TJ, Sims CA (1977) Business cycle modelling without pretending to have too much a priori economic theory. In: Sims CA (ed) New Methods in Business Cycle Research. Federal Reserve Bank of Minneapolis, Minneapolis MN 55480
Shorrocks AF (1978) The measurement of mobility. Econometrica 46(5):1013–1024
Singer B, Spilerman S (1976) Some methodological issues in the analysis of longitudinal surveys. Annals of Economic and Social Measurement 5:447–474
Stokey NL (with Edward C. Prescott), Robert EL Jr (1989) Recursive methods in economic dynamics. Harvard University Press, Cambridge MA

First version received: March 1995
Final version received: November 1995

IV Public Services, Money, and Growth Linkages

Estimating the Impact of Government Consumption on Growth: Growth Accounting and Endogenous Growth Models

STEVE DOWRICK[1]

Centre for Economic Policy Research, The Australian National University, Canberra, Act 0200, Australia

Abstract: Panel data is analyzed on government consumption and GDP growth in 116 countries, 1950–90. The purported positive impact of government growth on GDP growth is due to simultaneity bias. The negative cross-national correlation between government size and economic growth reflects in part an equilibrium relationship. Growth is a non-monotonic function of government size (measured at current domestic prices). Growth rates are increasing in government consumption expenditures up to a level around 12 percent of GDP.

Key Words: Government consumption, productivity, investment, economic growth

JEL Classification System-Numbers: H50, O50

1 Introduction

This paper attempts a thorough re-examination of the diverse cross-country evidence concerning the relationship between the provision of public services (as measured by government consumption in the national accounts) and the processes of economic growth. An anomaly within the empirical literature is evident: while GDP growth is commonly found to be positively correlated with the rate of growth of government (Ram 1986), it is negatively correlated with government consumption levels, as in Landau (1983), Barro (1991), Easterly and Rebelo (1993)[2] and Barro and Lee (1994).

These standard econometric findings are in fact evident to visual inspection of the aggregate data, as illustrated in Figures 1 and 2. There is a strong positive relationship between real GDP growth and the growth rate of government, with

[1] Helpful comments have been received from Robert Barro, Colin Hargreaves and participants at a seminar held at the Australian National University.

[2] Easterly and Rebelo (1993) also report a positive growth impact of public investment in transport and communication. This evidence on public *investment* is quite separate from the evidence presented here on public *consumption*.

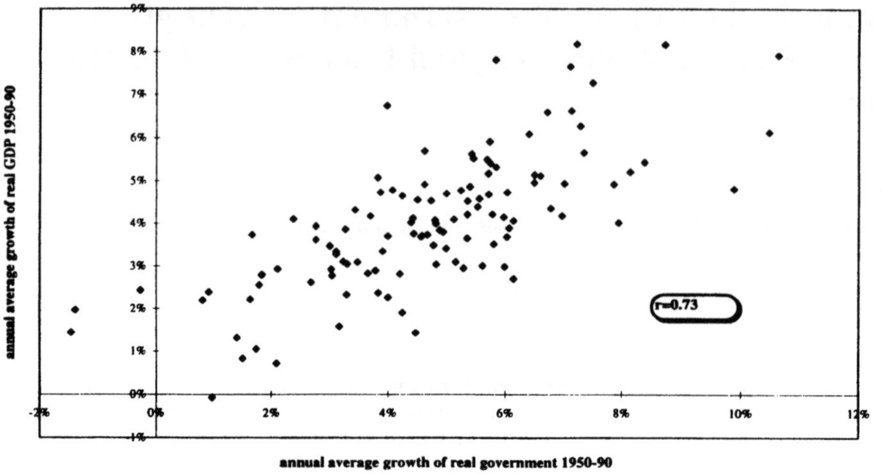

Fig. 1. Growth of real government and real GDP: 116 countries, 1950–90

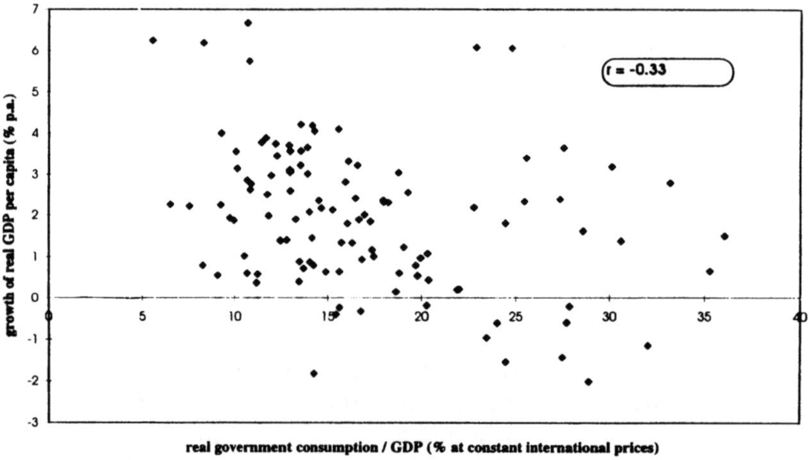

Fig. 2. Real government size and economic growth 1950–90

a simple correlation coefficient of 0.73. There is a somewhat weaker negative correlation between per capita growth and the size of government, but it is still statistically significant with a partial correlation of −0.33.

These apparently contradictory pieces of evidence can, however, be reconciled by econometric testing of models which take account of reverse causation and variations in relative prices of government services, controlling for other unobserved country-specific factors which affect both growth and the demand for government.

The first part of this analysis demonstrates that the positive correlation between growth rates is largely due to simultaneity bias, the demand for government services rising in response to both population growth and real income growth. The second, less obvious part, is to demonstrate that once we control for unobserved country-specific factors and for variations in the relative price of government services, then the impact of government consumption levels on GDP growth is indeed, as predicted by Barro's (1990) model, non-monotonic. Amongst countries with small government sectors, growth is actually an increasing function of government activity as measured by nominal public consumption.

This latter analysis highlights the distinction between real (constant price) measures of government activity and the nominal size of government, measured at current prices. Theories about growth-reducing effects of government expenditures are usually concerned with the distortionary effects of taxation. The Penn World Tables, from which many studies take their data, express real government consumption as a percentage of GDP at constant international prices, but taxes are of course raised to fund actual expenditures at current domestic prices. Fortunately, the latest version of the Penn World Tables, PWT5.6, has corrected previous errors in the measurement of relative prices, so it is now possible to calculate the price of government services relative to the price of GDP. Figure 3 displays this relative price. As expected, we observe that labour-intensive government services are relatively cheap in low-income, low-wage countries.

Figure 4 plots per capita GDP growth against the average level of nominal government consumption. It is interesting to note that the negative bivariate correlation, between growth and constant price government, now disappears. Indeed, there is some hint of the non-monotonic relationship which we investi-

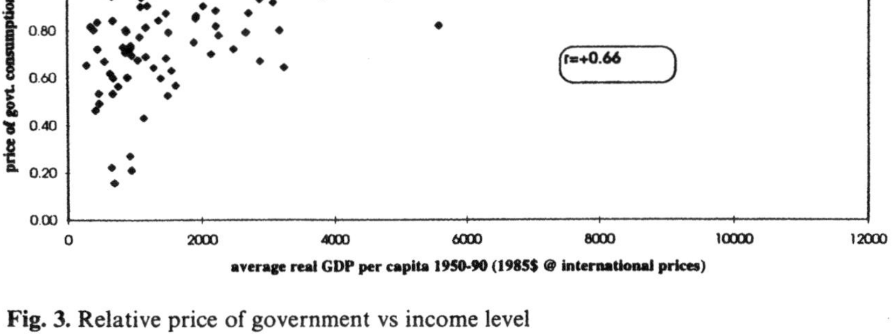

Fig. 3. Relative price of government vs income level

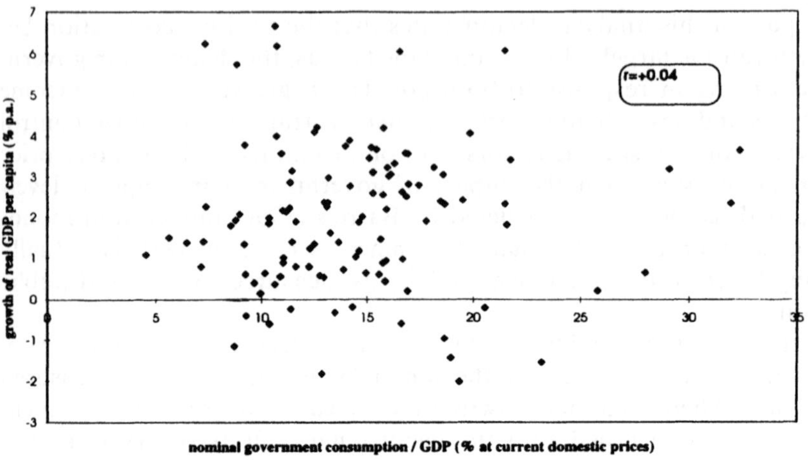

Fig. 4. Nominal government size and economic growth

Table 1. Growth rates of countries by nominal size of government sector

Quintile	Nominal size of government sector	Government size at constant international prices	Average growth of real GDP per capita
	% GDP, 1950–90, at current domestic prices	% GDP, 1950–90, at constant international prices	
q1	8.8	17.3	1.6
q2	11.4	15.8	2.1
q3	13.9	15.5	2.2
q4	16.2	19.2	2.3
q5	21.8	25.5	1.6

gate econometrically later. Grouping the observations in Figure 4 by quintiles (according to the average size of nominal government consumption, i.e., along the horizontal axis), Table 1 shows that growth rates of GDP per capita are highest for those countries with intermediate government consumption *measured at current domestic prices.* The underlying data are given in Appendix 1.

This preliminary examination of the aggregate data is of course merely suggestive. Section 3 of the paper reports a thorough econometric investigation of these relationships, disaggregating each country's data into five-year averages to take advantage of within-country variation, using panel estimation techniques to control for initial conditions and for unobserved country-specific factors. Interestingly, though, the econometric results are broadly in line with the very simple cross-tabulations of Table 1: growth rates are highest for countries with intermediate government size.

Two classes of economic models are examined in Section 2 to see what light can be shed on these relationships and on the important question of causality. The first class is based on the growth-accounting approach, assuming exogenous technological progress. If we postulate externality effects from government on the private sector, and/or systematic productivity differentials between the sectors in productivity levels, this model predicts a systematic relationship between economic growth and the *rate of growth* of government. The model is readily extended to allow for systematic sectoral differences in rates of technical progress, predicting a relationship between economic growth and the *size* of government. The principal drawback of these growth-accounting models is, however, that they rely on mechanistic and ad hoc relationships between public- and private-sector productivity.

The second and more satisfactory class of models is concerned with the properties of growth where agents make inter-temporal optimizing decisions. Government services may, ceteris paribus, influence rates of economic growth as in the first class of models – but the relationship works through increased incentives for private investment in response to the provision of a public good. On the other hand, the taxation required to finance government services reduces incentives for investment. So the relationship between government services and growth may be non-monotonic, as in Barro (1990). Moreover, if government services are set optimally, then observation across economies may reveal a spurious negative correlation between government and growth – spurious in that, rather than reflecting a direct causal relationship, it is induced by the effects of underlying technological differences on the choice of both government size and growth.

There are several potential sources of bias in econometric estimation of these models. To the extent that economic development affects the size of government, so there may be bias in single equation estimation which assumes that causality runs exclusively from government to economic growth. Furthermore, if country-specific factors affecting growth, such as the natural resource base and cultural values, are omitted from economic data sets, and if these omitted variables are correlated with the size of government, then simple cross-country regression is liable to bias.

This study attempts to deal with these problems by exploiting the time-series dimension of the Penn World Tables, as well as the cross-section dimension. Averaging the annual time series of data over five-year periods gives observations which are purged of most of the effects of short-term business cycle fluctuations, yielding a panel drawn from 116 countries with over eight hundred observations of medium-term growth rates. The availability of lagged variables makes it possible to test and control for endogeneity. Analysis of the within-country variation as well as the across-country variation in the data makes it possible to control for unmeasured country-specific effects.

Two further methodological points are dealt with. If investment and employment rates are influenced by government, then single equation estimates which treat factor supplies as exogenous, as in Ram (1986), may underestimate the full impact of government on growth. Finally, since the relative price of government services varies considerably across countries, it is important to distinguish between the real level of government services and the nominal expenditure which has to be financed by potentially distortionary taxation.

An important preliminary finding is that the rate of growth of government consumption is strongly endogenous to the rate of economic growth. This reverse causation imparts a positive bias and spurious statistical significance to single equation estimates of the impact of government growth. Our preferred specification therefore deals with government as an explanatory variable in terms of the nominal level of public consumption, controlling for endogeneity as well as for fixed country and time effects. The findings support the Barro hypothesis that public expenditures can have a non-monotonic impact on economic growth.

2 Modelling the Impact of Government Growth

We can draw together some of the recent analyses of economic growth under two broad headings. First, the simple growth accounting approach wherein factor supplies, including government, are assumed to reflect random or exogenous choices. Second, equilibrium growth models where government size and factor supplies are modelled as choice variables in an inter-temporal optimisation problem. In the latter case government and growth are jointly dependent on underlying tastes and technologies, albeit with some random influence of other factors.

2.1 The Simple Growth-Accounting Approach

There are several avenues within the growth-accounting approach whereby government size may influence measured rates of economic growth. These can be divided into hypotheses concerning differentials in either the level or the rate of growth of productivity between the public and private sectors, hypotheses concerning the external effects of government activity on productivity in the public sector, and hypotheses about the impact of government on factor supplies.

One of the simplest hypotheses is the proposition that measured productivity levels may differ systematically between government and private sectors. This difference might reflect a real productivity gap arising from the lack of market incentives and signals in the public sector. Alternatively, measured productivity in the public sector might lag that in the public sector simply because of the difficulties involved in measuring the true value of non-marketed public sector output. It is a common practice in national accounting to simply equate the value of such output with the value of the inputs, often with the level of employment[3], so denying the possibility of measuring any true productivity growth within the public sector.

It is often suggested that the government sector can have positive external effects on the private sector. Government can produce pure public goods such as information, security and social cohesion which promote private sector productivity. Government can also provide physical and human capital infrastructure which act as complementary inputs into the production process or the private sector.[4] While the empirical study presented in the next section deals only with the current services of government, as defined by national accounting procedures, some of these services such as public education may well be investments which produce a flow of services over an extended period.

It is quite possible, of course, that public sector activity may have negative external effects, particularly if viewed from the perspective of public choice theory wherein government activity may be directed according to the interests of special groups rather than the collective interests of the society.

In order to formally model these possible effects, I follow Ram (1986) and Dowrick and Gemmell (1991) in adapting Feder's (1983) approach to inter-sectoral transfer of resources within an aggregate accounting framework. I extend Ram's treatment by allowing for different rates of technical progress between the government and private sector, and show that this allows us to integrate his approach with that of Landau (1983). The model is based on separable production functions for the production of government output $G(L^G, K^G, t)$ and private sector output $P(L^P, K^P, G, t)$ where K and L refer to capital and labour services and t indexes time. Aggregate output $Y = G + P$.

Hypotheses concerning productivity differentials between the sectors can be captured by assuming that the marginal factor productivities differ systematically across the two sectors. In particular it is usual to impose a simplifying restriction that the productivity differential is a constant, δ, which is the same for each factor. Denoting marginal products by subscripts, we can write these restrictions as

$$G_L/P_L = G_K/P_K = 1 + \delta \ . \tag{1}$$

---

[3] See ABS (1989, section 4) for a description of Australian national account practices and references to the practices in other OECD countries.

[4] Carr (1989) argues that national accounting procedures misrepresent a substantial portion of government services as final outputs instead of intermediate inputs, so overestimating real final output and inducing a spurious correlation between the growth of government services and the growth of measured national output. Such arguments do not discount the possibility that government activity may indeed promote real output. The use of instrumental variables and measuring government in levels should reduce the likelihood that spurious correlation problems are significant.

The externality hypothesis is captured by assuming that government output enters into the private sector production function. Imposing constant elasticity gives

$$P_G \cdot G/P = \theta \ . \tag{2}$$

I assume that the rate of technical progress in the government sector, λ^G, is consistently above or below that found in the private sector, λ^P, so that

$$\lambda^G = (1 + \delta)(\gamma + \lambda^P) \ , \tag{3}$$

where γ is a constant which is, in the case of $\delta = 0$, simply the difference between government and private sector rates of innovation. Finally, let the rate of technical progress in the private sector be composed of a technological catch-up factor $\lambda \cdot \log(y/y^*)$, where y is per capita GDP and the star indicates the country with the highest level of y, a time-specific component, λ^t, a country-specific component, λ^i, and a randomly distributed error term ε.

$$P_t/P = \lambda \cdot \log(y/y^*) + \lambda^t + \lambda^i + \varepsilon \tag{4}$$

Differentiation of the production functions and substitution of (1) to (4) gives the following expression for the growth rate of aggregate output, $\hat{Y} = dY/Y$.

$$\begin{aligned} \hat{Y} = {} & \alpha\hat{L} + \beta\frac{dK}{Y} && (\textit{factor input growth}) \\ & \lambda^t + \lambda^i + \lambda \cdot \log(y/y^*) + \varepsilon && (\textit{private sector innovation rate}) \\ & + \frac{\delta}{1+\delta}\frac{G}{Y}\hat{G} && (\textit{factor productivity effect}) \\ & + \theta\frac{P}{Y}\hat{G} && (\textit{production externality effect}) \\ & + \left[\frac{\lambda^G}{1+\delta} - \lambda^P\right]\frac{G}{Y} && (\textit{innovation effect}) \end{aligned} \tag{5}$$

where $\alpha = LP_L/Y$ and $\beta = P_K$.

The last three terms in (5) show the way in which the various effects of government can enter the growth accounting relationship. If factor inputs are systematically less productive at the margin in the government sector than in the private sector, then government expansion that withdraws factors from the private sector will lower aggregate growth – but the magnitude of this effect will be small unless the government sector is of a substantial size in the first place. The externality effect is also dependent on the rate of growth of government output and on the relative size of the two sectors. In this case, however, the effect is larger the smaller the relative size of government – since the greater the size of the private sector, P/Y, the more widespread is the externality effect. The technological change effect, on the other hand, is a function only of the size of the government sector, not of its rate of growth.

It is important to be clear about the structure of the error term in equation (5). OLS estimation is valid only under the usual white noise assumptions. With a panel data set, containing a number of observations for each country, there may be country-specific effects which are not captured by the explanatory variables, in which case the error term will be autocorrelated within a set of country observations. Greene (1990) explains how it is possible to test for such effects and to obtain unbiased estimates if they are present. The Least Squares Dummy Variable (LSDV) estimates, corresponding to a model of fixed country-specific effects, are obtained by adding to the Ordinary Least Squares (OLS) regression a dummy variable for each country or by first differencing the data and estimating by GLS.

In other words, if there is evidence that a country is consistently above or below the regression line, we may infer that there are some unmeasured features of that country (e.g., its political and business institutions) which are systematically affecting its performance. If these unmeasured features are correlated with government size, then OLS cross-section estimates may be biased. The effect of the LSDV procedure is to ignore the cross-sectional variation in the mean values of the regression variables. While this procedure avoids bias, there is a cost of potential inefficiency due to the loss of the aggregate cross-section information.

It is worth comparing the growth equation (5) with that derived by Ram (1986, p. 1992, eq. 5). Expressing the externality effect in terms of $\hat{G}$, as Ram does, simply leads to a more complicated coefficient on the variable $(G/Y)\hat{G}$, but is algebraically equivalent to (5).[5] On the other hand, Ram's omission of technological growth from the sectoral production functions leads to his omission of the term in G/Y and to his unjustified criticism of Landau's (1983) specification which does include this term. So equation (5) is a general specification which nests both the Landau and Ram models.

Before we proceed to estimate (5) we should critically examine some of the assumptions which have been built into this model. Most fundamentally, equations such as (5) are growth accounting relationships which explain and/or help to measure the different components of aggregate growth without necessarily attributing causality. If we wish to isolate the contribution of government in a causal rather than an accounting sense, we need to examine some further assumptions which are implicit in much of the previous work. These assumptions concern the effects of government on factor supplies and the effects of economic growth on government.

First consider the relationship between government and the employment of labour services. A simplistic interpretation of the growth accounting relationship takes the employment of labour as exogenous. In this case any expansion of the government sector necessarily takes labour away from the private sector and may reduce aggregate growth. On the other hand, if government expansion

5 This is because $(P/Y)\hat{G} = (1 - G/Y)\hat{G}$. This point is due to Falvey and Gemmell (1988).

involves the employment of otherwise idle labour, there is a positive net productivity effect on aggregate growth even if marginal productivity is higher in the private sector. In terms of the growth accounting equation (5), this would be captured by the effects of an increase in labour utilization, $\hat{L}$. Unfortunately much of the empirical work carried out suffers from an absence of data on labour and capacity utilization. It is common practice to proxy labour utilization with aggregate employment data or even with population data. Without more detailed data, it then becomes impossible to say whether any positive productivity coefficient is measuring the differential between government and the private sector or between government activities and idle resources.

Similar reasoning suggests that we should also consider the effect of government on investment rates (I/Y). Treating investment as exogenous, as Ram (1986) and others have done, may underestimate the true impact of government in either a positive or negative direction. On the one hand, to the extent that the size of the public sector is an effective tool of Keynesian demand management, government expenditure may stimulate activity, expectations and investment. On the other hand, to the extent that government funding absorbs savings and distorts private returns to investment, government size may crowd out private investment. In either case, we expect investment to be related to nominal government expenditures, $p^g G/Y$, where p^g is the price of government services relative to the price of GDP.

A further important question is whether or not the growth of the economy exerts some systematic influence on government. If demand for government rises with output and income, then fast-growing economies will tend to produce faster-growing government. This positive reverse causation implies an upward bias in the estimation of the impact of government growth on economic growth.[6] On the other hand, to the extent that adjustment costs cause the supply of government services to lag behind growth in demand, a fast-growing economy may experience (temporarily) smaller government size than another country which has reached the same level of development but has been growing at a slower growth rate. If so, this negative reverse causation implies that estimates of the impact of government size (G/Y) on economic growth may be biased downwards.

The potential endogeneity of both factor supplies and government services suggests that as an alternative to the simple growth accounting model we should look to more recent attempts to model the interaction between these variables – in particular, to the models of endogenous growth.

2.2 Government and Endogenous Growth Models

Barro (1990) analyzes the role of government services in a model of endogenous growth. Growth is driven by investment which is modelled as the inter-temporal

---

[6] This point has been made forcibly by Rao (1989).

optimization decision of a representative consumer/producer in a closed economy. Public services, g, are an input along with the stock of capital, k, into a production process captured by a production function $y = k\phi(g/k)$, $\phi' > 0$ and $\phi'' < 0$ – measuring input and output on a per capita basis and assuming constant returns to scale. Government raises revenues through a flat-rate tax τ. Barro derives an expression (his equation 13) for the steady-state rate of growth of output, γ, as a function which can be simplified for our purposes to[7]

$$\gamma = (1 - \tau)\cdot[\phi(g/k)\cdot(1 - \alpha)] \tag{6}$$

where α is the elasticity of output with respect to government services and the expression in square brackets is the marginal product of capital.

Here I extend Barro's treatment by introducing the price of government services relative to the price of output as an exogenous variable, p^g. The government budget equality is now $\tau = p^g g/y$.[8]

Barro's essential result carries through, namely that the relationship between government size (now interpreted as the nominal size, τ) and growth is non-monotonic. On the one hand, government services are productive and they raise the marginal product of private capital, thereby stimulating investment and growth. On the other hand, government services have to be funded out of taxation which reduces private incentives to accumulate.

In the case of Cobb-Douglas technology, with $\phi(g/k) = (g/k)^\alpha$, the effect of increasing τ is

$$d\gamma/d(\tau) = \phi\cdot[\phi' - p^g]/p^g \;. \tag{7}$$

Concavity of ϕ implies that for some low levels of government expenditure the marginal impact of government is positive and that growth is maximized by the choice of τ which sets $\phi' = p^g$. It follows that, for a given p^g, growth is first increasing and then decreasing in government size and that the tax rate which maximizes growth is $\tau = \alpha$.

This is the first important prediction of the Barro model: that within a country, growth is a non-monotonic function of government size. The second prediction seems contradictory, that across countries we should expect to observe a monotonic negative relationship, but the argument can be illustrated readily.

Country A in Figure 5 faces a non-monotonic trade-off between government size and growth, given by the hump-shape line A in the figure. Country B, having more need for public services (a higher α in the Cobb-Douglas technology case), faces the trade off given by line B. The crucial result is that the highest growth rate that B can achieve, b^*, is lower than the highest growth rate A can achieve. An intuitive interpretation is that country B faces more severe 'public

---

7 I have simplified Barro's equation (13) by defining $\gamma = \sigma\gamma^* + \rho$, where γ^* is his growth rate, ρ is the discount rate and σ is the elasticity of marginal utility.

8 Reference to p^g as a relative price implies a multi-agent model with trade. In the representative consumer/producer model, p^g could, however, be interpreted as a measure of wastage in the process of tax collection with $p^g = 1$ representing no wastage and $p^g > 1$ representing the case of wastage.

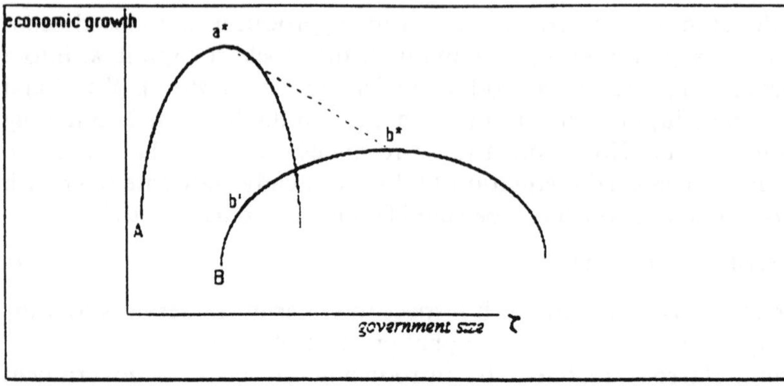

Fig. 5. Economic growth and government size in the Barro model

goods problems' (a higher α) than country A, so it is optimal for B to choose a larger public sector. At the same time, the need to impose higher distortionary taxation ensures that B cannot grow as fast as A. The implication is that if each country chooses government size to maximize growth, we should observe a negative cross-country relationship between government and growth: observing points a^* and b^* in Figure 5.

This predicted negative correlation across countries does not reflect, of course, a direct causal relationship. Indeed, if B was to reduce its government sector, its growth rate would fall. Rather, the negative correlation reflects the result that maximum attainable growth is decreasing in the extent of the 'public goods problem', α, whilst the optimal tax rate is increasing in α.

In practice, of course, government size may vary over time around a mean which might or might not correspond to the growth maximizing level. In this case, we should be able to observe *within* any one country that growth is a non-monotonic function of the size of the government sector. Utilizing time-varying data within countries, I parameterize this non-monotonic relationship as

$$\gamma_{it}(\tau, \alpha) = \psi_1 \cdot \log(\tau_{it}) + \psi_2 \cdot \tau_{it} + f(\alpha_i) \ , \qquad (8)$$

where i indexes countries, t indexes time periods and $f(\alpha_i)$ captures country-specific technological and demographic effects. Allowing for exogenous population growth and technology transfer as discussed in the context of the growth accounting model, suggests the following specification:

$$\hat{Y}_{it} = \alpha_1 \hat{P}_{it} + \alpha_2 \log(y_{it-1}) + \psi_1 \log(\tau)_{it} + \psi_2 \cdot (\tau)_{it} + \lambda_i + \varepsilon_{it} \ . \qquad (9)$$

We expect to find $\psi_1 > 0$ and $\psi_2 < 0$ in order to give the concavity of $\gamma(\tau)$ as in (7).

3 Data and Estimation

I use the data set of Summers and Heston (1991) updated to PWT5.6 which provides annual series for real GDP on an internationally comparable basis. GDP is broken down into investment, government consumption and private consumption. The time series start wherever possible from 1950. In order to abstract from short-term cyclical fluctuations, the data have been averaged over five-year periods, e.g., 1950–54, 1955–59, ..., 1985–89. Observations with missing variables have been deleted, the centrally planned economies and the principal OPEC members have been omitted, and the first five-year period has been omitted to allow for lagged instrumental variables. There are 703 observations covering 116 countries. All data are expressed as annual averages with shares of government and investment expressed as percentages of GDP.

F-tests for parameter stability on the various models suggest that there are three distinct sub-samples of countries ranked in order of per capita GDP 1970–74. The "poor" group comprises 42 countries, mostly from sub-Saharan Africa, for which there are 230 observations. The "middle" group is made up of 30 countries with 182 observations. The "rich" group has 44 countries with 291 observations. Sample means for some of the key variables are given in Table 2.

The first model tested is the growth accounting version of the "production externality" model represented by equation (5), with country specific factors, λ^i, assumed to be zero. Since the two variables measuring the growth of government in (5) are highly collinear, coefficient estimates are unstable. Accordingly I simplify the specification of (5) to include a single variable capturing the growth rate of real government, dG/G.

The estimated coefficients and *t*-statistics for the government variables are reported in the first rows of Table 3. The results are comparable to those reported by Ram (1986): there is a very strong partial correlation between output growth and government growth, with a *t*-statistic of 14. The government and investment variables are found, however, to be strongly endogenous. Re-estimation using the Two Stage Least Squares (2SLS) procedure provides a much weaker estimate, $t = 2.4$.

When country dummies are included in the regression, row 3, the OLS estimate, $t = 11$, is similar to the previous OLS estimate. Again, however, the test for endogeneity is highly significant. Re-estimation using 2SLS provides a negative estimate of the partial correlation between growth of government and growth of GDP, not significantly different from zero.

This evidence suggests that previous findings of a strong positive correlation between government growth and economic growth are due to reverse causation and omitted variable bias. It appears that the growth accounting model cannot tell us much about the impact, if any, of the growth of government on economic growth.

I proceed to investigate the alternative endogenous growth model. In this model, economic growth is affected not by the rate of growth of government but

Table 2. Descriptive statistics

Variable[1]		whole sample mean (s.d.) $n = 703$	poor sample mean (s.d.) $n = 230$	mid sample mean (s.d.) $n = 182$	rich sample mean (s.d.) $n = 291$
growth of real GDP (% p.a.)	$\hat{Y}$	3.9 (3.2)	3.5 (3.2)	4.5 (3.7)	3.9 (2.7)
growth of population (% p.a.)	$\hat{P}$	2.0 (1.1)	2.6 (0.8)	2.4 (1.0)	1.3 (1.0)
growth of workforce (% p.a.)	$\hat{L}$	2.0 (1.4)	2.3 (1.6)	2.4 (1.1)	1.3 (1.0)
per capita $GDP_{(1985\ US\ \$)}$	y_{t-1}	3660 (3600)	837 (338)	2217 (963)	6794 (3634)
investment ratio (% of GDP @ 1985 international prices)	I/Y	17.0 (9.0)	9.7 (6.7)	15.7 (6.7)	23.5 (6.8)
real government consumption (% of real GDP @ 1985 international prices)	G/Y	18.5 (7.8)	22.5 (7.6)	19.6 (8.6)	14.7 (5.3)
price of government/price of GDP	p^g	0.86 (0.30)	0.66 (0.25)	0.82 (0.22)	1.05 (0.28)
nominal government consumption (% GDP at current domestic prices)	τ	14.7 (5.8)	14.0 (5.6)	15.6 (7.3)	14.7 (4.7)
growth in real government (% p.a.)	$\hat{G}$	4.6 (4.6)	4.6 (5.4)	5.1 (5.0)	4.2 (3.5)

Source: Summers and Heston (1991) updated to PWT5.6. Nominal government consumption is CGDP × *PG/PY*.

[1] Observations are annual averages over the 7 periods, 1955–59, ..., 1980–84 and 1985–89.

by the size of the government sector, in nominal terms, relative to its optimum size. Results are reported in Table 4 for estimation of equation (9).

We find that the coefficients have signs as predicted by the Barro model of endogenous growth. Regression 1 of Table 4 replicates the standard result that real government size, G/Y, is negatively correlated with growth. Substituting nominal government size, τ, in regression 2 gives a similar result. These negative cross-country correlations are consistent with the cross-country equilibrium relationship predicted by the Barro model.

The subsequent regressions include country dummies to take account of country-specific factors that might affect both growth and the optimal size of the public sector. To allow for a non-monotonic, within-country relationship, regressions 3–7 include both nominal government consumption, τ, and its logarithm. $\log(\tau)$, as explanatory variables. There is no evidence of endogeneity, so OLS estimates are reported. The model is estimated with and without period dummies and for each of the three sub-samples as well as for the whole sample.

Table 3. The growth accounting model
Estimates of the impact of government growth on productivity growth. Estimating equation (5) with growth of real government consumption (dG/G) substituted for the two collinear terms in dG/G. $n = 703$.

Estimation Procedure	dummies	coefficients (t-statistics[1])					s.e. of estimate	adj. R^2	exogeneity test[2]
		dG/G	G/Y	I/Y	dP/P	$\log(y_{t-1})$	% p.a.		
1. OLS	period	0.32*** (14.5)	– 0.029*** (−2.2)	0.085*** (6.0)	0.16 (1.6)	−0.005 (−3.4)	2.44	0.4056	$F_{3.688} = 23$ ***
2. 2SLS	period	0.31 (2.4)	0.006 (0.2)	0.050 (2.3)	0.14 (1.0)	−0.002 (−0.8)	2.46	0.3922	
3. OLS	period & country	0.27*** (11.4)	−0.01*** (−0.6)	0.074*** (3.0)	0.08 (0.6)	−0.04 (−7.4)	2.27	0.4847	$F_{3.573} = 9.7$ ***
4. 2SLS	period & country	−0.06 (−0.4)	−0.125 (−1.2)	−0.02 (−0.4)	0.27 (1.5)	−0.04 (−5.6)	2.70	0.2764	

[1] Adjusted for heteroscedasticity-consistent covariance matrix.
[2] The test for exogeneity is a variant of the Hausman test as described by Beggs (1988) applied to the government and investment variables. The instruments are lags of the government and investment variables and prices.
*** indicates significant endogeneity at the 1% level.

Table 4. The endogenous growth model
Estimates of the impact of real (g/y) and nominal (τ) government size on economic growth

Estimation procedure	coefficients (t-statistics)					τ^* (s.e.)	s.e. of estimate	adj. R^2	exogeneity test on govt variables
	G/Y	τ	$\log(\tau)$	dP/P	$\log(y_{t-1})$		% p.a.		
1. OLS $n = 703$	−0.10 (−5.0)			0.24 (1.7)	−0.042 (−3.5)		3.07	0.0557	$t = 0.7$
2. OLS country dummies		−0.074 (−3.1)		0.20 (1.4)	−0.004 (−0.5)		2.67	0.0248	$t = -1.4$
3. OLS country dummies		−0.26 (−2.5)	0.031 (2.0)	0.13 (0.7)	−0.035 (−9)	11.9% (2.4)	2.67	0.2892	$F_{2.581} = 0.9$
4. OLS country & period dummies		−0.20 (−2.0)	0.019 (1.3)	0.20 (1.2)	−0.041 (−7)	9.7% (3.6)	2.54	0.3545	$F_{2.575} = 1.0$
5. OLS country dummies poor sample: $n = 230$		−0.26 (−1.7)	0.047 (2.1)	−0.15 (−0.4)	−0.056 (−5.9)	18.0% (4.1)	2.79	0.2444	
6. OLS country dummies mid sample: $n = 182$		−0.12 (−0.5)	−0.021 (−0.6)	0.23 (0.8)	−0.028 (−4.0)	–	3.19	0.2590	
7. OLS country dummies rich sample: $n = 291$		−0.18 (−1.5)	0.027 (1.2)	0.28 (1.1)	−0.035 (−6.5)	14.9% (6.0)	2.12	0.3723	

The overall conclusion is support for the predicted non-monotonic, within-country relationship. The coefficient on $\log(\tau)$ is positive in all cases except one (for the middle-income countries). But estimates of the size of government which maximizes growth, $\tau^* = -\psi_1/\psi_2$, are statistically significant and range between 10 and 18 percent of GDP.

Alternative non-linear specifications of the government-growth relationship come up with broadly similar estimates. For instance, a cubic specification yields coefficient estimates of $.513\tau - 2.78\tau^2 + 3.9\tau^3$, implying maximum growth at $\tau^* = 12.5\%$.

A further test of this model of endogenous growth is provided by estimating the impact of nominal and real government services on investment. Unfortunately, the data on investment aggregates public and private. Nevertheless, it is of some interest to report the results of the investment equation implied by the Barro model. The form of the investment equation is essentially the same as that of the growth equation, since it is endogenous investment which drives growth. I include the log of the price of investment goods, $\log(p^i)$ as an explanatory variable and allow for nonlinear income effects on savings and investment by including log GDP, ly, and its square. OLS results are reported because they differ hardly at all from Instrumental Variable estimation.

$$I/Y = 6.4\ (t = 3.6)\log(\tau) - 0.32(-2.8)\tau - 10.7(-21)\log(p^i) + 10.0(4.1)\log(y) - 0.45(-3)[\log(y)]^2 + \varepsilon_{it}$$

adj. $R^2 = 0.7004$; s.e. $= 4.9\%$; $n = 703$; 116 countries, 1955–59, ..., 1985–89.
$\tau^* = 19.8$ (s.e. $= 2.4$)

These results for aggregate investment across the whole sample are supportive of the endogenous growth and public goods model. The implication is that government services do tend to stimulate private investment, but financing such expenditures crowds out private investment. The crowding-out effect appears to dominate only when the public sector is particularly large, above 20 percent of GDP.

4 Concluding Comments

The simple growth accounting approach has been shown to lead to quite misleading results about the positive impact of government growth on economic growth. The strong positive correlation between the two growth rates is largely due to rising demand for public services consequent on economic growth, rather than vice versa.

We find support for the view that the negative cross-country correlation between real government size and economic growth is more an indication of an equilibrium relationship than of a direct causal relationship, perhaps reflecting the need for larger public sectors in those economies characterized by substantial market failures in the provision of public goods.

The negative cross-country correlation between growth and the size of government disappears when we control for the cost of government services and exploit the time-series dimension of the panel data to take account of unobserved country-specific differences in growth rates. Rather, the evidence is broadly consistent with the predictions of Barro's (1990) model of the role of public good provision in promoting private investment and endogenous growth. We find a statistically significant non-montonic relationship. The crowding-out effect of public finance dominates the positive public good aspect of public services only when government consumption expenditure is above some critical level. Estimates of that critical size of the public sector are imprecise, but they tend to lie in the range from 10 to 18 percent of GDP. This range encompasses some two-thirds of the 116 countries in our sample.

Appendix 1

Average values 1950–90; countries are listed in ascending order of the ratio of nominal government consumption to GDP (at current domestic prices)

	nominal government % GDP at current domestic prices	real government % GDP at constant international prices	growth of real GDP per capita % p.a.	price of government	growth of real government % p.a.	growth of real GDP % p.a.	real GDP per capita \$1985 ICP
	τ	G/Y	dy/y	p^g	dG/G	dY/Y	y
1 NEPAL	5.3	36.7	0.016	0.135	0.061	0.039	746
2 GUATEMALA	7.1	9.3	0.008	0.767	0.046	0.037	1966
3 BANGLADESH	7.2	31.5	0.013	0.231	0.060	0.037	1085
4 HONG KONG	7.2	6.5	0.058	1.119	0.071	0.077	7650
5 PARAGUAY	7.2	15.2	0.013	0.477	0.024	0.041	1590
6 MEXICO	7.4	7.3	0.024	1.000	0.065	0.051	4044
7 GUINEA	8.4	12.0	0.011	0.706	0.038	0.024	653
8 INDIA	8.6	26.8	0.019	0.320	0.048	0.040	818
9 UGANDA	8.7	19.2	0.001	0.459	0.021	0.029	623
10 COLOMBIA	8.8	10.9	0.020	0.807	0.054	0.045	2252
11 JAPAN	8.9	11.6	0.058	0.833	0.040	0.067	6677
12 PHILIPPINES	9.0	15.2	0.020	0.594	0.050	0.047	1386
13 SIERRA LEONE	9.1	30.0	0.003	0.303	0.016	0.022	1072
14 INDONESIA	9.2	13.0	0.038	0.708	0.057	0.059	1053
15 HAITI	9.3	17.3	−0.004	0.536	0.014	0.013	897
16 ZAIRE	9.3	21.1	0.006	0.440	0.031	0.033	518
17 CAPE VERDE IS.	9.8	7.3	0.027	1.437	0.099	0.048	684
18 MALI	10.3	20.4	0.000	0.505	0.033	0.023	484
19 ARGENTINA	10.3	11.7	0.004	0.897	−0.014	0.020	5142

Appendix 1 Continued

	nominal government % GDP at current domestic prices	real government % GDP at constant international prices	growth of real GDP per capita % p.a.	price of government	growth of real government % p.a.	growth of real GDP % p.a.	real GDP per capita $1985 ICP
	τ	G/Y	dy/y	p^g	dG/G	dY/Y	y
20 SRI LANKA	10.3	20.3	0.017	0.508	0.040	0.037	1392
21 BENIN	10.4	22.8	−0.006	0.467	0.008	0.022	1081
22 ETHIOPIA	10.4	18.7	0.009	0.542	0.058	0.035	284
23 DOMINICAN REP.	10.5	13.2	0.021	0.796	0.039	0.047	1659
24 PERU	10.6	15.5	0.009	0.684	0.039	0.033	2457
25 SPAIN	10.6	10.3	0.040	1.030	0.054	0.049	5435
26 SINGAPORE	10.7	9.1	0.065	1.176	0.087	0.082	5273
27 KOREA, REP.	10.8	12.4	0.058	0.894	0.058	0.078	2351
28 GHANA	10.9	16.4	0.001	0.726	0.053	0.029	900
29 THAILAND	10.9	14.2	0.036	0.769	0.064	0.061	1548
30 NIGER	10.9	24.3	−0.003	0.453	0.027	0.026	649
31 ECUADOR	11.0	16.6	0.021	0.663	0.046	0.049	2106
32 EL SALVADOR	11.1	19.4	0.010	0.569	0.048	0.035	1726
33 HONDURAS	11.1	15.5	0.008	0.715	0.051	0.041	1226
34 PAKISTAN	11.1	16.9	0.021	0.657	0.052	0.048	900
35 SWITZERLAND	11.3	8.5	0.022	1.321	0.032	0.031	11770
36 BRAZIL	11.3	12.0	0.029	0.944	0.057	0.055	2725
37 MAURITIUS	11.4	13.8	0.014	0.841	0.050	0.034	3508
38 TURKEY	11.4	11.4	0.031	1.002	0.054	0.056	2286
39 CAMEROON	11.7	20.3	0.022	0.576	0.060	0.047	983
40 BOLIVIA	11.7	19.1	0.012	0.612	0.046	0.037	1658
41 CHILE	12.0	21.5	0.014	0.559	0.031	0.033	3269
42 RWANDA	12.2	21.7	0.011	0.561	0.058	0.042	640
43 BURKINA FASO	12.2	17.4	0.004	0.694	0.042	0.028	438
44 CYPRUS	12.4	17.7	0.042	0.744	0.038	0.051	3813

45 SOUTH AFRICA	12.4	17.9	0.013	0.686	0.049	0.038	2870
46 URUGUAY	12.5	12.4	0.007	1.040	0.032	0.016	4165
47 PORTUGAL	12.8	14.8	0.046	0.879	0.065	0.050	3396
48 MADAGASCAR	12.8	15.7	−0.019	0.845	0.021	0.007	984
49 COSTA RICA	13.0	20.1	0.022	0.637	0.058	0.053	2716
50 TANZANIA	13.0	32.2	0.020	0.403	0.070	0.049	446
51 LUXEMBOURG	13.1	10.1	0.023	1.299	0.030	0.029	9851
52 MOROCCO	13.1	15.7	0.024	0.857	0.079	0.049	1387
53 ICELAND	13.4	13.9	0.031	0.944	0.056	0.046	7856
54 NICARAGUA	13.4	14.5	0.003	0.974	0.056	0.030	1923
55 TRINIDAD & TO-BAGO	13.4	7.4	0.023	1.888	0.070	0.042	7117
56 JAMAICA	13.5	10.8	0.018	1.263	0.060	0.030	2287
57 NEW ZEALAND	13.6	14.2	0.014	0.954	0.030	0.028	9185
58 ITALY	14.0	13.2	0.038	1.084	0.034	0.043	7171
59 BARBADOS	14.0	11.4	0.037	1.205	0.048	0.041	5074
60 SUDAN	14.0	27.9	−0.004	0.501	−0.003	0.024	836
61 GREECE	14.1	13.0	0.039	1.092	0.042	0.047	3986
62 BELGIUM	14.2	11.6	0.027	1.214	0.035	0.031	8144
63 KENYA	14.6	19.0	0.011	0.788	0.068	0.044	739
64 PUERTO RICO	14.7	14.0	0.038	1.065	0.066	0.051	5486
65 AUSTRALIA	14.7	11.4	0.019	1.282	0.044	0.038	10174
66 FIJI	14.8	19.0	0.021	0.782	0.054	0.042	2976
67 IVORY COAST	14.8	8.3	0.003	0.821	0.061	0.041	1595
68 NETHERLANDS	14.9	14.1	0.026	1.094	0.028	0.036	8526
69 FINLAND	15.1	13.8	0.035	1.081	0.044	0.040	7954
70 ZIMBABWE	15.2	15.0	0.006	1.097	0.079	0.040	1115
71 IRELAND	15.3	14.7	0.031	1.034	0.030	0.035	5013
72 MALAYSIA	15.4	15.7	0.040	0.980	0.067	0.066	2620
73 AUSTRIA	15.5	15.2	0.037	1.047	0.028	0.039	7456
74 NAMIBIA	15.7	21.8	0.016	0.675	0.054	0.036	2912
75 ALGERIA	15.8	17.8	0.016	0.896	0.055	0.044	2240
76 MYANMAR	15.8	21.5	0.025	0.741	0.047	0.045	405
77 PANAMA	15.8	25.2	0.020	0.622	0.045	0.046	2399

Appendix 1 Continued

	nominal government % GDP at current domestic prices	real government % GDP at constant international prices	growth of real GDP per capita % p.a.	price of government	growth of real government % p.a.	growth of real GDP % p.a.	real GDP per capita $1985 ICP
	τ	G/Y	dy/y	p^g	dG/G	dY/Y	y
78 SOMALIA	15.9	17.2	−0.010	0.937	0.061	0.027	891
79 TUNISIA	15.9	18.0	0.032	0.882	0.057	0.054	1941
80 CENTRAL AFR. REP.	15.9	29.6	−0.007	0.556	−0.015	0.014	683
81 FRANCE	16.0	15.9	0.031	1.024	0.033	0.039	8696
82 MALAWI	16.1	21.7	0.012	0.752	0.060	0.041	460
83 NORWAY	16.1	14.5	0.031	1.102	0.047	0.037	8762
84 GAMBIA	16.5	21.3	0.009	0.821	0.049	0.038	806
85 GABON	16.7	12.5	0.026	1.392	0.074	0.057	3884
86 GERMANY, WEST	16.8	15.2	0.036	1.103	0.037	0.042	8852
87 CANADA	16.8	13.0	0.025	1.301	0.044	0.041	10769
88 YUGOSLAVIA	17.0	17.3	0.029	1.024	0.017	0.037	4001
89 TAIWAN	17.0	18.4	0.057	0.940	0.072	0.082	2872
90 SENEGAL	17.1	23.6	0.003	0.728	0.018	0.028	1132
91 MALTA	17.3	20.4	0.052	0.852	0.055	0.055	3046
92 CONGO	17.4	36.7	0.023	0.475	0.057	0.052	1757
93 U.S.A.	17.7	14.9	0.018	1.205	0.033	0.030	12832
94 GUYANA	18.3	30.7	−0.012	0.585	0.015	0.008	1674
95 SYRIA	18.3	15.0	0.030	1.244	0.073	0.063	3131
96 EGYPT	18.5	29.8	0.023	0.622	0.057	0.047	1209
97 ANGOLA	18.6	25.5	−0.010	0.732	0.045	0.014	879
98 ZAMBIA	18.9	31.3	−0.007	0.609	0.040	0.023	984
99 U.K.	19.1	19.8	0.022	0.979	0.018	0.026	8583
100 MOZAMBIQUE	19.1	30.7	−0.014	0.619	0.017	0.011	1148
101 LESOTHO	19.5	15.6	0.038	1.284	0.105	0.061	712
102 DENMARK	19.5	18.4	0.024	1.044	0.038	0.029	9193

103 TOGO	19.8	75.4	0.019	0.789	0.041	0.048	576
104 MAURITANIA	20.2	55.3	0.000	0.802	0.009	0.024	874
105 SWAZILAND	20.2	26.9	0.025	0.757	0.046	0.057	2309
106 GUINEA-BISS.	20.4	24.2	0.010	0.842	0.048	0.030	644
107 BOTSWANA	21.2	25.8	0.047	0.829	0.106	0.079	1355
108 COMOROS	21.5	94.6	0.001	0.872	0.052	0.031	633
109 SWEDEN	21.6	80.0	0.023	1.066	0.037	0.028	10109
110 CNAD	21.9	28.5	−0.021	0.766	0.010	−0.001	593
111 SEYCHELLES	22.3	28.6	0.038	0.763	0.084	0.054	2155
112 ISRAEL	25.5	31.1	0.041	0.797	0.075	0.073	5691
113 SURINAME	26.1	24.4	0.005	1.070	0.049	0.019	2877
114 PAPUA-N. GUINEA	27.9	38.2	0.005	0.738	0.018	0.028	1703
115 REUNION	33.0	30.5	0.033	1.144	0.081	0.052	2253
116 JORDAN	33.2	27.2	0.043	1.256	0.071	0.066	1240

References

ABS (1989) Development of multifactor productivity estimates for Australia. Australian Bureau of Statistics, cat 5229.0, Canberra

Barro RJ (1990) Government spending in a simple model of endogenous growth. Journal of Political Economy 98(5:2):S103–S126

Barro RJ (1991) Economic growth in a cross-section of countries. Quarterly Journal of Economics 56:407–443

Barro RJ, Lee J-W (1994) Losers and winners in economic growth. Proceedings of the World Bank Annual Conference on Development Economics 1993, 267–303

Beggs JJ (1988) Diagnostic testing in applied econometrics. Economic Record 64(185):81–101

Carr JL (1989) Government size and economic growth: Comment. American Economic Review 79(1):267–271

Dowrick S, Gemmell N (1991) Industrialisation, catching up and economic growth: a comparative study across the world's capitalist economies. Economic Journal 101(405):263–275

Dowrick S, Nguyen DT (1989) OECD comparative economic growth 1950–85: catch-up and convergence, American Economic Review 79(5):1010–1030

Easterly W, Rebelo S (1993) Fiscal policy and economic growth: An empirical investigation. Journal of Monetary Economics 32(3):417–458

Falvey RE, Gemmell N (1988) Government size and economic growth. Mimeo, Australian National University, Canberra

Feder G (1983) On exports and economic growth. Journal of Development Economics 12:59–73

Greene WH (1990) Econometric Analysis. New York, Macmillan

Landau D (1983) Government expenditure and economic growth: A cross-country study. Southern Economic Journal 49:783–792

Ram R (1986) Government size and economic growth: A new framework and some evidence from cross-section and time-series data. American Economic Review 76(1):191–203

Rao VVB (1989) Government size and economic growth: Comment. American Economic Review 79(1):272–284

Summers R, Heston A (1991) The Penn world table (Mark 5): An expanded set of international comparisons, 1950–88. Quarterly Journal of Economics 106(2):327–368

First version received: March 1995
Final version received: November 1995

Growth and the Neutrality of Money

PAUL EVANS

Department of Economics, Ohio State University, Columbus, Ohio 43210-1172, USA

Abstract: Using two simple stochastic growth models that nest both exogenous and endogenous growth, this paper shows that money should not be neutral in the long run if it is not neutral in the short run and if growth is endogenous. By contrast, if growth is exogenous, money should be neutral in the long run. The paper also tests whether money is neutral in the long run, finding no contrary evidence. Given that money is not neutral in the short run, this finding indicates that exogenous growth cannot be rejected in favor of endogenous growth.

Key Words: Growth theory, endogenous growth, exogenous growth, monetary theory, neutrality of money

JEL Classification System-Numbers: O40, C40

I Introduction

Recent years have witnessed an enormous resurgence of interest in formulating growth models and testing them empirically. Following the seminal articles of Paul Romer (1986) and Robert Lucas (1988), the theoretical growth literature has primarily sought to endogenize the trend growth rate, which had been treated as an exogenous parameter in the earlier vintage of growth models formulated by Robert Solow (1956) and David Cass (1965) *inter alia.*

This paper makes two contributions. First, using two simple stochastic growth models that nest both exogenous and endogenous growth, the paper shows that money should not be neutral in the long run if it is not neutral in the short run and if growth is endogenous. Indeed, the long-run effect of money on output should approximately equal its short-run effect. By contrast, if growth is exogenous, money should be neutral in the long run.

The intuition for this result is straightforward. Suppose that workers supply an unusually large amount of labor following a permanent increase in the money supply. Some of the resulting increase in output is accumulated as reproducible factors of production since households wish to smooth their consumptions. If reproducible factors experience constant social returns to scale as in endogenous growth models, this accumulation creates no force leading households to decumulate the extra reproducible factors. Output therefore rises permanently in response to the permanent increase in the money supply. With diminishing returns, by contrast, the rate of return on reproducible factors is depressed, inducing decumulation until their original levels are restored.

The second contribution of the paper is to test whether growth is exogenous by testing whether money is neutral in the long run. No evidence is found that money positively affects output in the long run. Given that it does positively affect output in the short run, one cannot reject exogeneous growth in favor of endogenous growth.[1]

Charles Jones (1995) has performed a similar test of endogenous growth theories against exogenous growth theories. Unfortunately, his test requires that the ratio of gross investment to gross output be difference-stationary, a restriction ruled out by all growth theories that predict balanced growth paths and rejected for the United States by Robert King, Charles Plosser, James Stock, and Mark Watson (1991).[2] The test employed here does not require this restriction.

Many other papers have tested whether growth is endogenous. Why should yet another test be performed at this point? The reason is that virtually all of these tests have used ordinary least squares to fit cross-sectional regressions relating the average growth rate of per capita output over some period to its initial value and country characteristics.[3] My 1995 paper shows that the resulting estimates are seriously biased and that the inferences based on them are unreliable.

The rest of the paper is organized as follows. Sections II and III formulate two simple stochastic growth models for demonstrating the basic theoretical result. Section IV employs the framework developed by Mark Fisher and John Seater (1993) to develop two tests for the long-run neutrality of money. Section V then performs these tests for 27 countries. Finally, section VI summarizes the paper and offers a few conclusions.

[1] Interestingly, Lucas (1980), who could not reject the null hypothesis that money in the United States is neutral in the long run, has provided strong evidence that growth is exogenous.

[2] He has also performed two other tests that are valid under much less stringent conditions. These tests, however, rely primarily the univariate stochastic properties of per capita output.

[3] A far from exhaustive list is Roger Kormendi and Philip Meguire (1985); William Baumol (1986); Bradford De Long (1988); Robert Barro (1991); De Long and Lawrence Summers (1991); Barro and Xavier Sala-i-Martin (1992); Gregory Mankiw, David Romer, and David Weil (1992); Robert King and Ross Levine (1993); Jose De Gregorio (1993); William Easterly (1993); Alberto Alesina and Dani Rodrik (1994); and Torsten Persson and Guido Tabellini (1994).

II Theoretical Discussion

This section lays out a simple and tractable stochastic growth model that nests both exogenous growth and endogenous growth. The model is special in many ways because several restrictive assumptions are made for the sake of tractability. Nevertheless, results similar to the ones derived below should hold in a wide class of models.

Consider an economy inhabited by a government and a constant unit population of identical households that live in periods $t = 0, 1, 2, \ldots$. Following Romer (1986), I assume that every household is endowed with positive stocks $\exp(k_0)$ and $\exp(m_0)$ of capital and money at the beginning of period 0 and a technology

$$y_t = (1 - \kappa)n_t + \kappa k_t + (\lambda - \kappa)\bar{k}_t + q_t \,, \qquad 0 < \kappa < 1 \,, \qquad \kappa \leq \lambda \leq 1 \,, \quad (2.1)$$

for producing gross output $\exp(y_t)$ using $\exp(n_t)$ units of labor, $\exp(k_t)$ units of own capital, and an average stock $\exp(\bar{k}_t)$ of capital held by all households. In equation (2.1), κ and λ are parameters, and q_t is a productivity shock. The parameter λ measures the extent to which the physical capital held by some households produces spillovers onto the productivity of other households. The case $\lambda = \kappa$ corresponds to no spillovers; $\lambda = 1$ results in endogenous growth as shown below; and $\kappa < \lambda < 1$ corresponds to positive spillovers too weak to produce endogenous growth because the reproducible factor capital continues to experience diminishing social returns so long as $\lambda < 1$.

Each household is composed of two agents: a worker that supplies $\exp(l_t)$ units of labor and a capitalist that demands $\exp(n_t)$ units of labor. Each worker sets w_t, the logarithm of the nominal wage rate, during period $t - 1$ so that l_t is expected to be zero conditional on all information known at the time and then supplies whatever quantity of labor is demanded by the capitalist during period t at the predetermined nominal wage rate $\exp(w_t)$. This method of making money nonneutral in the short run has been widely used in the literature since the seminal article of Stanley Fischer (1977). It has been justified on the basis of three casual observations: nominal wage rates appear to be predetermined; short-run employment and hours decisions appear to be left to the discretion of employers; and such a process might conceivably be the outcome of optimizing behavior in the presence of transaction costs that make spot markets in labor prohibitively expensive to operate. It is not without critics, however; e.g., Barro (1977). I adopt it primarily because it is analytically tractable.

The timing within each period is as follows. Households begin the period with the stocks of capital and money that they acquired in the previous period. Next, Walrasian spot markets for goods and money open. Households then demand and supply labor, produce output, consume and invest, and demand money. After the markets have cleared, they close. Households then set the nominal wage rate for the next period. Finally, all households receive identical cash transfers from the government. The size of the transfer is uncertain until the government actually gives it.

Taking this environment as given, each household maximizes the objective function

$$E_0 \sum_{t=0}^{\infty} \beta^t[c_t + \omega(m_t^d - p_t)] , \qquad 0 < \beta < 1 , \qquad \omega > 0 , \tag{2.2}$$

subject to the sequence of budget constraints

$$\begin{aligned} &\exp(c_t) + I_t + [\exp(m_t^d) - \exp(m_t)]/\exp(p_t) \\ &\quad \leq \exp(y_t) + \exp(w_t - p_t)[\exp(l_t) - \exp(n_t)] , \qquad t = 0, 1, 2, \dots ; \end{aligned} \tag{2.3}$$

the sequence of accumulation equations

$$\exp(k_{t+1}) \leq (1 - 1)\exp(k_t) + I_t \tag{2.4}$$

and

$$\exp(m_{t+1}) \leq \exp(m_t^d) + \tau_{t+1} , \qquad t = 0, 1, 2, \dots ; \tag{2.5}$$

a sequence of production functions of the form (2.1); and a sequence of solvency constraints. In equations (2.2)–(2.5), $\exp(c_t)$ and I_t are the household's consumption and gross investment during period t; $\exp(m_t)$ and $\exp(m_t^d)$ are the stocks of money carried into and demanded during period t; τ_{t+1} is the cash transfer received from the government at the end of period t; p_t is the logarithm of the price level during period t; and β and ω are parameters. The household takes p_t, w_t, k_t, m_t, τ_t, $\bar{k}_t$, and the distributions of their future values as given.

Analyzing the neutrality of money would not be sensible without a demand for money. For this reason, real money balances enter the objective function in order to induce a demand for money. Three simplifying assumptions in this model are noteworthy. First, the production function has the Cobb-Douglas form. Second, momentary utility is separable and logarithmic in consumption and real money balances. Third, capital depreciates completely in a single period; see equation (2.4). These assumptions are required in order for the model to be tractable.

The first-order conditions for each household's problem are

$$1/\exp(c_t) = \beta E_t\{[1/\exp(c_{t+1})][\kappa \exp(y_{t+1} - k_{t+1})]\} , \tag{2.6}$$

$$\ln(1 - \kappa) + y_t - n_t = w_t - p_t , \tag{2.7}$$

$$\begin{aligned} &E_t\{\omega \exp(p_{t+1} - m_{t+1}) \\ &\quad - [\exp(p_{t+1} - p_t)\kappa \exp(y_{t+1} - k_{t+1}) - 1][1/\exp(c_{t+1})]\} = 0 , \end{aligned} \tag{2.8}$$

and

$$\begin{aligned} &\exp(c_t) + \exp(k_{t+1}) + [\exp(m_{t+1}) - \exp(m_t) - \tau_{t+1}]/\exp(p_t) \\ &\quad = \exp(y_t) + \exp(w_t - p_t)[\exp(l_t) - \exp(n_t)] . \end{aligned} \tag{2.9}$$

In addition,

$$E_{t-1} l_t = 0 \tag{2.10}$$

and

$$l_t = n_t \ . \tag{2.11}$$

Finally, solvency requires the following transversality condition:

$$\lim_{i\to\infty} E_t \beta^i \exp(k_{t+i+1} - c_{t+i}) = 0 \ . \tag{2.12}$$

The sole activity of the government is to print money and distribute it as equal lump-sum cash transfers to all households. Its budget constraint is therefore

$$\tau_{t+1} = \exp(m_{t+1}) - \exp(m_t) \ , \tag{2.13}$$

where m_t is the logarithm of the money supply.

I assume that m_t and q_t are generated by the processes

$$\Delta m_t = \pi + \mu_t \tag{2.14}$$

and

$$q_t = \gamma + \sum_{i=1}^{n} \psi_i q_{t-i} + \zeta_t \ , \tag{2.15}$$

where π, γ, and $\psi_1, \psi_2, \ldots, \psi_n$ are parameters for which $\exp(\pi) > \beta$ and all roots of $1 - \sum_{i=1}^{n} \psi_i L^i$ lie on or outside the unit circle;[4] and μ_t and ζ_t are identically distributed error terms that are serially and mutually independent with zero means and finite variances.

Equilibrium is characterized by the stochastic processes (2.14) and (2.15) for m_t and q_t; fixed initial conditions for k_0, m_0, w_0, and $q_{-1}, q_{-2}, \ldots, q_{-n+1}$; and functions that map $k_t, m_t, w_t, q_t, q_{t-1}, \ldots, q_{t-n+1}$ onto $n_t, l_t, y_t, c_t, k_{t+1}, m_t^d, p_t$, and w_{t+1} and that satisfy equations (2.1), (2.6)–(2.8), (2.10)–(2.12), and the following equilibrium conditions:

$$m_t^d = m_t \ , \tag{2.16}$$

$$k_t = \bar{k}_t \ , \tag{2.17}$$

and

$$\exp(c_t) + \exp(k_{t+1}) = \exp(y_t) \ . \tag{2.18}$$

---

[4] A natural decomposition of the productivity shock is

$$q_t = (1 - \lambda) a_t + z_t \ ,$$

where a_t is difference-stationary and z_t is stationary. The term a_t contributes a Harrod-neutral stochastic trend to q_t if, and only if, $0 < \lambda < 1$, while the term z_t contributes a Hicks-neutral component. In that case, the polynomial $\psi(L)$ has no roots on the unit circle if $\lambda = 1$ and exactly one root if $0 < \lambda < 1$. The text refers to the latter case as exogenous growth because all growth is generated by the exogenously given stochastic trend a_t. Note that the above form for q_t is the only one that permits balanced growth under both $0 < \lambda < 1$ and $\lambda = 1$.

According to equations (2.16)–(2.18), each household chooses to demand the money supplied by the government, to hold capital equal to the average held by all households, and to consume and invest its gross output. Note that equations (2.9), (2.11), and (2.13) imply equation (2.18).

The above model implies that[5]

$$c_t = \ln(1 - \beta\kappa) + y_t \tag{2.19}$$

and

$$k_{t+1} = \ln \beta\kappa + y_t \ . \tag{2.20}$$

Applying the operator E_{t-1} to both members of equation (2.7), noting that w_t is known in period $t - 1$, and substituting equations (2.11) and (2.10) into the resulting equation yields

$$w_t = \ln(1 - \kappa) + E_{t-1}(p_t + y_t) \ . \tag{2.21}$$

Plugging equation (2.21) into equation (2.7) and rearranging produces

$$n_t = (p_t + y_t) - E_{t-1}(p_t + y_t) \ . \tag{2.22}$$

Equations (2.1), (2.17), (2.20), and (2.22) then imply that

$$y_t = \lambda \ln \beta\kappa + \lambda y_{t-1} + (1 - \kappa)[(p_t + y_t) - E_{t-1}(p_t + y_t)] + q_t \ , \tag{2.23}$$

Substituting equations (2.19), (2.20), and (2.23) into equation (2.8) and rearranging results in

$$\begin{aligned}
&E_t\{\omega \exp(p_{t+1} + y_{t+1} - m_{t+1}) \exp(-y_{t+1}) \\
&\qquad - [\exp(p_{t+1} - p_t)\kappa \exp(y_{t+1} - \ln \beta\kappa - y_t) - 1] \\
&\qquad \times \exp[-\ln(1 - \beta\kappa) - y_{t+1}]\} \\
&\quad = E_t\{\omega \exp(p_{t+1} + y_{t+1} - m_{t-1}) - (1 - \beta\kappa)^{-1} \\
&\qquad \times [\beta^{-1} \exp(p_{t+1} + y_{t+1} - p_t - y_t) - 1]\} \exp(-y_{t+1}) \\
&\quad = E_t\{\omega \exp(p_{t+1} + y_{t+1} - m_{t+1}) - (1 - \beta\kappa)^{-1} \\
&\qquad \times [\beta^{-1} \exp(p_{t+1} + y_{t+1} - p_t - y_t) - 1]\} \exp\{-\lambda \ln \beta\kappa - \lambda y_t - (1 - \kappa) \\
&\qquad \times [p_{t+1} + y_{t+1} - E_t(p_{t+1} + y_{t+1})] - q_{t+1}\} \\
&\quad = [\exp(-\lambda \ln \beta\kappa - \lambda y_t)/(1 - \beta\kappa)] E_t \exp(-q_{t+1}) \\
&\qquad \times [1 + (1 - \beta\kappa)\omega \exp(p_{t+1} + y_{t+1} - m_{t+1}) - \beta^{-1} \\
&\qquad \times \exp(p_{t+1} + y_{t+1} - p_t - y_t)] \\
&\qquad \times \exp\{(\kappa - 1)[p_{t+1} + y_{t+1} - E_t(p_{t+1} + y_{t+1})]\} = 0 \, .
\end{aligned} \tag{2.24}$$

[5] Equations (2.6) and (2.18) become identities if equations (2.19) and (2.20) are substituted into them.

According to equation (2.14), m_t is a random walk. For this reason, a change in m_t does not affect the distributions of Δm_{t+1}, Δm_{t+2}, Δm_{t+3}, ... conditional on the information known during period t. One might therefore expect that a parameter ρ exists such that

$$p_t + y_t = \ln \rho + m_t \ . \tag{2.25}$$

Canceling $\exp(-\lambda \ln \beta\kappa - \lambda y_t)/(1 - \beta\kappa)$ from both members of equation (2.24) and substituting from equations (2.25) and (2.14) produces

$$\begin{aligned} &E_t \exp(-q_{t+1})[1 + (1 - \beta\kappa)\omega\rho - \beta^{-1} \exp(\Delta m_{t+1})] \\ &\qquad \times \exp[(\kappa - 1)(m_{t+1} - E_t m_{t+1})] \\ &\quad = E_t \exp(-q_{t+1})[1 + (1 - \beta\kappa)\omega\rho - \beta^{-1} \exp(\pi + \mu_{t+1})] \exp[(\kappa - 1)\mu_{t+1}] \\ &\quad = E_t \exp(-q_{t+1}) E_t\{[1 + (1 - \beta\kappa)\omega\rho] \\ &\qquad \times \exp[(\kappa - 1)\mu_{t+1}] - \beta^{-1} \exp(\pi + \kappa\mu_{t+1})\} = 0 \ . \end{aligned} \tag{2.26}$$

The third line of equation (2.26) derives from the mutual independence of the error terms μ_t and ζ_t in equations (2.14) and (2.15). Hence, equation (2.25) holds with

$$\rho = \{\beta^{-1} \exp(\pi) E_t \exp(\kappa\mu_{t+1})/E_t \exp[(\kappa - 1)\mu_{t+1}] - 1\}/[\omega(1 - \beta\kappa)] \ . \tag{2.27}$$

which is constant since μ_t is independently and identically distributed. Finally, substituting equation (2.25) into equation (2.23) yields

$$y_t = \lambda \ln \beta\kappa + \lambda y_{t-1} + (1 - \kappa)(m_t - E_{t-1} m_t) + q_t \ , \tag{2.28}$$

Money is said to be neutral if an unexpected permanent change in the money supply leaves all real variables unchanged. Such an intervention can be performed in the above model by changing μ_t by, say, 1 while holding everything else constant. Equations (2.14) and (2.28) then imply that $E_t y_{t+i}$ increases by $(1 - \kappa)\lambda^i$ for $i = 0, 1, 2, \ldots$. Money is clearly not neutral in the short run. In the long run, it is neutral or not according as growth is exogenous ($\lambda < 1$) or endogenous ($\lambda = 1$).[6]

Even though this result has been obtained in a very special model, it should hold in a wide class of models. The reason is plain to see. Without diminishing returns, no force leads households to decumulate (accumulate) reproducible factors following periods in which workers mistakenly supply too much (little) labor. By contrast, with diminishing returns, the return to reproducible factors falls (rises), inducing decumulation (accumulation) until their original levels are restored.

---

6 This model also implies that if $\lambda < 1$, money is superneutral in the long run. I do not emphasize this result because it can be easily overturned. By contrast, long-run monetary neutrality is a very general property of exogenous growth models.

III Further Theoretical Discussion

The theoretical discussion of the previous section was carried out using what has been called an AK model. In many ways, such a discussion is quite general since endogenous growth occurs if, and only if, some set of reproducible factors of production is produced with constant social returns in terms of themselves. Nevertheless, it may be useful to demonstrate that the same result holds in a model in which technology evolves endogenously over time. This section carries out such a demonstration.

The model considered here is identical to the one considered in the previous section except for the technology. I assume that

$$y_t = (1 - \kappa)(n_t + x_t) + \kappa k_t \ , \qquad 0 < \kappa < 1 \ , \tag{3.1}$$

with

$$x_t = \delta + v n_{t-1} + \lambda x_{t-1} + q_t/(1 - \kappa) \ , \qquad v > 0 \ , \qquad 0 < \lambda \leq 1 \ , \tag{3.2}$$

where κ, λ, δ, and v are parameters and q_t is an error term with the properties specified in the previous section. If $\lambda = 1$, growth is endogenous in the sense that the average growth rate of output depends on the average employment of labor. By contrast, if $\lambda < 1$, the average growth rate of output equals the mean of Δg_t, an exogenous parameter.

Equation (3.1) states that $\exp(y_t)$, gross output, is related to $\exp(n_t + x_t)$, the effective units of labor, and $\exp(k_t)$, the stock of capital, by a Cobb-Douglas production function with shares $1 - \kappa$ and κ for labor and capital. According to equation (3.2), the technology factor $\exp(x_t)$ is related to its value in the previous period and to the labor employed then. For the purposes of this section, equation (3.2) is best regarded as describing learning by doing that is entirely external to individual capitalists. Alternatively, it can be regarded as the "reduced form" for a model in which the labor allocated to R&D is increasing in its aggregate employment.

Analysis and manipulations similar to those in the previous section produce

$$(1 - \lambda L)(1 - \kappa L)y_t = (1 - \lambda)\kappa \ln \beta\kappa + (1 - \kappa)\delta$$
$$+ (1 - \kappa)[1 + (v - \lambda)L](m_t - E_{t-1}m_t) + q_t \ , \tag{3.3}$$

where L is the lag operator. Equation (3.3) has implications similar to those of equation (2.28). In particular, money is not neutral in the short run and is neutral or not in the long run according as growth is exogenous ($\lambda < 1$) or endogenous ($\lambda = 1$).

This result holds for reasons similar to those given in the previous section. If technology (a reproducible factor here) can be accumulated without diminishing returns, no force leads to decumulation (accumulation) following periods in which workers mistakenly supply too much (little) labor. By contrast, with diminishing returns, the return to technology in its own production falls (rises), resulting in decumulation (accumulation) until its original level is restored. Given that this result should hold quite generally, one should be able to test whether growth is exogenous by simply testing whether money is neutral in the long run. Section IV formulates such a test, and section V performs it.

IV Econometric Specification

Suppose that y_{it} and m_{it}, the logarithms of gross output and the money supply for country i during period t, are observed for $i = 1, 2, \ldots, I$ and $t = -r + 1, -r + 2, \ldots, T$. Suppose further that they are difference-stationary and are not cointegrated with each other, a natural assumption for two reasons. First, it is highly implausible that y_{it} is integrated with an order larger than one, that m_{it} is integrated with an order less than one, and that the logarithms of the *nominal* money supply and *real* output are cointegrated with each other. Second, Fisher and Seater have demonstrated that money must be neutral (nonneutral) in the long run if the order of integration of m_{it} is greater than (less than) that of y_{it}. Consequently, if both possibilities are to be nested, y_{it} and m_{it} must have the same order of integration, which most plausibly equals one.

Given that this supposition holds, the processes generating each pair of variables y_{it} and m_{it} can be approximated to any desired accuracy by

$$\Delta y_{it} = \sum_{j=1}^{r} \varphi_{i11j} \Delta y_{i,t-j} + \sum_{j=0}^{r} \varphi_{i12j} \Delta m_{i,t-j} + u_{it} \tag{4.1}$$

and

$$\Delta m_{it} = \sum_{j=0}^{r} \varphi_{i21j} \Delta y_{i,t-j} + \sum_{j=1}^{r} \varphi_{i22j} \Delta m_{i,t-j} + v_{it} \tag{4.2}$$

for some sufficiently large integer r. In equations (4.1) and (4.2), the φs are parameters and $[u_{it}, v_{it}]$ is a serially uncorrelated error vector with a zero mean vector and the covariance matrix diag$[\sigma_i^2, \varsigma_i^2]$.[7] Stationarity requires that all of the roots of the polynomial $(1 - \sum_{j=1}^{r} \varphi_{i11j} L^j)(1 - \sum_{j=1}^{r} \varphi_{i22j} L^j) - (\sum_{j=0}^{r} \varphi_{i12j} L^j)(\sum_{j=0}^{r} \varphi_{i21j} L^j)$ lie outside the unit circle. In addition, I posit that all of the roots of the polynomials $1 - \sum_{j=1}^{r} \varphi_{i11j} L^j$ and $1 - \sum_{j=1}^{r} \varphi_{i22j} L^j$ lie outside the unit circle. This econometric model for y_{it} and m_{it} is structural in the sense that the covariance between u_{it} and v_{it} is zero but φ_{i120} and φ_{i210} need not be zero.

[7] For simplicity and without loss of generality, I do not include intercepts in equations (4.1) and (4.2). By contrast, I included them in all estimated regressions.

Fisher and Seater have shown that θ_i, the long-run effect of an exogenous increase in m_{it} on y_{it}, is given by

$$\theta_i = \sum_{j=0}^{r} \varphi_{i12j} \Big/ \left(1 - \sum_{j=1}^{r} \varphi_{i11j}\right) . \tag{4.3}$$

The theory developed in the previous section therefore implies that the null hypothesis

$$\mathscr{H}_{0i}: \theta_i = 0$$

holds if growth is exogenous and the alternative hypothesis

$$\mathscr{H}_{1i}: \theta_i > 0$$

holds if money is not neutral in the short run and growth is endogenous. Indeed, θ_i should approximately equal the short-run effect of money on output, a potentially substantial magnitude. For example, the model of the previous section implies that θ_i is labor's share.

Suppose that ordinary least squares is applied to equation (4.1) with a sample consisting of observations for periods 1, 2, ..., T and initial conditions for periods 0, $-1, \ldots, -r+1$ and that the estimator

$$\hat{\theta}_i = \sum_{j=0}^{r} \hat{\varphi}_{i12j} \Big/ \left(1 - \sum_{j=1}^{r} \hat{\varphi}_{i11j}\right) \tag{4.4}$$

is calculated from the estimators $\hat{\varphi}_{i120}, \hat{\varphi}_{i121}, \ldots, \hat{\varphi}_{i12r}, \hat{\varphi}_{i111}, \hat{\varphi}_{i112}, \ldots, \hat{\varphi}_{i11r}$. It is straightforward to show that[8]

$$\operatorname*{p\,lim}_{T\to\infty} \hat{\Phi}_i = \Phi_i + \xi_i \sigma_i^2 \begin{bmatrix} H_{i11} & H_{i12} \\ H_{i21} & H_{i22} \end{bmatrix} e ; \tag{4.5}$$

where Φ is the $(2r+1) \times 1$ vector whose jth entry is φ_{i11j} for $j = 1, 2, \ldots, r$ and $\varphi_{i,1,2,j-r-1}$ for $j = r+1, r+2, \ldots, 2r+1$; $\hat{\Phi}$ is the estimator of Φ;

$$\begin{bmatrix} H_{i11} & H_{i12} \\ H_{i21} & H_{i22} \end{bmatrix} \equiv \begin{bmatrix} Q_{i11} & Q_{i12} \\ Q_{i21} & Q_{i22} \end{bmatrix}^{-1} ;$$

Q_{i11} is the $r \times r$ matrix whose (j, k)th entry is $p \lim_{T\to\infty} \sum_{t=1}^{T} \Delta y_{i,t-j} \Delta y_{i,t-k}/T$; Q_{i12} and Q'_{i21} are the $r \times (r+1)$ matrix whose (j, k)th entry is $p \lim_{T\to\infty} \sum_{t=1}^{T} \Delta y_{i,t-j} \Delta m_{i,t+1-k}/T$; Q_{i22} is the $(r+1) \times (r+1)$ matrix whose

[8] By construction $p \lim_{T\to\infty} \sum_{t=1}^{T} \Delta y_{i,t-j} u_{it}/T = p \lim_{T\to\infty} \sum_{t=1}^{T} \Delta m_{i,t-j} u_{it}/T = 0$ for $j = 1, 2, \ldots, r$. Stacking equations (3.1) and (3.2) and premultiplying by the inverse of the matrix

$$\begin{bmatrix} 1 & -\varphi_{i120} \\ -\varphi_{i210} & 1 \end{bmatrix}$$

produces the vector autoregressive system whose error term in the second equation takes the form $\xi_i u_{it} + v_{it}$, where ξ_i is the (2,1)th entry of the inverse; that is, the right-hand member of equation (3.6). Hence, $p \lim_{T\to\infty} \sum_{t=1}^{T} \Delta m_{it} u_{it}/T = \xi_i \sigma_i^2$.

(j, k)th entry is $p \lim_{T\to\infty} \sum_{t=1}^{T} \Delta m_{i,t+1-j}\Delta m_{i,t+1-k}/T$; e is the $(2r+1)\times 1$ vector whose $(r+1)$th entry is one and remaining entries are zero; and

$$\xi_i \equiv \varphi_{i210}/(1-\varphi_{i120}\varphi_{i210}) \;. \tag{4.6}$$

Letting b_{ij} be the $(j, 1)$th entry of H_{i12} for $j = 1, 2, \ldots, r$ and g_{ij} be the $(j+1, 1)$th entry of H_{i22} for $j = 0, 1, \ldots, r$, one can rewrite equation (4.5) in the form

$$\underset{T\to\infty}{p \lim}\, \hat{\varphi}_{i11j} = \varphi_{i11j} + \xi_i\sigma_i^2 b_{ij} \tag{4.7}$$

and

$$\underset{T\to\infty}{p \lim}\, \hat{\varphi}_{i12j} = \varphi_{i12j} + \xi_i\sigma_i^2 g_{ij} \;. \tag{4.8}$$

Finally, substituting equations (4.7) and (4.8) into equation (4.4) results in

$$\underset{T\to\infty}{p \lim}\, \hat{\theta}_i = \left[\sum_{j=0}^{r} \varphi_{i12j} + \xi_i\sigma_i^2\left(\sum_{j=0}^{r} g_{ij}\right)\right] \Bigg/ \left[\left(1-\sum_{j=1}^{r}\varphi_{i11j}\right) - \xi_i\sigma_i^2\left(\sum_{j=1}^{r} b_{ij}\right)\right] . \tag{4.9}$$

Equation (4.9) reduces to

$$\underset{T\to\infty}{p \lim}\, \hat{\theta}_i = \theta_i \tag{4.10}$$

if $\xi_i = 0$; that is, if money is predetermined in country i. Therefore, if money is neutral in the long run for the countries $1, 2, \ldots, I$ and is also predetermined, the $\hat{\theta}$s for these countries should tend to be zero. Moreover, standard methods of inference can be used to test whether money is neutral in the long run for each country.

The condition that money is predetermined might not be satisfied for every country. Suppose instead that the median of $\xi_1, \xi_2, \ldots, \xi_I$, is zero.[9] Suppose further that the denominator of equation (4.9) is positive for all countries.[10] Finally, suppose that the θs are either all zero or all positive; that is, either the null hypothesis

$$\mathscr{H}_0\colon \theta_1 = 0 \wedge \theta_2 = 0 \wedge \cdots \wedge \theta_I = 0$$

or the alternative hypothesis

$$\mathscr{H}_1\colon \theta_1 > 0 \wedge \theta_2 > 0 \wedge \cdots \wedge \theta_I > 0$$

---

9 If I is even, the middle two ξs are assumed to be zero.

10 The assumption that all roots of $1-\sum_{j=1}^{r}\varphi_{i11j}L^j$ lie outside the unit circle implies that $1-\sum_{j=1}^{r}\varphi_{i11j} > 0$. The denominator is therefore positive on some interval $(\underline{\xi}_i, \overline{\xi}_i)$ such that $\underline{\xi}_i < 0 < \overline{\xi}_i$. This assumption merely requires that $\underline{\xi}_i < \xi_i < \overline{\xi}_i$ for every $i = 1, 2, \ldots, I$.

holds. Equation (4.9) then implies that $\tilde{\theta}$, the median of $\hat{\theta}_1, \hat{\theta}_2, \ldots, \hat{\theta}_I$, converges in probability to zero under $\mathscr{H}_0$ and a positive value under $\mathscr{H}_1$.[11] Therefore, applying standard methods of inference to $\tilde{\theta}$ should enable one to test $\mathscr{H}_0$ against $\mathscr{H}_1$.

V Empirical Analysis

The data employed in the empirical work come from the CD-ROM IFS0594 provided by the International Monetary Fund. I obtained annual data on the monetary base and real GDP (or GNP) for the countries satisfying the following criteria: (i) they have market economies; (ii) their populations exceeded one million in 1960; (iii) their primary output is not oil; (iv) inflation was not so severe that the IMF writes their monetary base in scientific notation; (v) the growth rates of their monetary bases appear to be stationary; and (vi) their data are available for the entire period 1960–1992. I adopted criteria (iv) and (v) in order to omit countries with nonstationary money growth. Applying these selection criteria resulted in a sample of 27 countries with data for the period 1960–1992.

Table 1 presents some evidence that the growth rate of the monetary base is stationary for each of the 27 countries. I applied the test of Phillips and Perron (1988) with windows of length 0, 2, 4, and 6 years, producing the test-statistics reported there. Their critical value is −2.95 at the .05 significance level. Clearly, much evidence exists that the growth rate of the money supply is stationary for each of these countries.

I used ordinary least squares to fit equation (4.1) to data for each of the countries. The choice of r in equation (4.1) must trade off two competing considerations. First, the larger r is, the more likely is the lag structure of equation (4.1) to capture the relationship between money and output and to whiten the error term u_{it}. Second, the smaller r is, the more precisely can equation (4.1) be estimated. I chose a value of 4 years, which is about the length of a business cycle yet still leaves 18 degrees of freedom to estimate each regression. I then plugged the estimates into equation (4.4) to obtain $\hat{\theta}_i$ for each of the 27 countries. Figure 1 reports the estimate of each θ_i as well as its asymptotic 95 percent

[11] Because the denominator of the right-hand member of equation (3.9) is positive, $p \lim_{T\to\infty} \hat{\theta}_i$ is negative, zero, or positive according as its numerator is negative, zero, or positive. Furthermore, the term $\sum_{j=0}^{r} \varphi_{i12j}$ is zero under $\mathscr{H}_0$ and positive under $\mathscr{H}_1$. Finally, the factor $\sum_{j=0}^{r} g_{ij}$ must be positive because H_{i22} is positive definite symmetric. Therefore, $p \lim_{T\to\infty} \hat{\theta}_i \gtreqless 0$ as $\xi_i \gtreqless 0$ under $\mathscr{H}_0$ and cannot be negative under $\mathscr{H}_1$ unless ξ_i is bounded from above by some negative value. In the former case, half of the $p \lim_{T\to\infty} \hat{\theta}$s are nonnegative, half are nonpositive, and $p \lim_{T\to\infty} \tilde{\theta} = 0$. In the latter case, if I is sufficiently large, $p \lim_{T\to\infty} \tilde{\theta} > 0$ because more than half must then be positive.

Table 1. Tests statistics for the stationarity of the growth rate of the monetary base

	Window Lengths			
Country	0	2	4	6
Australia	−7.03	−7.06	−6.98	−7.02
Costa Rica	−6.45	−6.37	−6.37	−6.46
Denmark	−8.07	−8.56	−9.18	−9.42
El Salvador	−6.55	−6.53	−6.98	−7.82
Finland	−4.91	−4.89	−4.87	−4.91
France	−4.47	−4.53	−4.45	−4.43
Germany	−3.92	−3.99	−3.79	−3.71
Ghana	−5.10	−5.19	−5.38	−5.57
Greece	−4.74	4.72	−4.79	−4.84
Guatemala	−4.61	−4.57	−4.59	−4.59
Honduras	−4.01	−3.99	−4.08	−4.00
India	−3.81	−3.78	−3.85	−3.91
Ireland	−3.68	−3.70	−3.92	−4.12
Italy	−5.08	−5.08	−5.08	−5.06
Japan	−2.85	−2.94	−2.90	−3.01
Korea	−4.15	−4.18	−4.14	−4.12
Mauritius	−5.38	−5.42	−5.50	−5.51
Mexico	−4.86	−4.87	−4.96	−5.14
Netherlands	−6.88	−7.10	−7.69	−7.75
Norway	−4.68	−4.75	−4.84	−4.89
Pakistan	−4.56	−4.56	−4.56	−4.57
Philippines	−5.90	−5.90	−5.89	−5.90
Spain	−6.07	−6.05	−6.05	−6.07
Sweden	−8.03	−8.06	−8.16	−8.27
United Kingdom	−5.13	−5.12	−5.12	−5.15
United States	−5.70	−5.71	−5.75	−5.86
Venezuela	−3.29	−3.31	−3.18	−3.03

Note. The .05 critical value of the test statistics is −2.95.

confidence band. The covariance matrices used for calculating the confidence bands are robust to heteroskedasticity in u_{it}.

Seven of the 27 point estimates reported in Figure 1 are statistically significant at the .05 level. The evidence would thus be fairly strong against long-run neutrality, were money really predetermined. The nonneutrality, however, would be about as likely to be negative as positive, a result inconsistent with endogenous growth and positive short-run effects of money on output. A more plausible interpretation is that money is not predetermined for every country considered. Suppose instead that it is predetermined for the median country. Given this assumption, one cannot reject the hypothesis that money is neutral in the long run for all of the countries because −.00337, the median of the $\hat{\theta}$s, is not statistically significant at any reasonable level. Moreover, the top of its 95 percent confidence band is only .142. The theory in section II suggests that the long-run effect should appreciably exceed this figure if growth is to be endogenous and money is to have appreciable short-run effects on output.

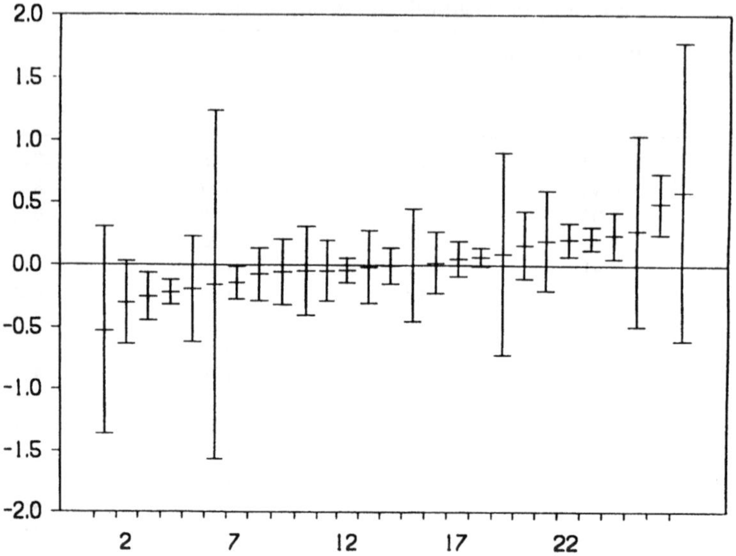

Fig. 1. Estimates and 95% confidence bands for theta

VI Conclusions

In a wide class of models, money is not neutral in the long run if it is not neutral in the short run and growth is endogenous. Although the class is wide, it is not universal because with sufficient ingenuity a model can surely be devised in which money alters relative prices in the short run, but the reproducible factors that can be produced with constant social returns in terms of themselves are accumulated independently of those relative prices. For example, if the real wage rate and real interest rate do not affect investment in R&D and technical knowledge can be produced with constant social returns in terms of itself, nominal wage contracting could conceivably make money nonneutral in the short run without affecting how technical knowledge evolves over time. Such a model would be highly contrived, however. For this reason, endogenizing the trend growth rate is a much more radical step than has been widely appreciated. Taking this step essentially requires macroeconomists to abandon their belief in either the short-run nonneutrality or the long-run neutrality of money. Few would welcome such a choice.

The empirical evidence reported in the paper does not support the joint hypothesis that money is not neutral in the short run and growth is endogenous. This conclusion can be sharpened, however, because compelling evidence exists that money is not neutral in the short run. For example, Milton Friedman and Anna Jacobson Schwartz (1963) examined many episodes in U.S. history, concluding that changes in the money supply produced appreciable short-run changes in output in the same direction. This evidence combined with that provided by this paper therefore offers essentially no support for endogenous growth.

References

Alesina A, Rodrik D (1994) Distributive politics and economic growth. Quarterly Journal of Economics 109:465–490

Barro RJ (1977) Long-term contracting, sticky prices, and monetary policy. Journal of Monetary Economics 3:305–316

Barro RJ (1991) Economic growth in a cross section of countries. Quarterly Journal of Economics 106:407–443

Barro RJ, Sala-i-Martin X (1992) Convergence. Journal of Political Economy 100:223–251

Baumol WJ (1986) Productivity growth, convergence, and welfare: What the long-run data show. American Economic Review 76:1072–1085

Cass DM (1965) Optimum growth in an aggregate model of capital accumulation. Review of Economics Studies 32:233–240

De Long, B (1965) Productivity growth, convergence, and welfare. Comment. American Economic Review 78:233–240

De Long B, Summers LH (1991) Equipment investment and economic growth. Quarterly Journal of Economics 106:407–444

De Gregorio J (1993) Inflation, taxation, and long-run growth. Journal of Monetary Economics 31:271–298

Easterly W (1993) How much do distortions affect growth? Journal of Monetary Economics 32:187–212

Evans P (1995) How to estimate growth regressions consistently. Unpublished

Fischer S (1977) Long-term contracts, rational expectations, and the optimal money supply rule. Journal of Political Economy 85:191–206

Fisher ME, Seater JJ (1993) Long-run neutrality and superneutrality in an ARIMA framework. American Economic Review 83:402–415

Friedman M, Schwartz AJ (1963) A monetary history of the United States, 1867–1960. Princeton New Jersey, Princeton University Press

Jones C (1985) Time series tests of endogenous growth models. Quarterly Journal of Economics 110:495–526

King RG, Levine R (1993) Finance and growth: Schumpeter might be right. Quarterly Journal of Economics 108:717–738

King RG, Plosser CI, Stock JH, Watson MW (1991) Stochastic trends and economic fluctuations. American Economic Review 81:819–840

Kormendi R, Meguire P (1985) Macroeconomic determinants of growth: Cross-country evidence. Journal of Monetary Economics 16:141–163

Lucas RE, Jr (1980) Two illustrations of the quantity theory of money. American Economic Review 70:1005–1014

Lucas RE, Jr (1988) On the mechanics of economic development. Journal of Monetary Economics 22:3–42

Mankiw NG, Romer D, Weil DN (1992) A contribution to the empirics of economic growth. Quarterly Journal of Economics 107:407–438

Persson T, Tabellini G (1994) Is inequality harmful? American Economic Review 84:600–621

Phillips PCB, Perron P (1988) Testing for a unit root in time series regressions. Biometrika 65:335–346

Romer PM (1986) Increasing returns and long-run growth. Journal of Political Economy 94: 1002–1037

Solow RM (1956) A contribution to the theory of economic growth. Quarterly Journal of Economics 70:65–94

First version received: December 1994
Final version received: June 1995

Subject-Index

MIX
Papier aus verantwortungsvollen Quellen
Paper from responsible sources
FSC® C105338

If you have any concerns about our products,
you can contact us on
ProductSafety@springernature.com

In case Publisher is established outside the EU,
the EU authorized representative is:
Springer Nature Customer Service Center GmbH
Europaplatz 3, 69115 Heidelberg, Germany

Printed by Libri Plureos GmbH
in Hamburg, Germany